Manichean Psychology

RACISM

AND THE

MINDS OF

PEOPLE OF

AFRICAN

DESCENT

Camara Jules P. Harrell

MANICHEAN PSYCHOLOGY

RACISM AND THE MINDS OF PEOPLE OF AFRICAN DESCENT

Camara Jules P. Harrell

HOWARD UNIVERSITY PRESS
WASHINGTON, DC
1999

Howard University Press, Washington, DC 20001

Library of Congress Cataloging-in-Publication Data

Harrell, Camara Jules P., 1949–
    Manichean psychology : racism and the minds of people of African descent / Camara Jules P. Harrell.
      p. cm.
    Includes bibliographical references and index.
    ISBN 0-88258-203-8 (alk. paper)
    1. Afro-Americans—Psychology. 2. Racism—United States—Psychological aspects. 3. United States—Race relations—Psychological aspects. I. Title.
E185.625.H38   1999
155.8'496073—dc21
                                     99-11024
                                       CIP

Manufactured in the United States of America

This book is printed on acid-free paper.

10 9 8 7 6 5 4 3 2 1

Contents

Introduction

The question seems straightforward enough. What mental consequences do people of African descent suffer because they live in a
racist environment? Nevertheless, if you pose it in a gathering of black
psychologists, you are likely to witness an argument that will continue
into the wee hours of the morning. Generations of behavioral scientists have struggled with this "nature of the effects" riddle. Certainly,
some of the most brilliant, energetic, and technically skilled African-
American psychologists have taken a turn or two at uncovering
oppression's effects on the personality of African people. But reaching
agreement on a definitive statement has proven to be a difficult task.
An empirical search for answers plunges one into contentious exchanges. These hot dialogues frustrate the individual researcher, strain
friendships, and provide additional brick and mortar for the walls
separating various intellectual traditions within the black community.

Studies of racial identification concern themselves with how African people who live in racist settings regard themselves. There was a
fascinating exchange among several leading investigators in the *Journal of Black Psychology* (Vol. 19, No. 3) on this topic. The authors
of these articles failed to agree on what aspects of black identity we
should measure and how we might measure them. This row showed
that the differences between several camps are quite fundamental. It
was clear that the participants were just warming up.

If we back up from this question, we can see that it is not simple
at all. It is a tangled, sticky web of propositions, fraught with sad
imponderables. Still, it has its lure, and its half-life is long. It beckons
to bright and vibrant young scholars in an almost mocking fashion.
Evidence, claims, and counterclaims mount. We move toward reso-
lution only in the sense that we are beginning to appreciate the complexity of the matter with which we are dealing.

The conventional psychological wisdom in the middle part of this
century was that in a society that despises African Americans, black
people would come to despise themselves. This notion was based on
early research that assessed racial attitudes using children's preferences for black and white dolls and figure drawings. William Cross

(1991), in *Shades of Black,* reviewed the empirical findings some psychologists cite as support for the "self-hatred" hypothesis. He came away somewhat unimpressed by this evidence. Cross seemed least enthralled by the interpretations some have made of the findings from the doll studies. He asserted that "had every single Black child in the earlier Clark or the more recent Powell-Hopson study selected 'white'. . ." this would be no "automatic indication of cultural pathology or poor mental health . . ." (116).

Banks (1976) and Baldwin (Baldwin 1979; Baldwin, Brown, and Hopkins 1991) were equally skeptical of the claims based on the self-hatred evidence. Banks found the studies wanting from a methodological perspective. He argued that the experiments failed to demonstrate that black children were showing anything but a random preference in the experiments where investigators asked them to select a black or white doll. Baldwin and his colleagues asserted that the problem with the self-hatred research extends far beyond methodological weaknesses. He criticized sharply, if not stridently, even those black scholars whose work tried to reform the self-hatred studies. Baldwin chided these researchers for "using European cultural definitions and European measures of self-conception in their efforts to refute the conclusions which these definitions and measures have been designed to confirm" (Baldwin, Brown, and Hopkins 1991, 156).

Cross is among those who distinguish between *personal identity* (PI) and *reference group orientation* (RGO). In their view, evidence from a number of studies compels us to conclude that people of African descent may think quite highly of themselves personally (PI) but harbor negative attitudes toward African people collectively (RGO). Thus, these two psychological orientations vary independently within the personality. If this is the case, the notion that racism leads to pervasive self-hatred in black people appears to be an oversimplification.

However, suggesting that a negative RGO can exist in an otherwise *healthy* African personality settles nothing. The proposition invites more controversy. Thus, Clovis Semmes (1992) suggested that Cross may have gone too far or perhaps was a little glib in his statements about the independence of RGO and PI. "It is simply not normal for a people to learn to devalue reference groups that look like them and that share a common social, cultural, and historical experience" (Semmes 1992, 110). Further, Wade Nobles (1991) and Baldwin, Brown, and Hopkins (1991) urged researchers to avoid ascribing meaning and importance to individualistic measures of the self-conception of African people. There is a growing consensus that African people gravitate toward a communal cultural orientation (Boykin 1986; Jones 1991; Baldwin, Brown, and Hopkins 1991; Nobles 1991). The writings that have come out of this camp make one suspicious of studies that measure the "effects" of racial oppression with questionnaire items that are personal and individualized. The healthy African self-conception is motion toward the collective. Thus, questions that tap feelings about the self on an individual basis are simply too restrictive.

Obviously, the controversy about the nature of the effects of racism involves much more than disputes about tests and statistical methods. At the core, the sides seem to differ on two enormous questions. The first is, What is the nature of the African personality in the absence of oppression? The other asks, What are the core features of a healthy African personality *at the present time*? At best, even with a firm grasp of the deep structure of African culture, we can only approximate an answer to the first question. Arguments over the second are likely to be interminable.

However, the situation is not totally blighted and bleak. The psychological instruments that researchers are developing to measure various facets of the personality of people of African descent are becoming increasingly sophisticated. Some address the effects question directly; others do so more tangentially. Burlew and Smith (1991) surveyed the literature on the measurement of racial identity and evaluated seventeen paper-and-pencil instruments that are in varying stages of refinement. Williams and Anderson (1996) developed a scale to measure "acculturative stress" (see also Anderson 1991), that is, the extent to which individuals experience anxiety and discomfort stemming from contacts with white individuals, institutions, or culture. Robert Sellers et al. (1997) is taking a sophisticated, multidimensional approach to measuring black identity. There seems to be some movement toward developing a set of instruments rich enough to assist in identifying the impact of racism on the African personality.

This book does not accuse the masses of African people of self-hatred or any other psychological disorder that might stem from racial oppression. I understand why Fanon (1967) wrote in the introduction to *Black Skin White Masks*, "Many Negroes will not find themselves in what follows" (12). Fanon knew that pointing a clinical diagnostic finger at any group or class of people is counterproductive and invites endless debate. I wish to avoid being locked away forever in the rooms with the nature-of-the-effects combatants. The purpose of this book is to address an issue that is slightly more answerable than the effects question. That is, *what are the conditions and circumstances that encourage African people to behave in a self-destructive or self-defeating fashion?* The foci become the processes involved in human mental activities and an external environment that is saturated with modern racism. The task at hand is to examine how each affects the other.

The first two chapters provide a foundation for the study. The first, a circuitous excursion treating matters of definition, history, and motivation, establishes scope and parameter. The theme underlying each discussion is that racism is not a slight tear at the edges in the garment of human interactions in societies touched by the West. Instead, it is a flaw that runs deep in the social fabric of these societies.

I have devoted the second chapter to putting on the table questions about various approaches to arriving at knowledge about racism and its effects. Psychologists pride themselves on their methodological sophistication. That is, they are proud of the rules they have generated that specify how one systematically uncovers facts and justifies claims about those facts. Psychologists have produced two grand traditions of research. One locates its roots in laboratory experiments where investigators control, measure, and manipulate variables systematically. The purpose is to establish cause-effect relationships between various factors and behavior. The other tradition concerns itself with the study of individual differences. Over the years, experts in the area of the measurement of human differences have generated advanced mathematical formulas, which are used to ascertain the extent to which psychological instruments are reliable and valid. Chapter 2 asks if we should accept knowledge about racism that is generated outside these two research traditions.

The body of this work is divided into discussions of material we can place under one of three headings. The first is environmental events and situations that may encourage the developments of racist thinking. The second is human information processing. The final area is the actual responses to racism that the oppressed evidence in a racist system. Chapter 3 takes up the discussion of the environment. It organizes the external circumstances into four classes. Specifically, I discuss the social ecology of the lives of oppressed people, popular culture, formal educational curriculum, and institutionalized religion. The chapter describes environmental events within each class that have the capacity to promote or foster racist thinking.

Chapter 4 is a finer-grained analysis of the environment. This chapter focuses less on the content of the environmental events than on several more abstract features of the external sources of racist thinking. The concern is with the intensity, subtlety, and patterns of the information that comes to us from the environment. The chapter also discusses how the temporal spacing of events might change the influence they have on individuals. In chapter 4 we are merging our discussion of situational causes with an introduction to what psychological research has shown about human responses to stimulation.

Chapter 5 shifts completely to an overview of a very small portion of the massive psychological literature on how humans process information. One can think of a grand continuum that is anchored at the extremes by the nouns *acquiescence* and *resistance*. Psychologists might find it useful to place behaviors of the oppressed at points along this continuum. However, in so doing, one would simply be looking at the spoils of a battle that takes place largely within the human mind. This hub of activity within the mind shapes the symptoms and behaviors that we might try to classify. Chapter 5 is a long exercise in speculation on the terms of an internal battle. It asks what we know about how the human mind works. The answers provide leads about the mechanisms by which racism persists in disrupting African lives.

The final two chapters address the responses of African people to racism. These two chapters take on a decidedly clinical tone. Chapter 6 discusses frameworks for organizing these responses. It is a study of several diagnostic systems. Chapter 7, the last chapter, discusses approaches to treating troublesome responses to racism. In chapter 7 I define treatment in very broad terms. Therapy ranges from activities that modify targeted behaviors of individuals to social movements aimed at overturning oppressive institutions. The healing process involves intervention on many levels.

At some point, perhaps when the early morning sun peeks over the horizon, argumentative but fatigued psychologists will grudgingly end their discussion of effects. They will reach for their coats and go out into a world where there is little room for debate regarding the gravity of the conditions African people face. On the ravaged African continent, natural and political disasters stalk the landscape. Black communities around the world struggle to resuscitate institutions that sustain life and advance cultural activities. Black children in many parts of the developing world are on the edge of physical starvation. In the developed world, the twins of these children starve for a mental sustenance that will provide meaning, vision, and purpose to their lives. This is not a clinical diagnosis. It is, rather, a statement of the precarious position in which African people find themselves on this, the eve of the twenty-first century. The present study, then, offered from the discipline of psychology, constitutes an analysis of some of the persistent forces that are the source of our peril.

References

Anderson, L. P. 1991. Acculturative Stress: A Theory of Relevance to Black Americans. *Clinical Psychology Review* 11: 685–702.

Baldwin, J. A. 1979. Theory and Research Concerning the Notion of Black Self-hatred: A Review and Reinterpretation. *Journal of Black Psychology* 5: 51–77.

Baldwin, J. A., Brown, R., and Hopkins, R. 1991. The Black Self-hatred Paradigm Revisited: An Afrocentric Analysis. In *Black Psychology*, 3d ed., ed. R. Jones, 141–66. Berkeley: Cobb and Henry.

Banks, W. C. 1976. White Preference in Blacks: A Paradigm in Search of a Phenomenon. *Psychological Bulletin* 83: 1179–86.

Boykin, A. W. 1986. Triple Quandary and Schooling of African-American Children. In *The School Achievement of Minority Children: New Perspectives*, ed. U. Neisser, 57–92. Hillsdale, N.J.: Erlbaum.

Burlew, A. K., and Smith, L. R. 1991. Measures of Racial Identity: An Overview and a Proposed Framework. *Journal of Black Psychology* 17: 53–71.

Cross, W. E. 1991. *Shades of Black: Diversity in African-American Identity*. Philadelphia: Temple University Press.

Fanon, F. 1967. *Black Skin White Masks*. New York: Grove Press.

Jones, J. M. 1991. Racism: A Cultural Analysis of the Problem. In *Black Psychology*, 3d ed., ed. R. Jones, 609–36. Berkeley: Cobb and Henry.

Nobles, W. W. 1991. Extended Self: Rethinking the So-called Negro Self-concept. In *Black Psychology*, 3d ed., ed. R. Jones, 295–304. Berkeley: Cobb and Henry.

Sellers, R. M., Rowley, S. A. J., Chavous, T. M., Shelton, J. N., and Smith, M. 1997. Multidimensional Inventory of Black Identity: Preliminary Investigation of Reliability and Construct Validity. *Journal of Personality and Social Psychology* 73: 805–15

Semmes, C. E. 1992. *Cultural Hegemony and African-American Development*. Westport, Conn.: Praeger.

Williams, D., and Anderson, L. P. 1996. The Acculturated Stress Scale: Preliminary Findings. In *Handbook of Tests and Measurements for Black Populations*, ed. R. Jones, 351–58. Berkeley: Cobb and Henry.

CHAPTER ONE

The Meaning and Impact of Racism

W hen the media brought us face to face with the "drug kingpin," a parade of *ifs* filled my mind. The man appeared to be in his early twenties. He was bronze, tall, and lean, but he was no more and no less regal than the more prominent of the young black men who live on my block. Unlike the young men in my neighborhood, however, the glide and rhythm in his gait were missing—hostage now to the leg irons fitted for him by the department of corrections.

My mind raced back to the time when those with power in this land locked chains on the legs of his and my ancestral grandparents. I wondered *if* his teachers had provided a lucid description of the horrific period of African enslavement in the United States. *If* they had taught him well, would he have opted to wade hip deep in the cocaine business? What *if* when he was just about to enter puberty, a mature man with hard hands and dark thick fingers had grabbed him by the scruff of the neck and said, "Come on son, help me change the oil in this ol' truck"? *If* he had been steeped in that kind of love, would the "kingpin" now be facing cameras and harsh lights, and even harsher faces? He continued to stare alternately at the cameras, at the faces, and at his own empty hands. Maybe *if* fate had favored him with three and a half inches more on his vertical leap, he might have become a basketball star. Eighty nights a year he would have soared above the rim in massive sports arenas, entertaining one segment of sedentary America and enriching another.

These thoughts buzzed furiously in my head. Then I heard myself say aloud the word "no." I resolved silently to invest all of the love, guidance, and time necessary to ensure other young people steer clear of the road this young man traveled. I knew my efforts would begin with my own children and with other children of African descent. Facing us was a man in his very early twenties who would soon begin serving a lifetime in prison with no possibility of parole, ever. This is how one is sentenced under the "drug kingpin law" in the District of Columbia and in many other of these United States. The *ifs* that flooded my mind ultimately took the form of questions, regrets, recriminations, and resolutions.

The facts of the matter were these. This young man had become much more affluent than his neighbors by selling some of them "crack" cocaine. He had bestowed gifts and favors on his family. In addition, he provided some members of his family and a few members of his community with employment opportunities. Thus they shared a portion of the financial gain accrued from his entrepreneurial activities. Drug pushing, however, is a dirty business. He dealt quite harshly with those who failed to acknowledge and respect his territorial imperatives, that is, the customers and trading avenues he designated his own. In the end, the U.S. Attorney would charge some of his family and friends with being accessories to his crimes. So, if indeed the young man had spread around some of his wealth, he had also spread around a whole lot of trouble and, quite likely, a good deal of death. Today he would talk to the press. For the first time, he was to speak his mind to the public and tell his side of the story.

Twelve African Americans comprised the jury of his peers. Maybe they found him imposing, bright, and capable. Indeed, this was the case with some of his neighbors that the defense had called as "character" witnesses. Certainly, the jury had found him guilty of all charges related to drug distribution. Quite understandably, he resented the guilty verdict. But his statement to the press described more than his anger. It revealed more about him than he and most of the members of the establishment press are likely to comprehend for a very long time.

The problem, as this young man saw it, was that his jury was all black. He reasoned that a white jury would have considered the intricacies of the legal arguments more carefully. The kingpin surmised that his downfall, that is, in his mind, his criminal conviction, was the fault of his own people. These people failed to or perhaps could not ponder the complexities of the charges he faced. Ironically, his attack on the intellectual capacity of the jury foreshadowed the outrage many whites would express toward a jury some years later. This anger was expressed when the jury handed down a "not guilty" verdict in the O. J. Simpson murder trial. Some felt that the predominantly black jury was either incapable of understanding the gravity of a "mountain" of DNA evidence or simply too emotional to render a rational judgment.

Evident in the words and actions of this doomed young man was an utterly disastrous mode of thinking. I was not surprised that he showed no understanding of the larger international, political, and economic context in which the drug industry in the black community is embedded (Adler 1995; Lusane 1991; Webb, 1998). Obviously and understandably, educational institutions in the society assiduously avoid teaching the alienated, wretched, and oppressed anything about the systems and the processes that make their lives utterly desperate. However, I was taken aback by the candid manner in which this young man belittled the thinking capacity of people of African descent. I was struck with how openly he elevated and adulated the mental capacities of white people. He had wittingly dealt death to his own people. Now his words uncovered at least a portion of the deep-seated rationale for his actions. This rationale was rooted in the core of his consciousness. In his mind, black people were not intellectually equal to white people. We had not quite yet measured up to the standard of human mental competence.

What is the nature, root, and active source of the cognitive framework through which this young man was socialized to operate? How did a cognitive system of this type come to govern the behavior of this extremely unfortunate individual? What were the modes through which this mindset was inculcated? These questions are the focus of this work. I contend that the cognitive operations of this young, distant son of Africa are prototypic of those fostered in the minds of the oppressed in modern racist societies. The press and the circumstances of the press conference had reduced him to an entertaining aberration. The magnitude of his success and, therefore, the magnitude of his fall were noteworthy. For me, however, his mind was the story. It was a rather remarkable extension of a socialization process that takes place in a society thoroughly saturated with racism. Therefore, to understand his mind, we must understand the nature of racism.

This opening chapter is concerned with establishing a definitional framework and a historical context for our study of racism's impact on people of African descent. First, the chapter will provide the conceptual foundation for an examination of racism. We will provide a working definition of racism and a sketch of the principal "cognitive" regions on which racism has its influence. The chapter gives the subsequent historical survey as support for the argument that racism is both an intractable and a pervasive phenomenon in modern life. Finally, we will consider the issue of motivation. What forces initiate and maintain racist actions and processes? Addressing the motivational issue puts us on tricky turf. Motivational theories make general statements about the psychological dispositions of Europeans and Africans. We will analyze these statements critically. In the conceptual system I am about to introduce, the historical antecedents of racism, as well as the psychological principle of individual differences, will guide our attempts to arrive at a motivational synthesis.

Understanding racism

Definition and conceptual frameworks

In 1972, James Jones, a young, energetic social psychologist, published a concise book entitled *Prejudice and Racism*. With that publication, psychologists lost their excuse for confusing the two distinct though related phenomena that composed the title of the book. Still, the field has persisted in doing so. Jones described prejudice as a "negative attitude toward a person or group based upon a social comparison process in which the individual's own group is taken as the positive point of reference" (3). Attitudes manifest themselves in the beliefs, feelings, and action tendencies of the individual. Jones pointed out that interpersonal forms of racial discrimination are the behavioral extension of prejudice.

Often psychologists, as well as people in general, assume that the cognitive, affective, and behavioral components of prejudice are fused or at least closely linked. For example, in the late 1980s and early 1990s, black students on predominantly white college campuses complained that their white counterparts were increasing their use of inflammatory speech. Along with sympathizers, some became involved in protest movements against this hate speech. Such movements examine the boundaries of the legal structures that sanction or permit these practices. Ultimately, the discussions that grew from these protests plumbed the limits of freedom of speech, as guaranteed in the Constitution of the United States. The intent of the protests, however, was to do away with a prejudicial form of behavior, that is, hate speech. The assumption was that when discriminatory behavior is prohibited by legal sanction, the cognitive and emotional components of prejudice will dissipate. That is, if laws forbid people from speaking in a racially inflammatory manner or if laws "protect" us from hearing such speech, eventually individuals will become less likely to feel or think in a prejudicial fashion.

In a similar vein, often television talk shows and race relations seminars are fraught with dialogue that attempts to destroy the cognitive and emotional components of prejudice. Hosts and facilitators challenge people to discuss their prejudices openly. The dialogue is intended to make clear how ludicrous these prejudices are. The hope is that the behavioral components will rot away in the process. If prejudice existed in a social vacuum or if it was merely an isolated individual pathology, the assumptions of the student protesters and the hopes of the hosts and facilitators might be justified. However, there is a more ominous phenomenon that limits the effectiveness of exercises that attempt to mitigate the impact of prejudice. The phenomenon is racism.

Jones (1972) argued that racism is the result of certain transformations of prejudice. These transformations are substantive, and they make it inappropriate to use the terms *racism* and *prejudice* synonymously. Racism involves "the exercise of power against a racial group defined as inferior by individuals and institutions with the intentional or unintentional support of the entire culture" (117). Power is the central ingredient in this conceptualization of racism. The transformation entails the institutionalization of prejudice. Racism marshals the full weight of social systems so that prejudicial thought and action can be specified, inculcated, and reinforced. Indeed, racism can be manifested on the individual level. However, its broader and deeper emanations from societal structures make it more pervasive and preemptive than prejudice or the racially discriminatory actions of individuals.

Jones went on to identify three forms that racism in modern society might take. The first of these, individual racism, is very similar to what is commonly called racial discrimination. Individual racism occurs when one holds beliefs of the racial superiority of one group over another and is able to engage in practices that reinforce or actualize the inferiorization of that group. Institutional racism, the second form of racism, can manifest itself in either of two ways. In some cases it is "the conscious manipulation of institutions to achieve racist objectives" (5). Or institutional racism can be a by-product or a natural extension of the practices of institutions that impinge on the rights and access of particular racial groups. Finally, Jones discussed the manner in which individual racism and institutional racism differ from a third form he called cultural racism. Cultural racism can be expressed institutionally or individually. It occurs when groups, societies, or individuals allege the racially based superiority of their cultural heritage. Indeed, institutions and individuals that wield power in the society are capable of buttressing these assertions.

Ani (1994) underscored the unique and fundamental importance of the concept of cultural racism. She put forth this argument in her book *Yurugu*. The text is an extensive, African-centered study of the impact of European thought and culture on African people. Ani introduced the notion of *asili*, which she defined as the center, seed, and organizing principle of a culture around which other elements of the culture revolve and cohere. She posited that control over all facets of existence is the central element of the European *asili*. On the other hand, according to Ani, the *asili* of African culture tends to see the world as inclusive of elements of spirituality. European cultural racism may involve something as circumscribed as elevating European forms of artistic expression and seeing corresponding African forms as primitive. However, Ani maintains that in its ultimate form, cultural racism involves an attack on the African *asili* and a promotion of the European *asili*. The attack may dislodge persons of African descent from their core cultural force, which includes a deep and fundamental appreciation of spirituality. If this occurs, Ani maintains that African people will engage in disordered and bizarre behaviors. Hence, according to Ani, we should not minimize or underestimate the thrust and potential impact of cultural racism. Attacks on the culture of people may uproot them from core elements of culture including ethos, values, and practices that will preserve them and ensure their growth.

Clovis Semmes (1992) explored the impact of Euro-American cultural hegemony on the fabric of the lives of black people. He defined cultural hegemony as the "systematic negation of one culture by another" (1). Obviously, Semmes is describing an active and destructive process, rather than the normal synergistic influence cultures may have on one another. He pointed out that "one culture bases its existence and well-being on the ability to absorb, redirect, or redefine institution building and symbol formation in the other" (1).

The cultural racism that Jones described is a subset of the activities that occur under cultural hegemony. There is no fundamental conflict between his analysis and that of Semmes. The differences in their analyses are rooted in the disciplines from which they address their subjects. Semmes's analysis of cultural hegemony is primarily sociological. It is a critique of social processes and social forces. Jones examines social psychological dynamics when treating the concept of cultural racism. He is more immediately concerned with what happens to the individual who is on the receiving end of cultural oppression.

An example may serve to clarify the various forms of racism Jones has defined. A mythical African-American college student described the following encounters. All four took place during her matriculation at a large, Midwestern university in the United States. On one occasion, she was touring the campus with her eight-year-old niece and four-year-old nephew. A carload of white male students drove by as the young woman and her charges waited at a pedestrian crossing. One student shouted to her "bet you don't know who the fathers are." This form of interpersonal meanness is racial prejudice. The young lady and her niece and nephew experienced the behavioral component of a prejudicial attitude, nothing more, nothing less.

On another occasion, a special seminar in this student's major was closed to further enrollment due to limited seating. The white professor granted a Caucasian student special permission to enter the course because it was in her major field. However, when the African-American student requested admission, she was rebuffed. The professor told her that the course would be extremely difficult and that she was better advised not to take it. Her academic record was outstanding, in fact, superior to that of the student whom the professor permitted to enter the course. Because of the power dynamic operating in this instance, we submit that the professor is engaging in racism on the individual level.

Upon completion of her third year of training, our very unfortunate student was considered for a special scholarship program. Her impressive academic record placed her among the top five candidates. However, her scores on several widely used tests were around the

50th percentile for a national sample. Educators had normed and standardized these tests on white populations. The tests were factored into the index that the selection committee used to choose the two recipients of the scholarships. The standardized test scores prevented this student from receiving the award, though her academic record in college was as strong as those of the two recipients. Institutional racism occurred in this circumstance. It is difficult to identify an intentional implementation of a racist agenda in this instance. Still, the selection practices and procedures tended to limit the access of black students to scholarship opportunities.

Our student has been bludgeoned sufficiently in our attempt to provide concrete instances of Jones's distinctions. Nevertheless, I will provide one final example. Unfortunately, the young lady waited until her senior year to take a required course in humanities. A class called "History of Civilization" was scheduled for a time that was ideal for her work hours. The focus of the material in the class was exclusively the history of Europe. The textbook and the instructor depicted the history of other regions of the world as minor terms in the record of the human story. At this point, the student is experiencing cultural racism. When an individual, or for that matter an institution, vested with some level of power, insists on a general superiority of Western culture, they are advancing cultural racism. Regardless of the scholarly tone of the assertion or the erudite tradition of the institution that allows such utterances, cultural racism is afoot.

Ten years after Jones (1972) articulated his definitions of racism, Maulana Karenga (1982) discussed racism in his very useful *Introduction to Black Studies*. He defined racism as the imposition of a system of dehumanizing forces based on the "specious concept of race" (209). Karenga focused on the manner in which power is manifested in the racist scenario. He contended that it takes three forms. First, power may entail conquest on the physical level. Initially, oppressors use trained military forces for this purpose. Eventually, the police, the military arm of civilian society, become the active participants in this primitive and bloody enterprise. A second, often ostensibly more cerebral manifestation of power in the racist context is the imposition of ideology, a system of ideas that tends to support the dehumanizing objectives of the oppressors. A good portion of our efforts in the present study will revolve around describing this ideology. The final manifestation of power within racist societies is the development of institutional infrastructure. Those with power develop and arrange social institutions so that they systematically support racism. The purpose of these institutions is to reinforce the racist ideology and, in ideal situations, reduce the need for further physical conquest.

Obviously, the definitions of Jones and Karenga are similar. Both see power as an essential component of racism. Additionally, their formulations highlight the central role institutions play in maintaining racism. They suggest that these institutions are not set up in a haphazard fashion. Rather, forces in the society arrange institutions systematically so they will function harmoniously for the effective operation of a racist system. Finally, both point up the cognitive element involved in the racist process. Karenga discusses the role of ideology directly. Significantly, Jones distinguishes cultural racism from other manifestations of racism emanating from institutional and individual forms. Thus he implies that racism may involve the propagation of an ideology. Specifically, and here is where Jones and Karenga would likely agree completely, racism will mandate that one racial group will claim superior mental functioning. The racist oppressor will insist that the history of thoughtful accomplishments; systems of values, philosophy, and world view; and virtually all higher-order human cognitive capacities are superordinate to those of the oppressed. In the context of racism, the setting forth of this hierarchy is crucial.

Far too often, psychological efforts to grapple with racism snag on matters of interpersonal relationships between members of different races. Sometimes these efforts can take the form of books and serious scholarship. Other times, therapists often address racism through the use of focus groups. Sessions are directed toward ameliorating the effects of racism or prejudice. The tendency in both the scholarship and the applied clinical setting is to explore the attitudes blacks, Native Americans, Latinos, Asians, whites, and other groups hold toward one another. The extension of this focus finds the scholars or the group participants examining the behavioral commerce between the various racial groups. They discuss at length the attitudinal surveys and explore or quantify the level of hostility or ill will that exists between the races. Often, the interactions that African people or others on the receiving end of oppression have had with sincere or benevolent whites are contrasted with negative racist or prejudicial encounters. The contrast is made inevitably when those facilitating multiracial encounter groups or writing scholarly works are excessively conscious of the sentiments of white participants and readers. The intent of discussion is to portray racism as a relatively evaporative and shallow phenomenon. The subtext of these explorations asks plaintively and simplistically, along with Rodney King, "Can't we all just get along?"

If we fail to appreciate fully the power dynamic that is operative in racism, discussions will consider only the individual forms. Usually, these discussions will confuse racism with prejudice. The ebb and flow of the feelings whites hold toward blacks (or vice versa) is of minor consequence at best. Attitudes may become more or less positive, rates of hate crimes will reach peaks and nadirs, and interracial marriages and alliances will slip in and out of vogue. In the face of all of these trends, institutional and cultural racism can flourish. Racism can thrive and a significant portion of the oppressed will lead miserable lives and die prematurely as long as those in the power structure, the principal socializing institutions of the land, continue to serve a racist order.

In a letter to Carl Jung, Sigmund Freud once lashed out at the "fallen away" disciple, Alfred Adler. In developing a theory of human personality, Adler advocated the study of the "ego" rather than the "id." According to Freud, the ego contains our perceptual and cognitive functions and the id houses instinctual strivings. Freud angrily wrote that "everyone knows that the ego is like the clown at a circus, trying to put in his oar to make the audience think that whatever happens is his doing" (Freud and Jung 1974). I like Freud's analogy, though I think the psychological content of his statement is incorrect. Admittedly, this is the usual form my evaluations of Freud's theory take. Race relations and interpersonal dynamics that take place in a modern racist system are but a small corner of the total picture. They act like the clown at the circus. They are not totally unimportant, but they should never command our full attention. We should not see them as primary causal agents. I think it is wise to take very seriously the distinctions Jones makes between racism and prejudice along with his taxonomy of the types of racism. In so doing we may avoid focusing on the "clown" while neglecting more important activities taking place in the center ring.

Racism and violence

Hussein A. Bulhan (1985) examined the work of the black psychiatrist Frantz Fanon. One of the remarkable aspects of Bulhan's book is that it was undertaken as a study of oppression from the vantage point of the victim. This change in perspective allowed Bulhan to avoid the trite, hackneyed treatments of Fanon that present his body of thought as a simple extension of Marxism on one hand or a glorification of violence on the other. Indeed, discussions of Fanon often gravitate toward debates about his controversial position on violence (see Onwuanibe 1983). Bulhan did not shrink from this debate. He joined it and brought to it the fresh perspective of one on the receiving end of racism. Accordingly, he refused to discuss the violent response of the oppressed without first framing oppression itself within the context of violent behavior. Therefore, it is extremely important that we allow Bulhan's presentation on violence to intersect the advances of Jones and Karenga in conceptualizing racism.

Bulhan's analysis broke with many traditional views of violence. In many instances, authors base their judgment of the violent or nonviolent nature of a behavior on the intent and emotional intensity of the act. Certainly when a teenage boy pulls the trigger, ending the life of one of his cohorts, all would agree that an act of senseless violence has occurred. The purpose was to destroy; the level of emotional intensity was high. But, perhaps in another part of the world, at the command of a superior officer, a trained American airman peers at a computer-enhanced image on a cathode ray display. He or she lines the crosshairs up on a target and pushes a button rather calmly. A "smart bomb" blows apart a building and human flesh several thousand feet below. We may find little intent to kill and a low level of emotional arousal. The act may appear as rational as taking a piece on a chess board. Still, the consequence is death. And in Bulhan's framework, the act is as violent as it would have been had the man gutted each victim with a dull machete.

Bulhan (1985) defined violence as "any relation, process or condition by which an individual or group violates the physical, social and or psychological integrity of another person or group" (135). Groups or individuals, invested with sufficient power, can carry out violent acts. The consequences for other groups or individuals may be physical or psychological. Surely, groups need not act as lynch mobs to engage in violence. They may express their violence through their social institutions. The crucial ingredient is the "violation of the integrity" of the individual who is the object of the violence.

When viewed through Bulhan's lens, the frameworks for understanding racism provided by Jones and Karenga lead us to conclude that racism is first and last, essentially and thoroughly, a violent phenomenon. At its core are the power and the willingness to violate and, as we will see, the history of violating human beings on the basis of their "race." In its various forms, individual, cultural, and institutional, the *intent* to violate may not be prominent. Still, the consequence is real. Racism might take the form of a crass invective from an individual, limiting another's personal access or liberty. In another instance, it is advanced as a published scholarly work downplaying gently the personal characteristics, values, or historical contribution of another group of human beings. In both cases, at its core, racism has violated the integral functioning of others. Therefore, in these instances and in all cases, it constitutes an act of violence.

Racism and white supremacy

It is necessary to address a second and perhaps more contentious issue related to the definition of racism. The last section argued that the role of power and violence must be inserted into the conceptual framework that we use to understand racism. I also find compelling Karenga's notion that physical conquest, along with the power or the capacity to control major social institutions, is essential to the implementation of racism. Inevitably, the question becomes, What individuals or groups wield such power? Approached from another angle and perhaps stated a better way, in modern and functional terms, it becomes, What manner of power is needed to impose racism?

Certainly on the level of individual racism, one might argue that any member of a racial group can behave in a racist fashion toward the member of another racial group, provided he or she is able to exercise sufficient power over some sphere of the injured party's life. Indeed, sometimes racial factors, wholly or in part, motivate interpersonally inept, rude, discriminatory, and uncivil behavior between people who are unequal with respect to some measure of power and personal influence. Individuals can engage in these acts regardless of race. However, the destructive racism that racks the lives of millions of oppressed people is not solely a function of the distribution of power in interpersonal relationships. Major societal institutions wield power for periods of time longer than the lifetimes of individuals. This power fuels racism and transcends the power of discrete individuals.

For example, the processes influencing whom an employer selects for a job extend past personal preferences. Other power-related forces operate. They include the criteria that society has come to use to index potentials and capabilities, as well as the myriad of training and socializing institutions that the job candidates have encountered. The power to decide whose historical and cultural perspective teachers will give to young people in schools is more than a matter of individual affinities and preferences. The existing corpus of thought will weigh heavily on the thinking of educators. However, a racist crucible shaped much of this material on the history and culture of the world's people. Thus, power may take the form of intellectual momentum and zeitgeist. The power to determine the nature of the images the media present lies only partly in the hands of the individuals in management positions. Long-standing oppressive conditions stultify individuals and communities. The images that result, even when presented objectively, are not attractive ones. Finally, there is the power to punish or coerce those who refuse to accept any of the above prerogatives. Individuals who would challenge institutional racism in job selection, cultural racism in the curriculum, or negative or stereotyped images of African people in the media risk being marginalized further by the society. This is the complex nature of the power residing at the core of racism.

Neely Fuller (1969) articulated the strong form of one answer to the "what manner of power" question. Fuller contended that, functionally, people of color do not exercise the kind of authority necessary to impose racism. This position has achieved some currency in African-American communities. Frances Welsing ([1970] 1991) agreed with this analysis, asserting that in modern times white supremacy and racism are synonymous. However, many individuals, black and white, still resist what appears to be an apparent notion that racism is wielded most effectively by the powerful.

In functional, not theoretical, terms, the position Fuller and Welsing take is compelling. In most instances, the argument that the power to impose racism is exclusively in the hands of white people holds for institutional and cultural forms. Indeed, Karenga (1982, 204) proposed that racism is the "denial and deformation of the history and humanity of third world people (people of color . . .)." As we will see, modern academic ideas of race are rooted in the slipshod thinking of sixteenth-century European intellectuals. Subsequently, history shows that it has been chiefly white people who have exercised the power that is necessary to deny, because of race, various peoples' expressions of their humanity and potential. This "violent legacy," as Bulhan (1985) pointed out, must be acknowledged when considering the impact of Europeans on the psychological development of people of color. Fanon's (1967) piercing, preparadigmatic statement is germane. "[T]he disaster of the man of color lies in the fact that he was enslaved. The disaster and inhumanity of the White man lie in the fact that somewhere he has killed man" (231). This statement illustrates Fanon's acute awareness of the historical realities that defined power relationships along the color line in the twentieth century. Also, Fanon, in this pithy remark, reminds us of the vast canyon that stands between frustrated resistance and efficacious, oppressive action. The stark difference between the tragedies Fanon described exemplifies the inequality between the power of black and white people to actualize their intentions.

Racism, then, in modern terms, entails sustained, institutionalized violence of a physical or psychological nature. If deemed necessary, those in power impose violence on both levels quite readily (Lindqvist 1996). In the real world, away from theory, the legacy of colonialism and slavery has left people of color the capacity to exercise racism only on the fringes. Racism's most vital manifestation is white supremacy. Indeed, I will employ the terms interchangeably in this text, but in a deliberate fashion. When white supremacy is used as a synonym for racism, we will be addressing institutional and cultural forms of racism. Concerning these forms of racism, the strong form of Welsing's and Fuller's thesis is essentially correct.

The Manichean order

Description

Racism infects multiple levels of society. Racist cultures generate and are supported in turn by social institutions that ultimately impact the perceptual, cognitive, and emotional lives of the individuals living within those cultures. Desmond Tutu (1985) provided an important insight into the impact of racism on the individual. His topic was the primitive manifestation of racism called apartheid. Tutu stated that the ultimate evil is that racism "can make a child of God doubt that he or she is a child of God" (26). Hence, after addressing topics related to racism in institutions, laws, and practices, the psychologist's attention remains riveted on racism's effects on the mind of the oppressed.

The present study is primarily psychological in nature. It is concerned with the cognitive activities and behaviors of individuals. Still, I acknowledge at the outset the complex cultural and institutional pillars that support racism. These supporting structures will continue to be a central focus. This is not to diminish any estimation of the impact racism has on the individual. I am concerned with racism on the societal level because I wish to avoid underestimating and misunderstanding its impact at the level of the individual. If unsuccessful at the level of the person, that is, if racist institutions fail to have an impact on the cognitive processes of the individual, those institutions will, over time, become threatened. There is then a rather symbiotic relationship between the institutions that support racism and the cognitive impact of these institutions at the level of the individual.

The total expression of modern racism creates a *Manichean* universe in which the oppressed are doomed to live out their lives. In his discussion of racism and psychopathology, Fanon (1967) used the term *Manichean* to describe the world of the colonized. In fact, the adherents of the teachings of Manicheaus in the third century A.D. saw an inherent conflict between light and darkness. The impact of this dualistic philosophy on Europe seems to be quite profound. The Manicheans conceived of blackness and things associated with it as evil. Whiteness, or light, became associated with good. It is not difficult to see how the Manichean order manifests itself along racial lines. People of African descent become associated with evil and inferiority. We come to see Caucasians as superior and inherently good.

The Manichean analogy is quite apt for describing the real conditions that racial oppression generates. Bulhan (1985) gave a stimulating account of the two levels of the ecology of the colonial situation. Philosophically speaking, the Manichean order means that "division is based not on reciprocal affirmations, but rather in irreconcilable opposites cast in to good versus evil, beautiful versus ugly, intelligent versus stupid . . ." (140). This philosophical reality has its counterparts in the daily grind of the oppressed. The oppressor lives where "houses are spacious and grand. The streets are brightly lit, the trees are well manicured and litter seldom seen. . . . There is, on the other hand, the ghetto in which the oppressed live on top of each other in dilapidated tenement houses, hovels and shacks. The streets, if they are paved, are rough and full of pot holes" (141).

The real conditions have their counterpart in the cognitive domain. Fanon (1967) explored the manner in which a Manichean ordering of the world has influenced semantics. Semantics is the study of the way in which language expresses meaning. In his words, African people endure a world where their color exists in associations with "blackness, darkness, shadow, shades, night, the labyrinths of the earth, abysmal depths, blacken someone's reputation; and on the other side, the bright look of innocence, the White dove of peace, magical, heavenly light" (189). The lexicon comes to reflect the racism

15

in the culture. Thus the Manichean order tends to permeate the entire phenomenological field of the oppressed. The saturation persists, from the physical environment through to one of the basic elements of thought itself, that is, the language.

St. Clair Drake (1987) cautioned against making invalid inferences based on cultural symbolic systems. He conceded that in many societies, cultural symbols polarize good and evil into distinct light and dark, or even black and white, hemispheres. However, he warned that we should not assume that in these societies conflicts between black and white people are inherent and universal. He designated Fanon and others "modern Manicheans." Drake pointed out that the error made by these writers involved accepting an assumption prematurely. The assumption is that where societies dichotomize cultural symbols along black and white lines, social reality within these groups will follow a similar cleavage. That is, the modern Manicheans, according to Drake, propose that there is an inherent link between universal manifestations of social and behavioral events and cultural symbols. Drake urged that those who employ the Manichean analogy be more deliberate. We should grant the notion that Manichean symbolism is associated with Manichean racial oppression the status of a hypothesis and not accept it as dogma.

On the one hand, with these cautions, Drake raises very complicated issues about the relationship between language and thought. Arguments that language determines thought (Whorf 1956) are extreme. Certainly, linguistic processes, especially the structure of meaning in a language, influence profoundly the manner in which we think about the world around us. I think that Drake is partially correct, however. We do not know the extent to which symbols influence our actions in any particular instance. We cannot be sure of this influence, even in the case where we can reduce symbols to language. Therefore, it is best that scholars phrase the possibility as a hypothesis. On the other hand, to expect that within a racist system, social forces will partition all facets of human endeavors and social relationships universally along Manichean lines is indeed asking too much of the analogy. The contours of human affairs and human cultures are rich. They preclude the existence of a perfect fit between the Manichean symbolic system and the social or physical conditions in the real world. Yes, there are instances in racist societies where whites will be attracted physically to blacks. Indeed, members within racist cultures will attribute certain positive characteristics to African people. However, notwithstanding Drake's criticisms, I find the term Manichean useful in characterizing general but not universal manifestations of mental, social, and physical realities that coexist with racism. Therefore, the term is used in this book in the adjective form. It is reasonably descriptive of the social environment and the cognitive structures of some of the oppressed.

Regions of impact

Racism affects three distinct domains of the cognitive activity of its victims. First, it influences the formation of beliefs about the efficacy and competence of human beings as a function of their race. Second, racist information influences standards of beauty and body image; that is, one's general preferences for physical features. Finally, the manner in which culture and history are viewed is vulnerable to influences from the Manichean world. I will describe each of these in turn.

Conceptually, dependency and doubt are distant cousins. However, in a Manichean universe they reside in the same house. The victim of racism learns to associate competent and effective behavior with the white world. Those living under white supremacy learn that "to get the job done right," one must enlist a white person to do it. The prevailing racist ideology is that ultimate authority should rest in white hands; otherwise, chaos will inevitably result. It was essential for the colonizer or the enslaver to inculcate this rather perverted logic into the minds of the oppressed. Those with power compelled the enslaved and colonized to believe that ultimate governance was vested, by a kind of divine decree, in the hands of the oppressor. Supreme earthly authority is white. By extension in the modern world, of course, the best doctor, the most competent lawyer, the most erudite professor, the most efficient accountant, the most thorough electrician, and the fairest merchant are all white. At least, they are not black. What is more important, they possess these superlative qualities because they are free of blackness.

Clearly, the Manichean system induces the oppressed to depend on the highly competent and skilled Caucasian. Doubt about their own racial or collective capacity for competent action solidifies as the dependency on whites grows. Du Bois (1903) wrote a lyrical dedication to the great educator Alexander Crummel. In it, Du Bois warned that one of the most crippling psychological consequences of racism is that black people begin to doubt their own competence. "[T]he temptation of Doubt. How he hated it, and stormed at it furiously! 'Of course they are capable,' he cried; 'of course they can learn and strive and achieve–' and 'Of course,' added the temptation softly, 'they do nothing of the sort' " (358–9). It is remarkable how these words and those of Bishop Tutu, mentioned above, agree so completely about the nature of doubt within a racist system. Tutu uttered his statement some eighty years after Du Bois wrote this passage.

This facet of Manichean thought strikes at the heart of a fundamental cultural presumption. A nation of people presumes that they are able to oversee their own survival, growth, and development. Notions are widespread under white supremacy that intellectual and behavioral proficiency is scarce in African people. The cause is a biogenetic "fact of blackness." The oppressed risk internalizing these notions in a cognitive area that we will designate the competence/ efficacy region. Manichean ideas in the competence/efficacy region pave the way for the oppressed to suffer not only the psychological but also the political consequences of racism.

Racist ideology has made much of facial features and other physical characteristics of the people of the earth. Historically, Europeans have ridiculed and deprecated the physical characteristics of African people. Listen to Thomas Jefferson's reflections on the body image question.

> The first difference which strikes us is that of color. Whether the black of the negro resides in the reticular membrane between the skin and scarf-skin, or in the scarf-skin itself, whether it proceeds from the color of the blood, the color of the bile, or from that of some other secretion, the difference is fixed in nature and is as real as if its seat and cause were better known to us. And is this difference of no importance? Is it not the foundation of a greater or less share of beauty in the two races? Are not the fine mixtures of red and White, the expressions of every passion by greater or less suffusions of color in the one, preferable to that eternal monotony, which reigns in the countenances, the immovable veil of black which covers the emotions of the other race? ([1861] 1964, 133).

Jefferson is a spokesman for the Manichean order. Many considered him an enlightened individual in his day. Even today, for some, he remains a hero. Plainly, an aesthetic emerged where the physical characteristics of the European, especially the skin color, facial features, and hair texture, were exalted. The physical counterparts of the African came to be viewed as ugly at best and often as evil and foreboding. In modern times, the aesthetic is less strident. Now, African people have hair, noses, eyes, and skin color that seem to be in need of some measure of "fixing." Technological manipulations that involve heat, chemicals, and surgery can effect these alterations. Racially mixed individuals, "blessed" with the features or an approximation of the features of Europeans, are allowed to approach the throne of beauty. Fate has bestowed on them a partial genetic fix.

A discussion of the body image question within present day Manichean thought is deceptively simple. Aesthetics intertwine with the matter of physical and sexual attractiveness. In addition, in the case of modern racist culture in the United States, the society is both sexist and sexual in nature. Consequently, the manner in which symbols and models of attractiveness and beauty are translated into reality differs between black men and black women. Over the past fifty years, black men have virtually punched and kicked in the door to the very lucrative sports market in the United States. Especially during the second half of this century, owners of teams found it impossible to continue to deny black men participation in several moneymaking sports entertainment businesses. Owners and managers first grudgingly allowed and then actively sought black athletes. Several factors caused this to occur. Morality and altruism played a minor role. The more compelling causes centered around the peculiar and profound nature of the economic gain associated with winning in sports. Inevitably, black male sport folk heroes came to have an enduring place in the consciousness of the U.S. public. They received a great deal of public exposure. In addition, they often performed remarkable athletic feats. Many became marketable commodities because they were associated with superior performance or with winning on the field or court. Physical prowess led some members of the general public to regard these men as attractive, regardless of the extent to which their features approximated the European standard. These black men spanned the skin color spectrum. Their facial features and body types have varied.

Some may wish to claim that, essentially, the black male athlete muscled, leaped, shot, and ran his way out of the confines of the body image dictates of the Manichean order. This is doubtful. Though seen as physically attractive or alluring, at best, it is more likely that the white public perceives these men no differently than Europeans viewed the "noble savages" at the time of Columbus (Sale 1990). Certainly, for the larger society they have emerged as exotics. In some instances, the general society sees them as possessing "animal magnetism." The white public considers them exceptional or exceptions to the laws of Manichean symbolism. Still, when considered on the grand scale, the alluring black athlete is no more than a mere curiosity.

19

And though several of these individuals have forced their moment on the stage of popular culture, it is a mistake to conclude that the standards of aesthetic judgment have been liberalized. They continue to be set in line with power relationships in the society. Without their athletic prowess or the financial means afforded by that prowess, these individuals would go unnoticed in the realm of aesthetics. The greater the extent to which they retain African physical features, the greater the likelihood they would be ignored aesthetically.

Similarly, the beauty, grace, and regal bearing of women of African descent simply could not be ignored in the world of fashion. The African woman displays a goddess-like gait and presence. The world could no more deny her a place on the modeling concourse than it could exclude the African man from a place in the world of sport. The gifts, in both instances, were too apparent. Designers have stumbled over themselves in an effort to hang their clothes on the stately frame of black women. Juxtaposed with the current attraction to black women in the fashion world is the sordid history of sexual exploitation of black women by European men. Bell hooks (1992), in an essay on the image of black female sexuality, made this paradox more comprehensible. The fascination with the body of black women in European culture and the equating of black women with sexual freedom are part of the long history of objectification of black female sexuality; hooks shows no comfort with the modern image of black women whose beauty in the fashion world is often "constructed not innate or inherent" (72). Those in the fashion world strive to reshape black beauty so that certain of its features will approximate white standards. Hooks is equally critical of the image of the female "sexual savage" (68) that business people use to sell records and movies, arguing that the image offers no resistance to the thrust of the racist history of the slave auction block.

Concerning body image, the exigencies of racism have been especially harsh and violent to black women. I think it necessary to press this point. Who has counted the number of full lips that have been ridiculed? How many of our darker sisters have been scorned by ignorant men of the same hue? What algorithm can estimate the number of hairs that are tortured by frying, dyeing, and chemical treatments? These tragedies occur ultimately because a racist aesthetic has not been authentically and persistently challenged. Insults that are finally rooted in the Manichean values related to body image have inflicted an inestimable number of wounds on the collective soul of black women. Fortunately, a burgeoning corpus of literature by black women describing this unique experience is beginning to make a scholarly mark (Guy-Sheftall, 1995; Evans 1984; Busby 1992). Still, a set of serious psychological studies of the compromised physical image and symbol of black women within white supremacy is long overdue. Certainly a rich literary tradition has prepared the way for these behavioral studies.

On the one hand, the subject of body image is a trivial matter when considered within the total life and death context of white supremacy. In some respects it is a tired topic, perhaps more appropriate for discussion in the most mundane of the tabloids and on the television talk shows. But on the other hand, we find that in modern societies, two matters related to body image are far from insignificant. The first is the virtual deluge of racist information that the popular culture transmits about body image. The second is the reality that African people often develop a mind-set that will accommodate the racist information about body image. Both the information and the mind-set may prove to be more than minor determinants of many facets of black people's psychological well-being and behavior. This is the case for several reasons.

First, especially in the West, there is a virtual obsession with surface, apparent, physical beauty. Hence, it is quite likely that values related to body image influence one's concept of self and self-esteem. Indeed, several traditional measures of self-concept include items that assess physical dimensions of self. These include ratings of one's physical appearance, physical competence, and physical attributes (Marsh 1990). A second sociocultural dynamic that makes body image an important cause of behavior in modern societies is the advanced level of commercialism that serves as the economic appendage of this obsession with the physical. Advertising and marketing directed toward the black community in the United States is wary of the body image issue. Dates (1990) described the oscillations in the physical features of black models in the popular magazine *Ebony*. Black models with Caucasian features gave way to a more representative sampling of African-American physical types in the 1970s. However, featuring the gamut of African people fell out of vogue quickly. According to Dates, by the 1980s "the pendulum had again swung in the other direction" (426). Obviously, clever business people are mindful that the physical appearance of product representatives buoys the interest of consumers in their goods. Further, working in concert with the racist underpinnings of the culture, businesses sell hair and skin products by convincing consumers they must alter some aspect of their physical appearance to bring it in line with the European standard. It would be deeply immoral and a brutal affront if African people spent one nickel to change their physical appearance to approximate the features of Europeans. The sad fact is that African people in the United States spend millions of dollars yearly trying to modify African hair, noses, and skin tones.

The body image component of Manichean thought is significant to the human personality, even beyond its relationship to self-concept. The standards that one uses to evaluate human physical characteristics emerge early. Parents and the media are the first influences. Commercial industries reinforce these standards for their own economic gain. The standards by which we judge our own beauty and that of others become an enduring, almost trait-like part of our personality. Consequently, it is very difficult and painful to question or reject these deep-seated preferences. People often see them as highly personal. Even when the preferences obviously reflect racist ideology, individuals will tend to view them as universal, congenital, or genetic. Otherwise enlightened African individuals who celebrate their "blackness" in political and cultural contexts cling to manifestations of negative body image.

Another instance of the impact of negative body image lies in a much more sensitive behavioral domain. Beauty standards influence, to some extent, our selection of mates. Physical attractiveness must play some role in this process. How do we explain to young black students the selection of white mates by many black leaders and scholars around the world? Often, students are initially excited by the written works or actions of these individuals. Later, they become perplexed when they learn of this aspect of their personal lives. On the one hand, the answer is quite simple. No one is compelled to give the world an explanation of his or her selection of a life partner and helpmate. This is a deeply personal matter. On the other hand, too often, outstanding African intellectual men parrot the lame lines mouthed by those in the entertainment and sports areas for the failure to turn to black women. "I couldn't find a black woman on my level," "love knows no color," or "when I look at her I don't see color." The fact is that Manichean ideas of beauty do not die easily, and they are at work in many aspects of our personal lives.

From a clinical perspective, the lesson is clear. When a person of African descent rejects the Manichean view of body image, there is no automatic assurance that all is well in the personality. However, rejection of European standards of beauty is evidence that a person of African descent has waged a valiant and probably protracted struggle against an onslaught of messages from a racist, highly organized, and sophisticated commercial enterprise. These forces persistently disparage non-European physical characteristics. The clinician would view positively the fact that one has engaged in such a struggle. It is a sign that the patient is committed to the process of healing a mind beset by Manichean ideas. It is likely that those who deal successfully with values centered around racist body image will be able to grapple with other facets of racist ideology. Conversely, waging a confrontation with white supremacy on a political or scholarly level provides no assurance a person has corrected the body image component.

Finally, the Manichean order reinterprets, diminishes, or destroys the historical and cultural memory of the oppressed. As Europe made its rise on the world stage, it tended to deny the history of African people and trivialize African culture. In a subsequent section, I present a short discussion of the factors that fueled the attack on African culture and history. In modern times, black scholars around the world find themselves plowing through a morass of remnants of historical evidence, artifacts, and papers. Their task is to reconstruct an accurate history and thus a proper posture toward elements of African culture (Chinweizu, 1987; Van Sertima 1994). This work includes some of the most important and indeed controversial activities in which those within the humanities are currently engaged. It is not an exaggeration to state that African behavioral scientists who are oblivious of these efforts are courting disaster. The work of the progressive historians will benefit behavioral scientists and the clients they may treat.

History and culture provide the launching pad from which an individual and a people propel themselves into the future. When a people internalize distortions and derogatory evaluations of their history and culture, their movement into the future founders, and their continued existence as a distinct people is at risk. This is precisely what occurs in the Manichean context. The accepted scholarly authorities write continental African history and even more localized renderings of the history of African people in the diaspora as footnotes to European history (see Karenga 1982). With rare exceptions, they are written from a white perspective, that is, through the eyes and the mind of a European or a Euro-American. Similarly, African culture is viewed through white eyes. African music and art are primitive. African social structures are seen in much the same light. Only the West can have democracy. That democracy that Chancellor Williams (1974) found among Africans is not authentic. In the United States, a truly classical music called jazz has struggled for survival as an art form. Many of the important innovators of African descent have had obscure and tragic lives.

Cultural racism, described by Jones (1972), targets the cognitive areas of oppressed people that include culture and history. Indeed, vain, brazen, and brash media, often in the name of commercialism, inculcate and reinforce Manichean body image. Also, scholarly books and papers shape and promote the destruction of oppressed people's views of their historical and cultural fabrics. Consequently, the books and courses that distort the history and culture of African peoples do so, in modern times, in a subtle, cloaked fashion. This is in contrast to the often obvious advertisements and images that encourage negative body image in African people. Racism masquerades as scholarly discourse and exchange. It becomes a plodding, erudite attempt to "discover truth." Concessions are made on minor points. However, the forces of cultural racism are firmly established, and the oppressed continue to be taught to see their own culture and history as inferior to that of Europe. Patient reformist scholars wait for a paradigmatic shift that can never arrive on its own power.

Table 1 summarizes the three regions affected by racism. The table lists, for each region, a primary and secondary source of the information. This information leads to the development of Manichean thinking in each area. These modes of inculcation are discussed in detail in chapter 3.

TABLE 1. Sources of Racist Thinking and Their Regions of Mental Impact

Cognitive Region	Primary Mode of Transmission	Secondary Mode of Transmission
Competence/Efficacy	Reality (decontextualized)	Formal education
Body image	Popular culture	Formal education
Cultural/Historical	Formal education	Popular culture

The origins of racism

Chancellor Williams (1974) and Aye Kwei Armah (1979), the former a historian and the latter a novelist, presented perspectives on the holocaust experienced by African people. This catastrophe was protracted; it included the East and West African slave trades. The writings of these two authors bear one remarkable similarity. Both discussed the events occurring on the African continent and within the African mind before the arrival of Arabs and Europeans. (Armah's terms are more descriptive; he speaks of events that took place before the "predators and destroyers.") To be sure, their formulations are complex and identify many reasons for the disaster. Their descriptions of causal events and psychological processes are not identical. For example, Williams surmised that climatic changes were among the central factors that weakened African societies and made them ripe for invasion. Armah tends to make much less of the impediments natural forces generated. Instead, he focuses primarily on the weakness in African societies that resulted from neglecting and abandoning time-honored cultural traditions. It is on this point that the novelist and the historian agree. Africans strayed from traditional mores and cultural practices. This led to internal psychological and political disarray and sometimes to collusion with invading forces. Indeed, some Africans fought, and fight, valiantly against tyranny from foreign elements and their surrogates. Still, history is a strident reminder that Africans failed to unify and mobilize in a decisive fashion in the face of invading Arabs and Europeans. The failure to repel these menaces has had cataclysmic consequences for African people and for the world.

Armah and Williams wrote in an expansive, often lyrical fashion. They provided glimpses into the ethos of African people. Their insights into "the way" bring into focus the ancient, awesome historical and cultural legacy of Africa. Both writers reveal an Africa that was fiercely democratic and committed to generative, spiritual values. At the outset, Armah openly challenges the reader to explore this legacy. "What has been cast abroad is not a thousandth of our history, even if its quality were truth. The people called our people are not the hundredth of our people" (2). Williams is equally clear in his challenge: "But the Black historian, member of a race under perpetual siege and fighting an almost invisible war for survival, dare not follow in these footsteps of the master. . . . The task of critical analysis and interpretation should begin. What were our strengths in the past? In what respects were we most vulnerable? Where did we go wrong?" (22–23). Indeed, African history, from the pens of individuals who challenge colonial lies and mythology, reveals itself to be rich and complex. The recent tragic moments are points and short segments on a very long temporal line (see Van Sertima 1994; Davidson 1991; Diop 1991; Du Bois 1947).

Additionally, and of equal importance, the analyses of Williams and Armah provide a window into the nature of the resistance that African people mounted in the face of the invasions: "and this their descendants must know and remember with pride: The Black resistance to White domination covered over 5,000 years" (C. Williams 1974, 316). We should not cringe from the fact of the matter. Black educators should require every African child, on the continent and in the diaspora, to demonstrate an understanding of the perspective and particular insights of Armah and Williams. Every child should know what these writers have said about the ethos of African people before the invasions, the forces that predisposed the holocaust of their people, and the nature of the struggle that Africans waged, even in a weakened state. Ultimately, the mental health of children depends on this understanding. A growing number of works show that if African history includes stories of individuals who colluded and collaborated with oppressive forces, it is also replete with stories of those who committed their lives to eradicating destructive forces (Davidson 1992; Lewis 1987).

The discarded and forgotten history of African people that a cadre of historians is exploring has universal implications. It is not much more than a naive and futile whimper to suggest that all who seek knowledge of the human spirit examine the pages of the human struggle. In a world free of the Manichean order, a reality distant from our day, such a request might be viable. However, presently, and for this study of the manner in which racism plays itself out in the lives of African people, I will follow the lead of the historian and the novelist. I will remember the rich, complex nature of African culture and history as we examine the fabric of racist forces. This will assist us in gauging the profound impact of white supremacy on the African world. Similarly, I will remain mindful of the nature of the resistance that continually influenced the forms and contours of racism. This history remains in the forefront of our thinking for these more immediate reasons, rather than for the universal importance of this history to the human family.

The study of the psychological impact of white supremacy requires that a second and more obvious historical question be addressed. A set of historical forces in Europe shaped and refined the terror that Europeans would unleash on inhabitants of the rest of the world. For our study of racism to be properly grounded, we must have some general appreciation of the nature of these events and circumstances. Previously, we argued that writers enrich their examinations of the impact of racism on African people when they consider the situation in Africa before and during the early moments of the invasions. Here I am arguing that it is equally important to examine the scene in Europe at the time of this crucial collision.

The lay person who listens at the door as historians debate their subject matter tends to form a conclusion that perhaps is inescapable. Historians are excellent detectives who dredge up an almost endless array of evidence and obscure facts. However, when they interpret the details of even large events, history becomes a highly subjective and uncertain scholarly exercise. In fact, no one can definitively paint the details of the picture describing Africa before the holocaust and Europe in the fifteenth century. Scholars and writers will debate the nuances of many events and the interpretation of these happenings perhaps forever. Historians continue to revise and refine both the African and European stories. I am less than a novice, a member of the untutored class with respect to the discipline. I will attempt to remain on reasonably safe ground by using a broad brush to paint five historical strokes. These broad swipes describe Europe at the time it assumed an aggressive posture toward the outside world. This is the period when Europe initiated exploitative contacts with Africans. The five general themes converged to shape the behavior of Europeans toward people outside of Europe. Therefore, they constitute the underpinnings of the encounters Europeans would have with people of color in general and with Africans in particular.

First, Europe in the fourteenth and fifteenth centuries, for a vast portion of its population, was far from a pleasant place to live out one's life. Robinson (1985) is instructive on this point. He noted that famine, disease, war, and rebellion were the order of the day. These catastrophes were "decimating the populations of the cities and countryside alike, disrupting trade, collapsing industry and agricultural production, leveling as it were, the bulk of the most developed regions of western European bourgeois activity" (17).

Sale (1990) described a fifteenth-century Europe in many of the same terms. He emphasized the terribly violent nature of Europe during this period. The violence that saturated societies existed on the level of petty criminals and highwaymen and continued to the "sanctioned violence"—part of the criminal justice system that was cruel and voyeuristic in nature (32). At another level, feudal conflicts between landowners were rampant. Meanwhile, the church sponsored the Inquisition. Finally, there existed the ever-present national wars between European states. Nature, with its infectious microorganisms, combined with the multilevel violence humans had generated. Sickness and plague loomed as invisible agents of premature death. Together, these forces produced a calamitous scene during this period.

Hatfield, Cacioppo, and Rapson (1994), in their discussion of emotional contagion, painted a rather bleak picture of the emotional tenor of the times in Europe before the 1700s. Their book discusses the manner in which emotional states seem to be passed from one person to another. It is not a history text, although the third author is a professor of history. The authors picture Europe prior to the eighteenth century as a land void of kindness and saturated with individuals whose emotions were rude and remote. They allow that not all historians agree with this portrait of the emotional state of Europeans at that time, although many contemporary sources indicate that negative emotions were pervasive. The "contagion seemed plentiful enough when it came to rougher and wilder emotions of fear, anger and hatred" (119). In general, the description of preindustrial Europe that Hatfield, Cacioppo, and Rapson (1994) extracted from the historical record is consistent with that of Sale and Robinson. Of the source of the depressive state of the European mind they remark: "The development of kindness in human life was inhibited by the ghastly conditions under which most humans labored before the coming of the Industrial Revolution—conditions that led to early death, nearly constant misery and a dark view of earthly existence" (Hatfield, Cacioppo, and Rapson 1994, 117).

Expansionism is the second general historical process that gripped Europe at the time of first contact with Africans. Expansion, or what Sale calls the "Columbian legacy," was, in part, an outgrowth of the unbearable conditions that existed in Europe. On the one hand, expansion was an avenue of escape, a kind of geographical solution to existing social chaos. On the other hand, expansion held the promise of facilitating economic recovery in Europe. Expansion opened new markets and provided new products. Sadly, as the world, especially the African world, would experience firsthand, expansion identified new sources of labor (E. Williams 1964).

The third broad historical statement is a bit more cryptic than the first two. Robinson (1985) wrote a compelling and detailed study of the radical tradition of black intellectual response to European advances. He argued that racism had its genesis in the interactions *among* European people. Indeed, Europe had an impressive history of war between distinct peoples. In his study, Robinson refused to limit the conceptualization of racialism to the ordering of relationships between Europeans and non-Europeans. In the sixteenth century, according to his thesis, war was central to the economy of many European states. As we have seen, the social order in this century was extremely violent. Robinson links a portion of this violence to the efforts of a middle class to establish its position in the social framework. Poorer classes, as well as foreign mercenaries, constituted standing armies for European governments. Also, nations commonly used foreign labor reserves in the nonmilitary economy as dock workers, field laborers, and domestic servants.

The crux of the argument Robinson advanced is that the military and nonmilitary economies of Europe had incorporated sizable segments of disenfranchised Europeans. The societies never intended to make these ostracized groups part of the emerging privileged class. Therefore, one born a member of the excluded caste could expect to participate at best marginally in the social and economic commerce of the society. That is, "racism" of sorts was at the core of the exclusion and exploitation of certain groups of people during this period. More powerful segments of the society assigned individuals to a permanent inferior status on the basis of the accident of belonging to a particular group at birth. Regarding the consequences of this practice, Robinson's words are frank: "The racialism and its permutations persisted, rooted not in a particular era, but in the civilization itself" (29).

The fourth theme treats the matter of religion. It should be viewed in combination with the first three, that is, extremely harsh conditions in Europe, a drive for expansionism, and the tendency toward "racial thinking." Religion and religious ideology and mythology are common to all of humanity. But the verdict of history seems to be that religion and its trappings exerted a peculiar influence on the mind of the European.

Looking at folklore and mythology, we can construct some of the fabric of a people's culture. In saying this, I confess to being under the influence of Sterling Stuckey, who has been especially attentive to folklore in his studies of African-American culture (1987). A strange religious myth haunted Europe for centuries. This myth provides an excellent insight into how religion would fit into the tragic drama that was to take place between Europe and the rest of the world. It shows us how religion functioned in the European mind. Finally, this myth provides a valuable lead as one searches for the factors that caused Europe's exploitation of others. The myth is the tale of Prester John.

The legend of Prester John appeared in twelfth-century Europe. As the story went, a Christian society flourished outside Europe. Some sources placed it in Ethiopia (Atvares [1540] 1961). Others anticipated that explorers would find the mysterious kingdom in the Far East (Boase 1971; Rowling 1968). In this kingdom, the corruption that beset contemporary Europe did not exist. People in the kingdom lived out the Christian ideal. Europeans came to believe that the kingdom would be an ally against infidels and that its ruler, Prester John, was poised to join forces with his Christian kith in Europe.

Robinson (1985) maintained that the myth had internal and external functions. Internally, Prester John came to set a standard by which the ordinary Christians in Europe would measure themselves. In fact, many would become obsessed with the standards set by this mythical kingdom. Devout Christians in Europe would gauge each failure and every corruption against the Prester John empire. Conversely, the external function of the myth was to provide the lens through which Europeans would view the lands beyond their continent. In the newly found lands where explorers failed to find the patient, vigilant Prester John, Europeans would deem the inhabitants' behaviors deviations from the standard set by the myth. Ultimately, non-European lands would lose their authenticity in European eyes. They would not exist on independent terms, as entities with their own preexisting purpose and organization. Rather, the "discovered" would be seen in terms of the myth and for their failure to be, quite literally, the subject of that myth.

Ultimately, scholars will list religion and the accompanying zeal with which it is actualized in the European framework among the major factors that would fuel Europe's conquest of many lands. Furthermore, religion and attendant mythology evidently had a profound impact on the shaping of the fatal encounters between Europe and the external world. Certainly Europe had invaded other lands and had been invaded by other lands in the name of religion. However, the mythology of Prester John provided a "stew" in which the dichotomous Manichean European view of the world would steep. At one pole of the dichotomy, other lands had the possibility of being glorious and worthy. If they embodied the characteristics of Prester John, Christian Europe would honor them accordingly. However, if Prester John did not reside in these lands and if the populations were people of color, Europeans might see the inhabitants at best as infidels or perhaps noble savages. But more often, as Sale (1990) shows, they would conclude that these people were savage beasts.

The historical record is remarkably clear on the fifth and final historical theme. An emerging European academic stratum provided the expanding political and economic forces an intellectual foundation for white supremacy (see Lindqvist 1996). Evidence supporting this theme is not difficult to find. Martin Bernal, who produced two important volumes related to the origins of ancient Greece, touched on the theme (Bernal 1987, 1991). These volumes argued that Afroasiatic cultures had extensive influences on the development of Greece. Their publication immediately stirred controversy in academic circles. The details of his argument and the supporting evidence he provided will be the stuff of scholarly exchanges for years to come. His argument is multifaceted and complicated. The evidence shows that there was extensive intellectual contact between the advanced African world and the Greeks. However, the question of interest is why European scholarship engaged in an intellectual about-face regarding the stature and influence of the more ancient African world. In a twisted sense of the word, this is the psychodynamic issue.

Occasionally, it is necessary to remind even the educated individual that Egypt, geographically speaking, is part of Africa. Du Bois (1947, 98) and later Diop (1974) and Bernal, might impose an additional shock to one's intellectual framework. These writers argued that, culturally speaking, Egypt was essentially African. Accordingly, when we speak of Egypt we are talking about an African country. Like other African countries it has suffered invasions and violations.

Bernal (1987) proposed that until the eighteenth and nineteenth centuries, European scholars taught that Egypt, not Greece, was historically the preeminent seat of knowledge. The deprecation of Egyptian thought and the denial of its influence on Greece coincided with the rise of white supremacy in Europe. Of course, it is understandable that Christian and Egyptian traditions had often experienced periods of contention and conflict. However, according to Bernal, this tension reached a peak in 1690. In that year, Isaac Newton published the *Chronology of Ancient Kingdoms Amended.* This text denied the claims of Egyptian antiquity and argued for the primacy of the Israelites. This position was more consistent with Judeo-Christian thinking. In fact, Christianity and a cadre of scholars formed an alliance and promoted Greece as a society detached from and devoid of Egyptian influences.

Indeed, an expansionistic Europe would crush many peoples of color on the earth. It would have been convenient for these exploitative actions to have an intellectual foundation. Still, it would be incorrect to suggest that the need for an intellectual tradition consistent with white supremacy was the only force leading to the denial of the contributions of the Nile Valley to Greek and European thought. To some extent, the denial of ancient Nile Valley influences stemmed from an emerging intellectual tendency to celebrate progress. To wit, intellectuals maintained that however important the ancient world had been in initiating academic disciplines, these advances were being nourished and made to flourish in Europe (Bernal 1987, 188). Ultimately, this spontaneous Eurocentrism would work in concert with the more vulgar racial proclamations that were to emanate from academic institutions.

The culmination of the academic world's contributions to Europe's headlong charge into a doctrine of white supremacy rests in several eighteenth-century treatises on race. Bernal (1987) listed several important race theorists at the University of Göttingen. Meiners in 1781–82 and J. F. Blumenbach in 1775, the latter who promoted the academic theory of zeitgeist, provided papers that were harmonious with the exploitative tenor of the times. Subjugation of the darker peoples of the world was, by that time, in full swing. These papers equated darker-skinned people with a lower status on the great chain of being.

Gould (1994) contrasted Blumenbach's *De Generis Humani Variete Nativa* with the 1758 *Systema Naturae*, written by Carolus Linnaeus. Blumenbach presented *De Generis* first as a dissertation in 1775. Later he published it in several editions. The later editions of Blumenbach's paper recognized five races of humans. Linnaeus cleaved humanity into fourths. Gould noted that where Linnaeus ascribed particular characteristics to each race, Blumenbach tended to rank-order the races. That is, Linnaeus described European races as cheerful and muscular, Asians as sad and stiff, Native Americans as easily angered and upright, and Africans as sluggish and relaxed. However, Blumenbach maintained that Caucasians represented the pinnacle of the species. For him, the other races departed from this, the most beautiful and the original form, because of environmental conditions. Gould (1994) argued that Blumenbach's purpose in his racial ranking was not to actively promote racial thinking. He sees Blumenbach as "largely passively recording the social views of his time. But ideas have consequences, whatever the motives or intentions of their promoters" (67). Clearly, by 1795, when the third edition of *De Generis* was published, the academic world was quite comfortable with the notion that the finest human qualities belong to the race called Caucasian and was equally comfortable with the notion that the lowest form of humanity was the African.

Wilhelm Wundt (1916) presented an analysis of the nature of human beings that contains elements of fairness when non-European peoples are viewed. Wundt and Harvard's William James are considered the fathers of modern psychology. In the main, Wundt's *Folk Psychology* extended and supported the notions of the primacy of white culture and the "primitive" nature of many black cultures. Wundt, a dedicated empiricist, does not try to deny that members of the ethnic groups in Africa that he designates "primitive" show sophisticated intellectual activities. Within their environments, Wundt admits, they evidence high levels of intellectual and moral behavior. However, calling the minds of these people primitive is essentially consistent with the treatises of the Göttingen schools. He views the thinking of the diminutive peoples of central Africa as restricted to the "concrete," after what is obviously a cursory study of their use of language. Rather than explore how the ethnic groups engage in abstractions, Wundt advanced the conclusion that they do not engage in extrapolation or thinking beyond the building of associations between one sensory event and another. Wundt's study in some ways is interesting and painstaking. Nevertheless, it stands as an excellent example of how interpretations based on a fair and proper utilization of empirical methods run the risk of being influenced by the racist tradition that runs deep in the veins of European academia.

This brief excursion into the disturbing and sordid past was not meant to quench the thirst of the serious student of history. Instead, with the five general historical arguments in mind, we can glean three important lessons. All three are quite germane to the psychological inquiry into racism. The first is that orthodox psychologists are a self-serving, ahistorical lot. The record is clear that Euroamerican psychology finds its roots in the deeply racist and violent traditions of European scholarship and European conquest. The majority of living psychologists seem to have at best a dim appreciation of these traditions and their insidious impact on the field. Robert Guthrie's (1976) *Even the Rat Was White* has been available to a generation of students. Bulhan (1985) and, more recently, Nobles (1986) provided additional reflections on the impact of white supremacy on the activities of the young science of psychology. Nevertheless, when overt, crass, and virulent forms of racism appear in mainstream psychological journals, psychologists are jolted and embarrassed. The articles published a few years ago by Rushton (1989), Miller (1993), and Rushton and Ankney (1993) are excellent examples. In fact, these publications are but extensions of a grand, racist scholarly tradition. As we have seen, this tradition emerged to support and justify the destructive conduct of a belligerent and beleaguered Europe. Those who know the discipline's history will express no surprise when sometimes vulgar, usually subtle racism surfaces in psychological journals. That psychology is historically linked to racism astonishes novices and professionals in the field. This is a symptom of what Bulhan aptly termed "the amnesia of Euroamerican psychology" (37).

The second lesson is related to the first. Bulhan's summation of the implications of the sordid history of Europe and of Western psychology was characteristically frank. His words remind us to be critical when using psychology to understand oppression. "The effort of exploring the psychology of oppression requires that we begin by at least sketching the history that determined the nature of social existence, the boundaries of individual biographies and the direction the discipline took" (37). Psychology, the very discipline that would provide the tools for the analysis, is itself an extension of a racist intellectual tradition. A failure to engage in the historical analysis, even the cursory kind just presented, leaves the inquisitor peering at the problem through an unfocused and tarnished lens. In the United States, the field of psychology has shown itself an impotent and pathetic player when addressing matters related to race and racism. In most instances, the field has come up short when it has attempted to conduct research, develop tests, or generate therapies that might anticipate or mitigate the effects of racism. For the most part, within the discipline, racism conceptually has become synonymous with prejudice. Psychologists deal with racism at the level of individual pathology. I submit that psychology's failures are an outgrowth of the ahistorical strategy used in studying racism. The failings stem from the refusal to recognize how racism affects preparadigmatic as well as paradigmatic questions in the field. The second lesson: employ this discipline with great care when analyzing racism.

The final lesson is most sobering. A reasonably careful reading of history throws caution flags in the face of anyone concerned with the psychological impact of racism. Racism unleashes forces that saturate each and every nook and cranny of human social existence. This is evident wherever Europeans and their descendants control the lives of people of African descent. The historical analysis reduces the likelihood that we will underestimate the dimensions and depth of racism. This analysis makes two points that speak to the gravity of racism. First, deep-seated structural problems in Europe fueled the aggressive posture Europeans assumed toward the rest of the world. Second, even before racist ideology as we know it today was codified, Europeans, through war, their economy, and their religious mythology, were prone to racist thinking. The disease of white supremacy is both chronic and pervasive. Harold Cruse (1987), in his complex book *Plural versus Equal,* called attention to the prophetic words journalist and organizer T. Thomas Fortune spoke in 1890. Fortune warned that mitigating the effects of slavery and analyzing the dimensions and effects of racism would in no form or fashion amount to "child's play." The lesson of history is that the "best intelligence of the race" will be needed to come to grips with its metastasis and to heal its deleterious effects.

This brief look at history is not intended to lead to a conclusion that the formal discipline of psychology is useless in studying racism. Psychology suffers from a criminally racist past, but so do other disciplines in the humanities, natural sciences, and social sciences. Each has its own bloody stick. Rather, the historical excursion demands that we gird properly for the task at hand. Robinson (1985) is probably correct. Europeans were inclined to engage in racism cognitively and behaviorally before coming across mass populations of Africans and other people of color throughout the world. Since the voyages of Columbus, social systems, institutions, and systems of thought have been constructed to support the order of white supremacy. That is to say, the very cultural fabric has become racist. That fabric is at least five centuries old. It is deadly folly to pursue psychology's prescription of addressing racism by measuring a prejudicial attitude here or tinkering with a twisted psychological state of mind there. Undoubtedly, white supremacy is a deep-seated cultural dynamic. Concerning the matter of racism, this is what history says to psychology.

he question of motivation

Rational but driven, technologically developing but doggedly pessimistic, pious but desperate, European man explored the world in the fifteenth and sixteenth centuries. These men would bring a new kind of devastation to the world in general. They would disrupt the lives of the people of the African continent fundamentally. Chinua Achebe's phrase was most appropriate; things, indeed, would "fall apart." The magnitude of that destruction was like none ever known in human history. The cost in terms of human lives is inestimable even if viewed in terms of the West African slave trade alone (Inikori and Engerman 1994). The magnitude of the loss of knowledge and the disruption of the growth of African culture is unthinkable. In a very real sense, this human devastation continues to this moment. In like manner, the havoc wreaked on the physical environment and on animal and plant life that followed in the wake of European expansion persists (Day 1981; Sale 1990).

Psychologists are often pressed to consider the very unsettling matter of motivation. The motivational issue is nettlesome because it asks the difficult question "why" (see Weiner 1992). One of the expressed purposes of the psychology is to explain and understand the forces that produce behavior. Applied to the phenomenon of white supremacy, the motivational question becomes, "What is the cause and source of racism?" Expressed more starkly, this query reads, "Why did Europeans find it necessary or expedient to 'kill man' (Fanon 1967) on such a mass scale?"

One can phrase the issue in a more precise and heuristic fashion when applying it to the situation of people of African descent. Indeed, the whole planet suffered under European expansions: animal, plant, soil, water, and air. Did Africans get in the way of a blindly destructive sequence of forces and events? Was this simply the worst instance in human history of being in the wrong place at the wrong time? If so, we can understand the motivation behind white supremacy by isolating factors in the mind of the European. But the reality is probably more complex. We have to proceed from an interactional perspective. That is, we must consider the possibility that there was something peculiar about African people that fanned the flames of destructive fires in the European heart. This is to propose that something beyond the need for labor and the African's capacity to work shaped the contours of racism. This conceptualization of the motivational issue suggests that, regarding the application of white supremacy to African people, there may have been a peculiar motivational dynamic at work. The prospect is most intriguing.

Two classes of theories address the motivational questions. *Material theories* tend to see African labor as the sole or at least the primary attraction for European expansion. African people served as one form of fodder for a burgeoning capitalistic system. Nothing in particular, save the capacity to survive the harsh physical requirements of the plantation system, qualified Africans for the treatment they were to receive. Europeans would perceive as weak and vulnerable any people who were unable to deter their thrust. They would merit treatment similar to that meted out to the Africans. They would have been enlisted in like service for the same purposes.

The second class of motivational theories proposes that deep within the European mind or nested within the interaction between Europeans and Africans is a peculiar psychological process. Anyone can be greedy or, for that matter, desperate. The *psychological theories* maintain that more than a universal human motivational dynamic was at work here. I will describe two psychological theories, though many forms have been advanced. These theories differ in several respects. Differences will include the extent to which the theory links the "peculiar psychological process" to biological and cultural dispositions and processes.

A final caution is necessary before discussing motivation. As we noted earlier, psychologists phrase and answer the motivational question in general terms. We must make very broad statements when addressing the reasons behind the exploitation of one people by another. Naturally, these generalizations miss their mark when applied to particular, selected individuals. Not all whites were in collusion with the various facets of racism. If there is one known fact in psychology, it is that people differ one from another with respect to their personalities and their behaviors. This may be the one consistent finding.

Our discussion of motivation, at certain points, may seem to fly in the face of this principle of individual differences. The reader should remember that I advance this motivational discussion in terms of major outcomes of the movements of people against people. In the language of psychological methods, the motivational issue generates a discussion of main effects and interactions and not of intersubject variability. The statements are not an accurate measure of all people. Indeed, the fact is that not all Europeans helped build the structure of white supremacy that exists today. Some avoided being placed under the sway of the forces that generated and sustained it. The actions of these individuals are only marginally relevant to our discussion of motivation. This discussion of motivation, and, indeed, this entire study of racism, is necessary because the mission of those well-meaning enlightened white souls was frustrated. Those who opposed the motives and actions of their countrymen as the evil-doers shaped and formed racism did not prevail against the violence that was to be visited on a significant portion of humanity. Perhaps they could not have prevailed—thus the need for this discussion.

Racism as capitalism's handmaid

Capitalism and Slavery, by Eric Williams (1964), provides the bedrock of the material hypothesis of racism. Most colleges in the Western Hemisphere do not require students to read this short, scholarly text as part of their liberal education. Williams reminds us that slavery provided early capitalism with centuries of wageless labor. "Negro labor [was] cheapest and best. . . . [Planters] would have gone to the moon if necessary for labor. Africa was nearer than the moon. . . ." (20). The average, college-educated individual in the United States might find this statement mildly offensive. Similarly, the liberally educated Westerner might recoil at Williams's assertion that this slavery served one real master, capitalism. Capitalism and slavery gave some the opportunity to accrue inordinate wealth. At the same time, this not-so-dynamic duo ensured that a portion of the population would remain poor. Sterling Brown's words from the poem "Strong Men" come to mind, reminding us that slavery gave only "a few gentlemen ease."

However, after reading Williams (1964), one is inclined to conclude that *greed* was the motivating force behind the European enslavement of Africans. Curiously, the protestations from the liberally educated citizen of the United States are likely to stop when one posits the greed hypothesis. Sheepishly, the graduates of most academies might concede to Dr. Williams that racist thought, practice, institutions, and cultures are an outgrowth of attempts to rationalize slavery. In fact, Western thinking has been liberalized to the point that it views racially biased thinking and ideology, at least crass forms of it, as anachronisms. Racist epithets and themes belong to that peculiar period of slavery during which that all-too-human of flaws, greed, simply ran amok. Indeed, under capitalism, greed becomes the intense drive to acquire wealth regardless of the cost to other humans. The proposition that greed was crucial as a determining force of racism is not difficult for mainstream America to swallow. Modern capitalistic societies view moderate levels of greed with ambivalence at worst, and often with admiration. The proposition that the motivating force behind racism was greed is likely to find a sympathetic ear in many quarters of educated America.

E. Williams's (1964) view was that "slavery was not born of racism: rather, racism was a consequence of slavery" (7). The reason for slavery was economic, not racial. "It had to do not with the color of the laborer but with the cheapness of the labor" (19). Williams's view of the relationship between capitalism and slavery is not an unsupported one. Others (Sale 1990; Robinson 1985) have thought of racism as a servant to a larger dynamic in European history, that is, a push toward the domination of the world and its resources. Racist institutions and practices buttressed the exploitative drive. The ideology would hold, quite coolly, that some people had to die, that others must work without compensation, and that all would have to come to see the white man as a superior being. Racist mythology rationalized certain untidy and inhumane facets of the conquest of people. Doesn't the ideology of racism suggest that "primitives" would fare better laboring, even slaving, within a modern society than wallowing in uncivilized acts in their own societies? And at the bottom of it all lay avarice, coupled with the terrible conditions that existed in Europe, fueling a desire to control the natural resources and lives of others.

From this motivational perspective, behaviorally speaking, racism is a conceptual category that describes a particular form of oppressive, inhuman action. Racist thinking is a convenient fiction, rationalizing exploitation. Nevertheless, in the view of those who support the material theories, the real player on the stage, the basic motivational force, remains the desire for the riches and resources of other lands. These fueled and motivated the destruction of humans based on race.

Of course, the matter of developing a racist mythology capable of belittling the culture and history of African people was not as simple as modern racism would lead one to believe. Premodern history, during which African history and particularly Nile Valley history had been viewed in strictly different terms, militated against racist mythology. Racists had to discredit what Bernal (1987) calls the "Ancient model's" claim that African civilization had predated and influenced Greek culture. In Robinson's (1985) phrasing, a "transmutation" of African people was mandatory. "The construct of Negro, unlike the terms African, Moor or 'Ethiope' suggested no situatedness in time, history, or space that is ethno or politico geography. The Negro had no civilization, no cultures, no religions, no history, no place and finally no humanity which might command

39

consideration" (105). Interestingly, the processes of denying African humanity and the construction of the Negro open the possibility for other kinds of motivational theses. These perspectives contend that there is an energizing dynamic behind the need to renounce the human capacity of African people in particular that functions partially independently of greed.

Psychological theories

The material motivational theory may tend to elicit grudging agreement from the average educated American. However, the first of the psychological theories that we will consider elicits anything but accord. In fact, no theory of racism tends to inflame and polarize discussions of the motivational question more than the theory known as the "Cress theory of color confrontation." Frances Cress Welsing ([1970] 1991), a psychiatrist, developed this alternative to the "greed" hypothesis. The most significant break with the greed hypothesis is its proposal that the principal dynamic involved in racism is not a motive shared in varying degrees by all humans. Rather, for Welsing, the motivating force for racism is the Caucasian race's effort to avoid genetic "annihilation" by people of color. It is the exploration of this "intrapsychic" dynamic that is perhaps the ultimate source of the spirited and often heated discussion this theory generates.

Welsing proposed that Caucasians represent a "genetically recessive" variation of the human species, born with reduced levels of the skin pigment melanin. She argued that whites are recessive in the sense that other "races" have significantly greater amounts of melanin. In Welsing's view, the offspring of the mating of a "recessive" white with a person of color will be an individual with melanin or one capable of producing an offspring with melanin. Accordingly, Welsing held that people of color threaten the physical existence of Europeans. Obviously, Africans, the people of color with the highest concentration of melanin, would constitute the most formidable threat.

The theory is quite specific. It proposes that the massive destruction of people of color during the early colonial period and the lynching and castration of black males in the United States were strategies whose ends included avoiding genetic destruction. In modern times, the strategies may take subtler forms, though the end is the same. They include the dominant society's attempts to control the population of people of color by promoting Western-style family planning strategies. Another modern survival strategy for white people is the jailing of a large segment of the black male population during their years of highest reproductive activity.

On the other hand, Welsing observed that white people often engage in behaviors that suggest that they are envious or jealous of people of color. In Freudian terms, a reaction formation develops in the white psyche. It takes the form of a repressed wish to produce offspring of color. The heinous expression of this wish was the sexual exploitation of women of color. Welsing argues that white men sexually desired and raped African women partly because of an unconscious wish to produce offspring of color. The reaction formation may take milder forms, including that of white people engaging in the common, dangerous practice of getting suntanned and the tendency of white culture to appropriate black music, dance, and linguistic styles.

Welsing's theory disturbs even progressive black psychologists. Cross (1991) made a veiled reference to theories like the Cress theory, calling them vulgar (222). Bulhan (1985) referred to it as reactive. Indeed, the theory shares several common elements with Freudian theory. One fundamental problem in the Cress theory is endemic to Freudian analyses of behavior. Freud proposed that the motivational forces fueling behavior are unconscious. Only extraordinary procedures can render these forces accessible to the conscious mind. These procedures include dream analysis and the interpretation of symptomatic acts, for example, slips of the tongue and showing up late for meetings. Usually, these procedures are employed during the course of psychotherapy. However, it is difficult to be certain that one has identified the correct unconscious dynamic or motive. Again, the motive is not available to the consciousness of the actor, so he or she cannot help us verify its role. It is risky to infer that we have isolated the correct dynamic or motive simply because the actor becomes uncomfortable when we mention it. Many white people may wince when told they have an unconscious fear of genetic annihilation. However, we should not take this as proof that, if this dynamic exists, it motivates racism. Their discomfort could result from innumerable causes.

In the case of the Cress theory, one can usually interpret the evidence used to support the existence of the motive in an alternative fashion. For example, Welsing discusses the savage practice of castrating black men that was often part of the lynchings that occurred in the United States in the first part of this century. She interpreted this act as a direct and unconscious attack on the "ultimate" source of threat to white people from the man of color (the organ of reproduction). Despite the internal consistency of this formulation, it involves conceptual leaps that are difficult to justify and leaves open alternative explanations that are highly competitive. For example, one might propose that the motive that led white men to castrate black men was quite conscious; that they removed the genitals to enhance the sense of fear and terror that they hoped lynchings would engender in the minds of the oppressed.

Still, white people engage in practices within the Manichean order whose motivation seems to go beyond simple greed. Caucasians' behaviors toward people of African descent cover the spectrum of comportment. The conduct ranges from unspeakable cruelty to actions that suggest a curious, persistent attraction, if not outright fascination. Indeed, some of the men during the enslavement period who professed great disdain for African people felt a strong physical attraction to African women. Welsing has been persistent, consistent, and courageous in her efforts to examine the motivation behind complex behaviors and events that occur as the practices of white supremacy evolve. The response of the academic community to her efforts has been to cast her in the role of pariah. Even many black behavioral scientists view her work as an embarrassment. However, had black scientists examined her propositions forthrightly, we would be much clearer today on the utility, validity, and explanatory limits of the Cress theory.

The ignoble treatment Dr. Welsing and the Cress theory have received at the hands of those who study racism is, at best, unfair. Her thesis regarding a sense of inferiority among whites is not radically different from motivational theories advanced by white scholars. For example, Welsing's theory shares some common elements with Mannoni's propositions of the 1940s and 1950s, later published in book form (Mannoni 1964). He proposed that a misanthropy among Europeans was an outgrowth of a sense of inferiority. Mannoni was simply less explicit about the source of this inferiority. Welsing located the source in a fear of genetic eradication. (Additionally, Mannoni argued that African people have a dependency complex, that is, a need to be colonized. Fanon (1967) debunks this notion in *Black Skin White Masks.*)

There are other examples of white scholars' using Freudian principles to uncover motivational forces behind racism. In a volume on the symbolic role of animals in American life, Mechling (1987) discussed a common theme in folklore and popular art of alligators striking terror in the hearts of black people. His explanation of this motif constitutes a motivational theory of white racist behavior. Mechling proposed that the alligator provided white males with a symbolic mechanism for castrating the black male. In addition, Joel Kovel's (1971) study concluded that racism was rooted in the intra-psychic conflicts Freud outlined. These conflicts change within the individual across the stages of psychosexual development. However, biological factors are ultimately responsible for the stages, and all humans experience them. Racism is a complicated set of fantasies and practices that provides Europeans with a mode for dealing with in-trapsychic conflicts. It is a peculiar way of dealing with universal conflicts, according to Kovel. Obviously, the work of Kovel and Mechling shows that it is not difficult to locate the progeny of Mannoni's Freudian approach to racism. In this respect, Welsing would seem to be on safe ground in advancing her theory.

Could it be that mainstream scholars renounce the Cress theory because a person of African descent is providing essentially a Freudian analysis of racism? Indeed, in 1927 a young E. Franklin Frazier, the noted African-American sociologist, spirited himself out of Atlanta with a .45-caliber pistol tucked in his belt. A paper he had written went beyond discussing the practice of racism in the South as a form of psychopathology. Frazier's paper considered racist behavior in terms of Freudian defense mechanisms. Friends concluded Frazier's life was in jeopardy because of this paper (Platt 1991). Also, history shows that Francis Sumner, a pioneering African-American psychologist, found his graduate career threatened in 1917. Sumner wrote what Guthrie (1976) called "an interesting psychoanalytic analysis of racism" (180). The treatise took the form of a letter to the editor of the local paper in Worcester, Massachusetts. Local and regional postal authorities called his analysis treasonous and threatened to put him on a list of government enemies. Perhaps history is repeating itself in the case of Dr. Welsing. White society, in and outside of the academy, is not uncomfortable with the psychoanalytic study of racism and colonialism. Rather, judging from the experiences of Frazier, Sumner, and Welsing, analyses of racism that employ Freudian principles appear to be off limits for black scholars.

The second psychological theory is rooted in the work of a physical anthropologist. Cheikh Anta Diop left his homeland, Senegal, in 1946, bound for Paris and graduate school. Brilliant and at the same time "proud, stubborn and independent," Diop would present three doctoral dissertations in the area of African history and culture before taking the terminal degree (Van Sertima 1986). His life would be a somewhat lonely intellectual sojourn. Other scholars ignored or scorned many of his ideas relating to the African nature of Egyptian society and culture. It is some consolation that toward the end of his life, a group of African researchers in the diaspora made Dr. Diop aware of the impact of his work. In a conference held at Morehouse College, they showed him the extent to which his ideas and work had reawakened and enlightened many people of African descent in the United States (Finch 1986, 29). However, of interest to us is his brief excursion into the question of motivation. He sketched a theory that describes the cause of the protracted conflict between Europe and Africa.

Diop's studies of Nile Valley civilizations required that he study early European history and culture. Hence, his knowledge of the literature and the language of both worlds was extensive. The political and social relationships that existed between Europe and Africa also intrigued Diop, who explored the source of these relationships. Diop (1974) proposed that at the core of the destructive encounters between Europeans and Africans were differences in "national character." We can discern national character, according to Diop, through an analysis of linguistic, psychological, and literary elements of a given people and their culture. Additionally, he had anticipated the current emerging consensus on the origins of humans. Converging evidence supports the hypothesis that *Homo sapiens* developed in Africa and then migrated to distal settings (Finch 1986). The source of this evidence includes molecular genetic studies (see Paabo 1995; Dorit, Akashi, and Gilbert 1995) and studies of the tools produced by early humans in Zaire around ninety thousand years ago (Yellen et al. 1995). However, Diop maintained that centuries of separation in distinct geographical cradles fashioned two distinct national characters. The discrete regions differed radically with respect to the exigencies of the physical environments. The demands inherent in the environment made all the difference. The cultural trajectories developed along different lines; therefore, the modal personalities for each group are distinguishable.

The northern cradle, located on the Eurasian steppes, was a harsh, erratic, and unforgiving setting. Cold winters, truncated growing seasons, and thin soils forced the inhabitants to lead nomadic lives. Possessions and status became important. A materialistic, patriarchal social system emerged. The people viewed their god as harsh and judgmental and became pessimistic and individualistic.

In the Nile Valley, the second of the two cradles, the climate was hospitable and nature was predictable. The seasonal flooding of the

Nile provided fertile soil for planting. Consequently, in Diop's thinking, the national character that emerged in this region was sedentary and more optimistic. A matriarchal social system nurtured this communal and highly spiritual personality. Diop (1974) contended that an understanding of the differences in character between Europeans and Africans is essential to identifying the source of the conflicts between them.

If Diop is even only partially correct, one is hard-pressed to imagine a more explosive and fatal confluence of historical forces. The opportunities for misperceptions between the two groups are virtually endless. Dreams of gold and the acquisition of other valuable materials that would ease the uncertainty and pain of their existence were the obsessions of Europeans. They were somber, driven, and warlike. They must have cut a strange if not pathetic profile in the mind of the African. The African, at home with, perhaps preoccupied with, the unseen, was more open, spontaneous, and effusive. Africans must have appeared equally odd and, perhaps more important, weak and vulnerable when viewed through the perceptual system of the European.

To be sure, the perception of differences does not provide sufficient ground for inferring a motivation dynamic for racist exploitation. But to understand Diop's position, we have to attend to the exact nature of the differences that were perceived. The northern cradle produced human beings bent on conquest. The pinnacle of their science entailed the perfection of weapons of destruction. Humans from the northern cradle were quick to conclude that novel entities, animate or inanimate, were hostile and foreign until proven otherwise. The African was physically unlike the European and different with respect to temperament. Conquest was not the central theme of existence, and so African military technology was less advanced. Not only would it be quite easy for the European to perceive the African as primitive but the African and the resources of Africa would also be seen as "there for the taking." Conversely, the African would be slow to become distrustful of the newcomers. Africans would not anticipate the Europeans' proclivity to look directly at the face of human beings and see something other than humanity. This fatal and fateful mix would motivate the development of oppression from the European sense of superiority and white supremacy.

Finally, Diop clearly supposed that the ethos and world views of Africans and Europeans energized the clash. Europeans surmised that the African was superstitious, earthy, and unrestrained. The rational and repressed European despised these traits. Of all the people they encountered in their expansion, Europeans found it most important to distance themselves from the Africans. Psychologically and philosophically, the African represented the clearly negative region of the Manichean universe that was already partially constructed in the European mind (Robinson 1985).

Diop's theory is viewed best as a set of hypotheses. It is more interesting for the questions it raises than for the ones it answers. His thinking sends us scurrying in search of historical, linguistic, and literary themes that have emerged from the two cradles. After reviewing the hypotheses, the psychologist interested in culture and personality must confront the status of assessment technology: Are there personality measures with sufficient sensitivity in both groups to identify the differences Diop anticipated? Finally, a portion of the lasting value of these hypotheses is in the general questions they raise regarding the manner in which the physical environment shapes culture and, by extension, personality.

Marimba Ani (1994) structured her discussion of the motivation behind racism around a meticulous critique of European culture. Ani extended Diop's observations on the national character of the residents of the northern cradle. However, Diop's comments are moderate and circumscribed next to Ani's detailed explication of core tendencies for control in European culture. If Ani's conclusions are valid, the world in general and Africa in particular had good reason to be alarmed when Europeans gained power on the world stage. Ani argued that European culture is unique in its consuming drive for control and power. The energizing force of European culture requires an "other" as a kind of fuel. The "other" becomes an object and a conduit for the expression of the thrust for power. Ani concludes that racism is "endemic to European culture and . . . the goal of White supremacy, European power over others, [is] the supreme goal of the culture. That is the statement that no other culture can make" (482). In any event, both Diop and Ani challenge scholars to examine core themes in European culture. They conclude that these studies will lead to an understanding of the motivation behind racism.

Motivational synthesis

It is not necessary to dismiss one general class of motivational hypotheses in favor of the other. Both material and psychological theories may have some explanatory power. To be sure, when Europeans set forth on their deadly duty, they came across some Africans ready to meet their challenge blow for blow. The Europeans would call those who resisted "savage beasts" (Sale 1990). Encounters with the defiant ones shaped certain details of the evolving racist mythology. The material hypothesis provides a fascinating and viable explanation of behaviors related to the initial explorations and often physically violent encounters between whites and Africans. This hypothesis provides cogent explanations of the centuries-long use of Africans as a labor force (E. Williams 1964). However, over time, white supremacy etched its details on the historical canvas. As it formed the fine points of cultural deprecation, the contours of racist institutions, and codes of interpersonal racism, the motivational question became more complicated. When we attend to these fine points, the motivation behind racism can best be discerned using both material and psychological theories. The advantage of the psychological theories is that they examine the interactions between the mind or character of the oppressor and particular cultural and physical characteristics of those targeted for oppression. In this respect, Diop's theory, Ani's extension of Diop's theories, and elements of Welsing's thinking provide interesting bases for further study.

onclusion

This chapter wandered through conceptual, historical, and conjectural issues related to racism. We have conceived of racism as a social phenomenon that is protracted and power based. Our focus is its impact on the cognitive structures of the oppressed. The institutional and cultural sources and struts of racism are responsible for its persistence. The less important, individual forms of racism and prejudice that white people express tend to ebb and flow. Indeed, the historical record shows that racism finds its roots deep in the fabric of European society. Violent interactions among Europeans may have predisposed them to racism before large-scale European excursions into Africa. Finally, a theoretical cornucopia providing explanations of the motivation behind racism is available. Scholars from a variety of disciplines have offered theories that are intriguing but fundamentally different. It may be that only as the oppressed dismantle racism will the motivation behind it become clear.

* * * * * * * * *

I am still haunted by the face of the young man holding his press conference before beginning a life sentence for pushing cocaine. I remember that moment when the volley of inane questions from the press finally subsided. The cameras no longer flashed. After what seemed an eternity, the shackled pusher was led away. Did he regret his actions? Did the thought of prison life intimidate him? For my part, I wondered if this individual had any idea what had hit him or, better, what had penetrated his mind. He knew the term "prejudice." But racism, his real foe, had gutted and decapitated his existence without his ever being able to draw a bead on even its most salient manifestations. Power was at issue. His personal influence had allowed him to move a quantity of crack into neighborhoods. When necessary, he could teach a violent lesson to a delinquent employee. However, buttressed by powers a thousand times more formidable than his, racism had ensured that his mind would construe the world in a fashion that would put him on a course toward self-destruction. During this time, racism cloaked its own existence effectively. It is the task of this study to rend the cloak and to examine the pathways and processes in which racism may have an impact on cognitive events.

References

Adler, W. M. 1995. *Land of Opportunity: One Family's Quest for the American Dream in the Age of Crack*. New York: Atlantic Monthly Press.

Ani, M. 1994. *Yurugu: An African-centered Critique of European Cultural Thought and Behavior*. Trenton, N.J.: African World Press.

Armah, A. K. 1979. *Two Thousand Seasons*. Chicago: Third World Press.

Atvares, F. 1961. *The Prestor John of the Indies*. 1540. Reprint, London: Cambridge University Press.

Bernal, M. 1987. *Black Athena: The Afroasiatic Roots of Classical Civilization. Vol. I: The Fabrication of Ancient Greece 1785–1985*. New Brunswick, N.J.: Rutgers University Press.

———. 1991. *Black Athena: The Afroasiatic Roots of Classical Civilization. Vol. II: The Archaeological and Documentary Evidence*. New Brunswick, N.J.: Rutgers University Press.

Boase, T. S. R. 1971. *Kingdoms and Strongholds of the Crusades*. Indianapolis: Bobbs-Merrill.

Bulhan, H. A. 1985. *Frantz Fanon and the Psychology of Oppression*. New York: Plenum.

Busby, M. 1992. *Daughters of Africa: An International Anthology of Words and Writings by Women of African Descent from the Ancient Egyptians to the Present*. New York: Pantheon Books.

Chinweizu. 1987. *Decolonising the African Mind*. Lagos, Nigeria: Pero Press.

Cross, W. E. 1991. *Shades of Black: Diversity in African-American Identity*. Philadelphia: Temple University Press.

Cruse, H. 1987. *Plural but Equal: A Critical Study of Blacks and Minorities and America's Plural Society*. New York: William Morrow.

Dates, J. L. 1990. Advertising. In *Split Image: African Americans in the Mass Media*, ed. J. L. Dates and W. Barlow, 421–55. Washington, D.C.: Howard University Press.

Davidson, B. 1991. *African Civilization Revisited*. Trenton, N.J.: African World Press.

———. 1992. *The Black Man's Burden: Africa and the Curse of the Nation-state*. New York: Time Books.

Day, D. 1981. *The Doomsday Book of Animals*. New York: Viking Press.

Diop, C. A. 1974. *The African Origin of Civilization: Myth or Reality*. Westport, Conn.: Lawrence Hill and Company.

———. 1991. *Civilization or Barbarism: An Authentic Anthropology*. New York: Lawrence Hill Books.

Dorit, R. L., Akashi, H., and Gilbert, W. 1995. Absence of Polymorphism at the ZFY Locus on Human Y Chromosome. *Science* 268: 1183, 1185.

Drake, S. 1987. *Black Folk Here and There*. Vol. *I*. Los Angeles: Center for Afro-American Studies.

Du Bois, W. E. B. 1903. *The Souls of Black Folk: Essays and Sketches*. Chicago: A. C. McClurg.

———. 1947. *The World and Africa: An Inquiry into the Part Which Africa Has Played in World History*. New York: Viking.

Evans, M. 1984. *Black Women Writers (1950–1980): A Critical Evaluation*. Garden City, N.Y.: Anchor Press/Doubleday.

Fanon, F. 1967. *Black Skin White Masks*. New York: Grove Press.

Finch, C. S. 1986. Meeting the Pharaoh: Conversations with Cheikh Anta Diop. In *Great African Thinkers, Vol. I, Cheikh Anta Diop*, ed. I. Van Sertima, 28–34. New Brunswick, N.J.: Transaction Books.

Freud, S., and Jung, C. G. 1974. *The Freud/Jung Letters*. Edited by W. McGuire. Princeton, N.J.: Princeton University Press.

Fuller, N. 1969. *The United Independent Compensatory Code/System/Concept*. Copyrighted, Library of Congress.

Gould, S. J. 1994. The Geometer of Race. *Discover* 15: 64–69.

Guthrie, R. 1976. *Even the Rat Was White: A Historical View of Psychology*. New York: Harper and Row.

Guy-Sheftall, B. 1995. *Words of Fire: An Anthology of African-American Feminist Thought*. New York: The New Press.

Hatfield, E., Cacioppo, J. T., and Rapson, R. L. 1994. *Emotional Contagion*. New York: Cambridge University Press.

hooks, b. 1992. *Black Looks: Race and Representation*. Boston: South End Press.

Inikori, J. E., and Engerman, S. L. 1994. A Skeptical View of Curtin's and Lovejoy's Calculations. In *The Atlantic Slave Trade*, ed. D. Northrup, 65–66. Lexington, Mass.: D. C. Heath.

Jefferson, T. 1964. *Notes on the State of Virginia.* 1861. Reprint, New York: Harper and Row.

Jones, J. M. 1972. *Prejudice and Racism.* New York: McGraw Hill.

Karenga, M. 1982. *Introduction to Black Studies.* Los Angeles: Kawaida Publications.

Kovel, J. 1971. *White Racism: A Psychohistory.* New York: Vintage.

Lewis, D. L. 1987. *The Race to Fashoda: European Colonialism and African Resistance in the Scramble for Africa.* New York: Weidenfeld and Nicolson.

Lindqvist, S. 1996. *"Exterminate All the Brutes."* New York: The New Press.

Lusane C. 1991. *Pipe Dream Blues: Racism and the War on Drugs.* Boston: South End Press.

Mannoni, O. 1964. *Prospero and Caliban: The Psychology of Colonialism.* Trans. Pamela Powesland. New York: Praeger.

Marsh, H. W. 1990. Confirmatory Factor Analysis of Multitrait Multimethod Data: The Construct Validation of Multidimensional Self-concept Responses. *Journal of Personality* 58: 661–92.

Mechling, J. 1987. The Alligator. In *Symbolic American Wildlife,* ed. A. K. Gillespie and J. Mechling, 90. Knoxville: University of Tennessee Press.

Miller, E. M. 1993. Could r Selection Account for the African Personality and Life Cycle? *Personality and Individual Differences* 15: 665–75.

Nobles, W. W. 1986. *African Psychology: Toward Its Reclamation, Reascension and Revitalization.* Oakland, Calif.: Black Family Institute.

Onwuanibe, R. C. 1983. *A Critique of Revolutionary Humanism: Frantz Fanon.* St. Louis: Warren H. Green.

Paabo, S. 1995. The Y Chromosome and the Origin of All of Us (Men). *Science* 268: 1141–42.

Platt, A. 1991. *E. Franklin Frazier Reconsidered.* New Brunswick, N.J.: Rutgers University Press.

Robinson, C. 1985. *Black Marxism: The History of the Radical Black Tradition.* London: Zed Press.

Rowling, M. 1968. *Everyday Life in Medieval Times.* New York: G. P. Putnam's Sons.

Rushton, J. P. 1989. Race Differences in Sexuality and Their Correlates: Another Look and Physiological Models. *Journal of Research in Personality* 23: 35–54.

Rushton, J. P., and Ankney, C. D. 1993. The Evolutionary Selection of Human Races: A Response to Miller. *Personality and Individual Differences* 15: 677–80.

Sale, K. 1990. *The Conquest of Paradise: Christopher Columbus and the Columbian Legacy.* New York: Knopf.

Semmes, C. E. 1992. *Cultural Hegemony and African-American Development.* Westport, Conn.: Praeger.

Stuckey, S. 1987. *Slave Culture: Nationalist Theory and the Foundations of Black America.* New York: Oxford.

Tutu, D. 1985. The Nobel Laureate and His Message. *New Directions: The Howard University Magazine* 12: 26–29.

Van Sertima, I. 1986. Introduction: Death Shall Not Find Us Thinking That We Die. In *Great African Thinkers, Vol. I, Cheikh Anta Diop*, ed. I. Van Sertima, 7–18. New Brunswick, N.J.: Transaction Books.

———. 1994. Editorial: African Origin of Ancient Egyptian Civilization. In *Egypt: Child of Africa*, ed. I. Van Sertima. New Brunswick, N.J.: Transaction Publishers.

Webb, G. 1998. *Dark Alliance: The CIA, the Contras, and the Crack Cocaine Explosion*. New York: Seven Stories Press.

Weiner, B. 1992. *Human Motivation: Metaphors, Theories and Research*. Newbury Park, Calif.: Sage.

Welsing, F. C. 1991. The Cress Theory of Color-confrontation and Racism (White Supremacy): A Psycho-genetic Theory and World Outlook. 1970. Reprinted in *The Isis Papers: Keys to the Colors*. Chicago: Third World Press.

Whorf, B. L. 1956. Science and Linguistics. In *Language, Thought and Reality: Selected Writings of Benjamin Whorf*, ed. J. B. Carroll, 207–19. Cambridge, Mass.: MIT Press.

Williams, C. 1974. *The Destruction of Black Civilization: Great Issues of a Race from 4500 B.C. to 2000 B.C.* Chicago: Third World Press.

Williams, E. 1964. *Capitalism and Slavery*. London: Andre Deutsch.

Wundt, W. 1916. *Elements of Folk Psychology: Outlines of a Psychological History of the Development of Mankind*. New York: Macmillan.

Yellen, J. E., Brooks, A. S., Cornelissen, E., Mehlman, M. G., and Stewart, K. 1995. A Middle Stone Age Worked Bone Industry from Katanda, Upper Semliki Valley, Zaire. *Science* 268: 553–54.

CHAPTER TWO

Methods of Study

Their eyes tell me I have made a connection. In basic psychology classes, for almost two decades, I have shared with students of African descent a small portion of the piercing insights left to us in the writings of W. E. B. Du Bois and Frantz Fanon. Usually I begin by providing these young people with a brief biography of the two men. Then I sketch a short introduction to the corpus of thought that each produced and left the world. Finally, I show my students how Du Bois and Fanon committed themselves holistically to coming to grips with the forces aligned against people of African descent. Gradually, inevitably, fidgeting stops, papers cease rustling, and the ubiquitous mumbling that drones through large university lecture halls fades.

Before taking my class, these students, mostly freshman generally but not exclusively educated in the United States, are only dimly aware of Du Bois. Most have never heard of Fanon. Hence, a conditioned genuflection that might follow the invoking of the name of Dr. Martin Luther King or, more recently, Malcolm X is not the root of their reaction. In addition, I doubt that intellectual intimidation quiets my students and brings a new level of intensity to their gaze. The glimpse I give them of the work of Du Bois and Fanon is too brief to elicit awe-filled silence from brash and energetic eighteen- and nineteen-year-olds. Rather, I think the light in my students' eyes burns from a sense of admiration. I believe that they appreciate the manner in which each of these men formed his portrait of the conditions of those oppressed by racism.

The writings of Fanon and Du Bois show that both used their formal training in Western empirical methods of discovery and analysis to gain insight into the sources and dimensions of the dehumanization of African people. At the same time, each transcended the conventional paradigms of his discipline to arrive at a deeper understanding of the world of oppression. Gifted with formidable intellects, they struggled to create conceptual frameworks that future scholars would use to depict, with greater accuracy, the forces impinging on Africans around the world. However, they engaged the world with every facet of their being. This constitutes the uniqueness of their contributions. They came to know their worlds by using intellect and affect, soul and spirit. In this holistic manner, they identified and conceptualized their respective realities. Then, each set forth an action agenda designed to address the consequences of being an African in a Manichean reality. The eyes of my students are changed by the unique epistemological posture these two sons of Africa assumed.

Guided by the life lessons of Fanon and Du Bois, this chapter will focus on the matter of epistemology. The purpose is to set forth the methodology we will use in this psychological study of racism. This discussion of methods of knowing enables us to specify the ground rules for evaluating evidence and claims about particular facets of racism and about its psychological effects. Initially, I will consider how black psychologists in the United States have approached the methodology, products, and applications of traditional Western psychology. Then, to provide both depth and breadth to this discussion, I will contrast the ongoing struggle on the African continent to develop an African philosophy with the efforts of the black psychologists in the United States.

Psychology is still a very young discipline in Africa. It is not feasible to contrast black psychology as practiced in the United States with the efforts of continental African psychologists. Nevertheless, the comparisons with African philosophy prove to be interesting and instructive.

Distinct schools of thought have emerged among the psychologists and the philosophers. I will position both the psychological and philosophical schools on continua that represent two orthogonal, that is, uncorrelated, facets of their functioning (see figure 1). The first, the *methodological continuum,* represents the posture the school assumes concerning the accepted methods in one's field. This continuum ranges from conservative to liberal. The more conservative views tolerate only the conventional methodological practices of the discipline. The second we have designated the continuum of *African sensibilities.* I am using the term *sensibilities* in the manner in which Kent (1972) defined it, that is, as a "means of sensing, apprehending; [one's] characteristic emotional, psychic and intellectual response to existence" (17). This continuum reflects the manner in which the adherents of a particular school evaluate the knowledge available to them either from a traditional African experiential base or from the unique vantage point of being on the receiving end of racist oppression. This continuum ranges from open to closed. The approaches that are intolerant of information obtained through African sensibilities are characterized as closed.

At first glance, it would seem that the second continuum is conceptually similar to the first. It appears impossible to be hospitable to traditional methods of an academic discipline and open to African sensibilities at the same time. Indeed, European epistemological bias saturates the methods of most modern academic disciplines. Still, we will see that scholars behave in ways that suggest these continua are independent.

In the subsequent section, we discuss the type and quality of the information and data that Western empiricism generates. We criticize the application of Western empiricism in providing data related to the effects of racism on people of African descent. The "scientific approach," as practiced in the behavioral sciences, is impressive in some respects. However, current practices harbor significant epistemological limitations. Sigmund Koch (1981) argued that psychology as a discipline only occasionally produces work that "may qualify as a science" (268). Koch scorned "ameaningful" thinking within the discipline, where "inquiring action is so rigidly and fully regulated by the rule that in its conception of inquiry it often allows the rules totally to displace their human users" (259). Clearly, we can find stinging criticism of the methods of psychology within the discipline itself.

Du Bois and Fanon conducted their scholarly lives in such a way that they were often able to transcend the limits of rigid Western scientific methods. I will describe instances where they broke with the constraints and conventions of their disciplines in the penultimate

FIGURE 1. Schools of Black Psychology and African
Philosophy Located According to Posture toward Methodology and
African Sensibilities

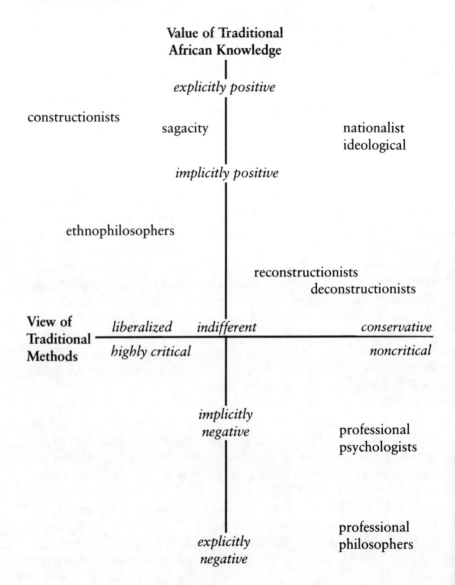

section. This discussion sets the stage for final comments describing the epistemological lens through which this book views the impact of Manichean reality.

Paradigmatic dilemmas in black psychology

Historical notes

Psychologists labor in a discipline that has a relatively short "modern history." In the United States, instructors teach students that in the year 1879, with activities in Wilhelm Wundt's laboratory in Leipzig, psychology became a distinct academic discipline. Some teach that the independent openings of William James's laboratory at Harvard and Wundt's Leipzig laboratory in 1875 signal the beginnings of the field (Crider et al. 1993). The history of people of African descent in the field predates the turn of the century. Leslie Hicks (1988), a black physiological psychologist, argued that the first empirical contribution to the behavioral sciences by an African American was the work of Charles H. Turner (1891). A biologist by training, Turner today would likely be designated either a comparative psychologist or neuroscientist. His studies of animal behavior were seminal in the early years of psychology. Additionally, Turner (1901) produced important statements addressing the role of education in the rebuilding of the African American. Interestingly enough, he called for the industrial training that Booker T. Washington proposed and the liberal arts training that Du Bois advocated. This is not dissimilar to the position Du Bois would take in 1930 (Du Bois 1973). By that time the dust surrounding his controversy with Washington had settled.

The first Ph.D. in psychology granted to an African American occurred when Francis Sumner received the degree from Clark University in 1920. Eventually, Sumner would go on to serve as the first head of a freestanding department of psychology at Howard University. In many historically black institutions, psychology departments amounted to service units for the larger, more dominant departments of education. Guthrie (1976) wrote a very useful history of the early involvement of African Americans in psychology. It is an essential introduction to the work of the first generations of black psychologists. I will relate my own personal contact with two of the earlier African Americans in the field. Guthrie speaks of the first of these individuals, James A. Bayton. He failed to identify the second,

Keturah Whitehurst, though he learned of Dr. Whitehurst's work by the end of the 1970s while visiting Virginia State College. My purpose is to give the reader a feeling for the kind and caliber of individuals who were of African descent and psychologists from the third decade of this century forward.

Sumner's thorough and demanding teaching had a strong influence on James Bayton. For fifty years, until his death in August of 1990, Bayton provided students at Howard University with firsthand recollections of the earliest days of black participation in psychology. Because of the demands placed on the field by World War I, the new discipline was transformed into a science that could be used to solve human problems. Bayton was part of this exciting period. Generations of fledgling psychologists sat at his feet to hear how psychology might address problems as mundane as choosing the most desirable flavor for orange juice to issues as lofty as eliminating racism from society (Bayton 1987). Bayton's love for the discipline never waned. I remember the excitement in his voice whenever he discussed statistical matters. He loved wrestling with old as well as new procedures. Hence, he always found time for the exchange with a student about the most appropriate manner to conceptualize a multifactorial analysis of variance designs. These designs have been a staple in psychological research since the 1930s. Similarly, he relished the opportunity to use path analysis, a statistical technique that did not become popular in psychology until the 1970s. We will discuss Bayton's orientation toward the field in more detail shortly.

South of Washington, D.C., at Virginia State College (later Virginia State University) in Petersburg, Dr. Keturah Whitehurst never let students forget that the history of Western psychology was quite brief. Dr. Whitehurst, who retired in 1977, had been a classmate of Dr. Bayton's at Howard during the 1930s. She obtained her master's degree at Howard in 1934. She prefaced her thesis with a brief expression of appreciation to a young, bright undergraduate named Kenneth B. Clark. Clark had assisted in collecting the data for the master's thesis (Whitehurst 1934). He would become widely known for his "doll studies" of the racial attitudes of black children, which Thurgood Marshall and others included in the *Brown v. Topeka Board of Education* desegregation lawsuit in 1954. In 1970, Clark became the first African-American president of the American Psychological Association. Dr. Whitehurst was the first licensed black clinical psychologist in the state of Virginia. On my first academic job, as an assistant professor at Virginia State, I recall her telling students of the lineage of four generations of psychologists. She traced this line back to the inception of the field. Dr. Whitehurst would explain that Wilhelm Wundt taught Edward Titchner, that Titchner taught E. G. Boring, and that Boring taught Whitehurst. Whitehurst had studied with Boring at Harvard University. She would add, "And now I am teaching you!" Dr. Whitehurst encouraged students to know the young discipline thoroughly and avoid a "creeping specialization" that would give them too narrow a perspective on the field. Bayton shared this sentiment for a generalist approach to the field and against overspecialization. He linked their orientation to the pedagogical philosophy Sumner brought to Howard. The thrust was to train students in the appreciation of all aspects of the new and vibrant discipline.

These early black psychologists, and a host of others described by Guthrie, were consummate professionals. In the main, they were well trained and deeply immersed in the scientific study of behavior. Additionally, many of these pioneers studied the impact of racism on black people. They dedicated their lives to using the discipline to enhance the lives of people of African descent. Dr. Whitehurst would say that the goal was "to use the discipline to do some good for our folks." Wilcox (1971) published a collection of papers that are a reasonable representation of the efforts and orientations of many black psychologists over the first half of the century. Most of the articles in this book are reports of studies where data were obtained from black subjects in the United States. In most of the studies, researchers administered conventional tests and measurements of personality or intellectual functioning to the participants. Nearly all of the articles were reprints that Wilcox took from mainstream journals of psychology or educational psychology. This enthusiastic orientation toward the traditional paradigms and practices in the field would change during the second half of the century.

A cadre of psychologists who viewed the discipline in a more critical fashion than the first group of professionals emerged in the late 1960s (see R. Williams 1974). They began publishing their work in the early 1970s. We can draw a contrast between these generations of psychologists by considering the postures several key players assumed toward methodology. However, it is an oversimplification to designate all psychologists trained before the late 1960s as uncritical of the discipline and all trained afterward as critical. Nothing could be farther from the truth. For example, Keturah Whitehurst, Robert L. Williams (n.d., 1974), Bobby Wright (1975), Reginald Jones (1991), and Edwin Nichols (1976) all received their training prior to the late 1960s. All are known to have offered critical and creative analysis of orthodox psychology. Arguably, this is not the case for far too many of the black psychologists trained during and after the 1970s. A good portion of this generation has swallowed the stale conceptual frameworks, content, and methodological dictums of the field hook, line, and sinker. Still, some sense of the history of the field of black psychology can be provided by looking at some key players chronologically. Considering several biographies might be enlightening.

James Bayton was, in the mode of Paul Robeson, a large man in physique, intellect, and voice. It is very doubtful that any psychologist living or dead, African or of other ethnic background, has trained more students of African descent in graduate statistics and research methods. Leslie Hicks summarized Bayton's view of methodology as a commitment to "do the thing right." Hicks was a student of Bayton's, and since 1968, he has been chair of the psychology department at Howard. Bayton believed the social sciences could achieve objectivity and that psychological methodology was essentially neutral (Bayton 1987). The issue for black psychologists in Bayton's estimation was to pose the right questions. Good use of the scientific method would ensure that we would find the truth.

For the first generation of black psychologists, represented by Bayton, Kenneth Clark, Herman Canady, and others named by Guthrie (1976), the challenge was to secure the time, space, and opportunity to use the fledgling methods and technology of psychology properly. In their estimation, if provided with the operating room, a competent psychologist could find the answers to the psychological problems suffered by black people. Excitement was in the air. Indeed, the newly emerging discipline psychology provided the means and the framework for addressing complex questions related to the causes and cures of many human behavioral problems.

As professionals, these black psychologists viewed the knowledge obtained from their discipline as special and exalted. The value of insights and knowledge gained from experiencing life as an African in America and from the fount of traditional wisdom that is part of the black experience was not directly deprecated by these individuals. On the whole, knowledge obtained outside of this spanking new discipline and its "scientific" methodology was simply out of the question. In their epistemology, one would come to know the world most accurately through the proper application of methods in the field. In figure 1, I have placed the *professional psychologists* in a quadrant representing a conservative posture with respect to methodology. They are, in general, closed to knowledge obtained from African sensibilities or from the perspective of the oppressed.

But as I suggested above, in the late 1960s and early 1970s a contingent of black psychologists who were disillusioned with traditional Western psychology found their voices. Sterling Plumpp (1972) was a graduate student in psychology during this period. His intellectual sojourn amounted to a lonely search for moorings in the field of psychology. In many respects it was emblematic of the search in which a significant number of psychology students of African descent engaged during those contentious years. As Plumpp phrased it, he was concerned that psychology be written from the "rats' point of view." He was not comfortable assuming the controlling posture of the experimental psychologist. Eventually, he would leave graduate school, opting for a career in creative writing over psychology. In his book *Black Rituals*, he asks if black psychologists will morbidly persist in attempts "to squeeze every ounce of value" (84) from white psychology. To Plumpp, the alternative to this rather demeaning enterprise of finding a drop of utility in the old paradigm was to begin the construction of a new psychology sensitive to the culture of black people. As we will see shortly, Plumpp was not alone in questioning and eventually rejecting the content, conceptualizations, and methodology of Western psychology.

Of course, the criticisms voiced by some during this period were more moderate. A. Wade Boykin completed his undergraduate work at Hampton Institute. He went on to train as an experimental psychologist at the University of Michigan in the late 1960s and early 1970s. Boykin (1977, 1991) argued for the retention of empirical methods in the new black psychology. However, according to Boykin, the top-to-bottom analysis of experimental enterprises in black psychology would include a critical look at methodology. Boykin thought that the theories, methods, results, conclusions, and the operationalization of constructions were susceptible to influence by racist thought. He deemed none of the levels of the research process sacrosanct.

There is a qualitative distinction between the positions of the early professionals of Bayton's generation and the critics that emerged en masse in the late 1960s and early 1970s. In the first chapter we argued that there is an independent, radical tradition in the African intellectual response to racism. The tradition has existed since the day the first Africans were kidnapped by Portuguese adventurers (see

Robinson 1985). As Robinson showed, in the beginning this tradition took the form of a bloody resistance to slavery and the development of independent, "marooned" societies and communities.

Later, the thinking of C.L.R. James, Henry Highland Garnett, W. E. B. Du Bois, and others would reflect the radical tradition whose influence would ebb and flow across the decades and centuries. In the late 1960s, this legacy of radical intellectual challenge simply spilled over into the consciousness of academically trained black psychologists. From that point forward, the face of black psychology in the United States changed. The discourse within the field took on a variegated and richer tone. Previously, debate might center around whether a psychological paper or book written about people of African descent was solid science and good psychology. The new black psychologists rephrased and refined the question to read: "Is Western psychology itself, and therefore any book or paper written from its perspective, capable of valid description of the forces influencing the behavior patterns of African people?" The stage was set for the emergence of several new schools of thought in black psychology.

Approaches in black psychology

Curtis Banks edited the *Journal of Black Psychology* between the years 1977 and 1987. As editor during this nascent but vigorous period, he coordinated the handling of the wide variety of manuscripts that a growing legion of black psychologists submitted to the journal. Banks demonstrated a strong penchant for philosophical and paradigmatic discussions. Accordingly, in a presentation at the annual meeting of the Association of Black Psychologists in Denver, Colorado, in 1981, he identified a framework for understanding the modern critical orientations within black psychology. Banks was concerned with the manner in which each of several approaches addressed methodological questions. Again, we will evaluate the position each approach takes to the traditional methods of the discipline. Also, we will estimate the extent to which each approach relies on knowledge generated outside of Western methodological prescriptions. Specifically, we will reveal the status each approach attributes to knowledge emanating from African sensibilities and the sensibilities of the oppressed (see figure 1).

Banks described the *deconstructionists* as strict methodologists in the traditional sense. To some extent, they embrace Western empiricism as much as the first group of professional psychologists. However, their intentions are different. They use the ground rules of traditional science to estimate the quality of the empirical evidence produced in studies of black people. Ironically, they debunk and falsify the claims advanced about black people in the standard journals of the discipline. The criterion is the extent to which these assertions measure up to the standards set forth by the scientific method (see Banks 1982). As deconstructionists go about their work, they examine the logical status of the claims of Western psychology. Subsequently, the deconstructionist inspects all facets of research methodology, including the conceptualization of the problem, operationalization of research constructs, data collection, analyses, and interpretation.

Banks himself was the preeminent deconstructive black psychologist until his untimely death in 1998. He scrutinized the empirical foundations for the commonly held beliefs that African Americans are unable to delay gratification (Ward, Banks, and Wilson 1991); generally expect the control over reinforcers in their lives to reside outside of their immediate influence (Banks et al. 1991); and prefer white dolls to black ones in studies of racial preference (Banks 1976). Additionally, Banks (1992) developed a cogent criticism of comparative paradigms in psychological research. Comparative studies are devoted to ferreting out differences between black and white subjects on measures of psychological dispositions, behavioral performance, and even psychophysiological reactions (see Harrell, Morris, and Rasayon 1996).

The deconstructive black psychologist agrees to play the game in the court of the Western empiricist, evaluating the empirical contentions and declarations of Western psychology according to a conservative interpretation of the rules of traditional methodology. Therefore, in figure 1, I have located the deconstructive approach in a region that represents an openness to traditional methods. To repeat, adherents of the deconstructive school do not criticize traditional methodology. Rather, they use it in a crafty and creative fashion as the principal tool in the process of debunking. A careful reading of Banks's work shows how this is done.

However, how the deconstructionists regard the psychological knowledge base that resides outside of Western psychology is not totally explicit. This is the knowledge that individuals process through African sensibilities from the perspective of the oppressed. Their posture toward this knowledge is best inferred from their scholarly actions. Certainly, the flaws, inconsistencies, and inadequacies of the research the deconstructionists target fuel and direct their efforts.

However, another motivational force is at work as the deconstructionistic black psychologists ply their trade. From the perspective of the victims of white supremacy, the claims made about black people in the trade journals of the profession are often oversimplifications and, in some cases, ludicrous. That is, certain statements appear outrageous not only because the data fail to support them but also to some extent because the experience of the deconstructionist insists that they are false. As a behavioral scientist of African descent, he or she simply knows better.

Ward, Banks, and Wilson (1991) provided a pithy statement before examining the empirical research regarding delay of gratification in people of African descent. They noted that "throughout the long and arduous struggle for freedom and equal opportunity, blacks in this country and abroad have demonstrated persuasively and in very real-life and practical ways their ability to forgo immediate gains of lesser value in favor of more highly prized and distant goals . . ." (167). The source of this particular insight is a sensibility that lies beyond the empirical psychological evidence at hand.

In short, part of the skepticism about the claims of Western psychology stems from the deconstructionist's reliance on African or oppressed sensibilities. Therefore, we cannot conclude, in my estimation, that the deconstructive black psychologist is completely hostile to insights and knowledge gained through sources residing external to Western empirical psychology. To be sure, the deconstructionist may not make use of these in a conscious fashion. The external knowledge may operate as a hidden hand in the deconstructionistic enterprise. The influence of this knowledge base is subtle but certain. Therefore, in figure 1, I have located the deconstructionist as moderate regarding the evaluation of knowledge gained from African sensibilities.

Banks identified a second approach, the *reconstructionistic* orientation in black psychology. Generally speaking, reconstructionists are more hospitable to the constructs and products of Western psychology than deconstructionists are. However, they are less accepting of the activities of Western psychologists than professional psychologists are. Reconstructionists modify what is produced in Western psychology so that its application in black populations is more appropriate. Reconstructionistic approaches share a portion of the critical posture of the deconstructionists. However, their efforts center around the production of a hybrid that incorporates salvageable elements of traditional psychology.

Robert Williams (n.d.), at Washington University in St. Louis, is known internationally for his work on test development. He has developed modified (reconstructed) versions of tests of intelligence and personality and structured them to capture nuances of black cultural life in the United States. In the reconstructionistic mode, Williams's Black Intelligence Test of Cultural Homogeneity and his projective test, Themes Concerning Blacks, do not challenge the construct of intelligence or the practice of intellectual assessment. Further, they leave the concept or custom of projective testing unassailed. The dismissal of either the practice or conceptual foundation of projective and intellectual testing might be the work of the deconstructionist, but it is not the purview of the reconstructionist. The reconstructionists challenge the uncritical application of the traditional psychological product to black populations. However, they implicitly hold that the product itself has sufficient value to warrant modification.

Most reconstructionists view traditional psychological methodology as salvageable. Still, certain facets of the methods of psychology would not escape modification. Boykin's (1991) words reflect this position: "while certain cautions should be exercised, the judicious deployment of experimental psychology can be a useful and worthwhile endeavor" (491). Though methods of inquiry have not escaped unscathed, the focus of the reconstructionists has been largely the content of the psychological enterprise. Therefore in figure 1, I have placed reconstructionism in the area reflecting a moderately hospitable posture toward traditional methods.

The reconstructionists are similar to the deconstructionists in that the origin of the critiques they advance is somewhat obscure. However, a portion of the insight and energy fueling the critical efforts originates in psychological knowledge rooted in African sensibilities. Certainly, the hard evidence often speaks to disastrous outcomes of the willy-nilly application of Western psychology in black populations (Campbell et al. 1996; Williams and Mitchell 1991). However, the reconstructionist senses that the fallibility of the application resides in instruments or procedures that tend to mismeasure black people. That is, the reconstructionist considers an independent knowledge of African people gained from a different source. This knowledge, obtained from the African living in a Manichean system, is the source of the critical insight of the reconstructionists. Indeed, they are tolerant of many central constructs of Western psychology. However, they retain some sense of appreciation of the knowledge obtained through the experience of racism. I have given them a place on the

African sensibilities continuum in figure 1 that reflects their partially open posture. Like the deconstructionists, usually the reconstructionists do not use this African knowledge base in a conscious or explicit manner.

The third approach in black psychology is *constructionistic*. Nobles (1986) traced the beginnings of this approach to an article published in the first volume of the *Journal of Black Psychology* (Clark et al. 1975). Those who identify themselves with the constructionistic school are in agreement with the thrust of that paper, which calls for the development of a new African psychology from an organic, authentically African epistemological and ontological base. The constructionists dismiss the philosophical premises of Western psychology. They reject what they see as a parade of ephemeral concerns, research fads, and bickering schools of thought. They usher out close behind the empirical methods and the tradition of logical positivism that undergird much of psychological inquiry. The constructionists are not comfortable with the notion that all knowledge will be publicly verified or justified by sets of objective facts or data. They suspect that some truths will elude that grand experiment or empirical exercise in data collection.

The strong form of the constructionists' thesis is consistent with the thinking of Molefi Asante (1990), the leading proponent of an Afrocentric approach to the study of African people. Indeed, constructionism in black psychology is an Afrocentric method where "African ideals and values [are placed] at the center of inquiry" (Asante 1990, 5). Wade Nobles (1986) and Na'im Akbar (1979) have presented seminal works in the development of the constructionistic view. The work of progressive historians of African descent including C. A. Diop (1974), J. H. Clarke (1990, 1991), and I. Van Sertima (1983) has influenced the efforts of the constructionists. Asa Hilliard is a leading constructionistic educational psychologist. He has emphasized the importance of Diop's work to the accurate writing of the history of African people (Hilliard 1986). Also, Hilliard sees Diop's historical writings as seminal in the development of constructionistic psychology. In fact, much of Hilliard's work in recent years has centered on examinations of misinformation about history found in public school curricula. In essence, he has studied one of the principal manifestations of cultural racism (Hilliard 1995).

I have located the constructionistic school at the ends of each continuum in figure 1. Constructionists are highly critical of Western methodology. To them, the portrait of human behavior that Western methods generate will be, at best, an insufficient representation of human functioning. Concerning the second continuum, constructionists place a high value on traditional African wisdom. Therefore, African epistemological sensibilities, whether they are culturally based or based on the experience of racist oppression, are deemed essential. In fact, constructionists have expended a great deal of effort uncovering the wisdom and the methods of inquiry of ancient African scholars (Akbar 1985). Developing a system that will allow one to view the world in general and behavioral processes in particular through an African lens is an essential element in this approach. Thus, in figure 1, it is fitting to see the constructionists residing in a far region of the left quadrant. This placement represents a critical posture toward traditional methods and an openness to knowledge gained through an African perspective.

Nobles (1986) provided some stimulating comments on Banks's framework for classifying the activities of black psychologists. He viewed the framework as useful at the present but anticipated that it might be discarded as the field of African psychology matures. Nobles predicted that as the field evolves it will be able to assert an emphasis on a communality of thinking. In a strong conciliatory statement, Nobles maintained that currently "each approach is equally important, complementary and necessary" (87).

Indeed, consensus and conciliation have their places in political and intellectual exchanges. Nobles's comments are valuable in that respect. Still, the distinctions among the three "critical approaches" in black psychology are significant. Additionally, the differences between the critical schools on the one hand and the professional psychologists on the other loom too large to be swept under the rug in the name of conciliation. Teachers must provide guidance to students and initiates in the discipline who must grapple with the issues and disparate critical analyses raised by these approaches. Of course, we should not expect splintered Western psychology to provide any kind of model for handling differences among schools of thought (notwithstanding the efforts of Staats [1981]). However, the retreat to a position of forced conciliation is dishonest.

A more appropriate and fruitful search for a model for handling differences among schools of thought might begin closer to home. The current works of the continental African philosophers are instructive. Fittingly, these philosophers are generating their body of thought from "beneath the veil" (Du Bois 1903) since white supremacy is a worldwide phenomenon. A people on the receiving end of racism are

67

developing the African philosophical intellectual tradition. We will show that continental African philosophers are engaged in intellectual wrangling that has certain implications for the activities of black psychologists. The approaches of continental African philosophers to their discipline, as well as the manner in which they are settling points of contention, are instructive to the black psychologist "in search of a paradigm" (see Bulhan 1985).

Schools of African philosophy

The constructionists introduced black psychologists to the notions of African ontology, epistemology, and cosmology. There are two cogent reasons that black psychologists in the Western hemisphere might wish to come to grips with continental African philosophical principles. First, even under the brutal conditions imposed under the European chattel slavery system, the level of retention of cultural elements by the kidnapped Africans was surprisingly high. These retentions are unmistakable in the Caribbean and in parts of South America. Indeed, they are evident even in North America where the slavery system was especially totalitarian (Holloway 1990; Stuckey 1987). The evidence shows that African people in the Americas have retained elements of an African worldview, and the influence of African cultural motifs is evident in a wide gamut of behavioral patterns. When analyzing the behavior of African people in the West, a psychologist ignorant of these retentions is apt to make erroneous interpretations and invalid attributions of cause.

The second reason to examine the continental African worldview reduces to a matter of simple practicality. One's analysis of behavior is very likely to be improved by considering the traditional African perspective. Behavioral scientists are likely to improve their perceptual and interpretive powers when they broaden their epistemological stance. The Western view of the world and of knowledge is only one among many. This, even basic psychology texts are beginning to acknowledge (see Zimbardo 1992). But as we will see, the weary traveler in search of a more eclectic epistemology finds no easy answers in the writings of the continental African philosophers. Instead, these writings are intriguing because of the substantive questions they raise regarding the African personality, the manner in which the philosophers respond to differences among themselves and critical statements made by other philosophers, and the similarities between their sojourn in search of a paradigm and that of the black psychologists in the United States.

One can discern four schools of thought among the African philosophers. These schools differ along many conceptual lines. However, we will discuss them in terms of the extent to which they use conventional Western philosophical methods (methodological continuum in figure 1). Additionally, we will examine their view of philosophical knowledge that is an outgrowth of African intellectual efforts independent of Western philosophy (African sensibilities continuum). Thus, the treatment of the philosophers will parallel our discussion of the approaches in black psychology. This approach allows us to place each school on the continua in figure 1. Serequeberhan (1991a) compiled a very readable collection of essays in which philosophers from the various schools described their positions. The spirited and rich dialogue in this anthology is the foundation of the following discussion.

The history of the participation of continental Africans in Western philosophy is an interesting one. Wilson Armistead ([1848] 1969) recounted for American readers the strange and fascinating tale of Anton Amo. Born in Guinea, West Africa, in the early eighteenth century, he was taken to Holland, a victim of the slave trade. Although a captive, he was provided educational opportunities. Amo eventually enrolled at Halle University in Saxony. He studied a wide variety of subjects and ultimately earned the doctorate of philosophy. He continued his studies at the University of Wittenberg, where he became active in the development of German philosophy and chair of philosophy at Wittenberg. Upon the death of Duke Anton-Ulrich von Braunschweig, the individual who had originally purchased Amo and allowed him to begin his studies, the African scholar decided to return to his homeland. Records of his life in this final period are sketchy. In 1753 an explorer recounted finding Amo living in an isolated setting with his father and sister. Apparently, Amo knew that his brother was enslaved in South America. But ultimately, his activities during these final years will likely remain shrouded in mystery forever. Scholars assume that his great intellect remained dormant and that he died a recluse. Who would not be reclusive in the face of a vicious commerce in human lives? Still, one wonders. Is it not foolish to surmise that Amo's powerful mind remained motionless once he returned to Africa? It is intriguing to imagine the kinds of reflection in which he must have engaged, the discourses he had with other sages, the possibilities he must have pondered, and the losses he was forced to contemplate.

This early African participation in Western philosophy would not alter one whit the absurd, self-serving, and dehumanizing portrait Western academics would paint of African people. As we saw in the first chapter, the mission of the West was conquest, domination, and exploitation of the human and land resources of Africa. Europe would have to reduce the African to a subhuman status. As Fanon (1967) wrote, "not a new man has come in, but a new kind of man, a new *genus*, why, its a Negro!" (116, emphasis mine). The African could certainly not be the kind of organism that engages in philosophical activities. This "transmuted African" (Robinson 1985) provided the free labor for the expanding of European capitalism (see E. Williams 1964). It was easier for Europeans to rationalize exploitation of the newly synthesized, brutish subhuman organism.

Father Palicids Tempels (1969), in his book *Bantu Philosophy*, presented a picture of the African that differed from the transmuted entity Europeans had used to rationalize colonial exploitation. So liberal was Tempels's view that the francophone African journal *Présence Africane* reprinted the entire manuscript in 1969. Tempels, a Belgian cleric, argued that Africans lived according to a complex philosophy and that this philosophy would influence their attitudes toward Western religion and culture.

African philosophers refer to Tempels's book and work inspired by it as *ethnophilosophy* (Hountondji 1991). John Mbiti's (1970) well-known *African Religions and Philosophies* is part of the ethno-philosophical tradition. Ethnophilosophy maintains that rituals, prac-tices, worldviews, and cultural artifacts of Africans are the markers of their philosophy. A scholarly examination of these allows one to glean the elements of African philosophy.

The ethnophilosophers sought to disprove the Western charge that Africans had no philosophy. Accordingly, Onyewuenyi ([1976] 1991) correctly placed the racist argument that Africans were without phi-losophy in the same camp as those theses that disfigured and distorted the ancient and more recent history of Africa. People of African de-scent in the United States have received the works of the ethnophiloso-phers amiably. Perhaps this favorable reception stems from the fact that this school actively confronts the intellectual dishonesty of many Western scholars. Generations of European writers distorted the rec-ord of African history and cultural achievements. The constructionists among the black psychologists frequently cite Mbiti (1970) and Jahn's *Muntu* (1967) (see Nobles 1986).

On the African continent, the ethnophilosophers have not enjoyed similar adulation. Criticisms have been substantive, methodological, and ideological. Ethnophilosophers have advanced what they consider to be manifestations of African philosophy. Often the substantive criticisms center around the extent to which a particular manifestation is universal or specific to particular ethnic groups. For example, Wiredu (1991) summarized criticisms of the African idea of time described by Mbiti. He argued that descriptors of time vary linguistically across ethnic groups. Thus critics dismiss the naive notions of unanimity across African ethnic promoted by ethnophilosophy. Still, normally, the flexible ethnophilosopher can accommodate substantive criticisms of this type. One might anticipate that there will be exceptions to general formulations. However, the methodological and ideological criticisms are more threatening.

Critics have asserted that African philosophy is not simply participation in African culture (Owomoyela [1987] 1991; Hountondji 1991). African philosophy, in the minds of these critics, includes a reflective element where individuals ponder facets of their own cultural motifs. Tempels and Mbiti implied that African people live out their philosophy without reflecting on it. To Hountondji (1991), the ethnophilosophers distort the definition and method of the philosophical discipline by reducing it to "a collective worldview, an implicit, spontaneous, perhaps even unconscious system of beliefs to which all Africans are supposed to adhere" (117). The destructive myth Hountondji identifies and stringently criticizes here is termed "primitive unanimity." Implicitly, it holds that African societies and people have not reached a cognitive level where reflection can lead to intellectual discourse, challenge, and disagreement.

The ethnophilosophers have allowed themselves a methodological departure. Hountondji (1991) points out that they have synthesized from their observations of the behavior patterns and practices of African people a philosophy that they call African. However, in the process they failed to question the "nature and theoretical status of their own analysis" (119). The philosophy of the cleric, anthropologist, philosopher, or scribe who is examining the practice of a particular ethnic group or nation is not necessarily the philosophy of the people being studied (Hountondji 1991). Implicit in these criticisms is an argument that a different, more authentic African philosophy exists among African people trained in philosophy or, perhaps, among traditional African thinkers. To refer to cultural artifacts and practices as the sole embodiment of African philosophy ignores the more deliberate contemplative activities of true philosophers.

Finally, Tempels's book and, to a degree, the ethnophilosophers in general have been criticized from an ideological perspective. Indeed, Father Tempels sought to liberalize the vulgar Western perspective holding that the African had no philosophy. But his thrust remained colonial. By excavating the structure of the philosophy of Africans, Europe could carry out the task of civilizing or converting "the native" with greater ease and efficiency. In short, Tempels and, to some extent, Mbiti have been criticized for adopting a position that did not challenge the perverted, destructive colonial mission of the West in a forthright fashion (Wamba-dia-Wamba 1991).

Though ethnophilosophy has borne the brunt of criticism from continental African philosophers, as we have said, it has not been without an international impact. Certainly, the work of the ethnophilosophers challenged the thesis that traditional African wisdom and philosophy did not exist. To be sure, their celebration of African knowledge and wisdom is muted since they still viewed Africans as unreflective, unpondering, and spontaneous beings. Accordingly, in figure 1 we have placed ethnophilosophy in the moderately open region on the African sensibilities continuum.

However, the ethnophilosophers broke with traditional practices in the discipline by looking for philosophy in cultural manifestations. The ethnophilosophers were probably not "self-conscious" in this methodological challenge to traditional practices in philosophy. Nevertheless, their actions represent a criticism and expansion of the existing paradigm. Thus we see them as a liberalizing force with respect to the traditional methods of the discipline and have placed them accordingly in figure 1.

A relatively new cadre of *professional philosophers,* formally trained in the discipline, have been among the most vocal critics of ethnophilosophy. Most of these philosophers work on the continent of Africa in university philosophy departments. One would expect that tension might develop between the ideas of these individuals, who have formal philosophical preparation, and the thinking of the clerics Mbiti and Tempels.

However, the literature generated by the professional philosophers has gone beyond criticisms of ethnophilosophy. Hountondji (1991) declared that a "literature produced by Africans and dealing with philosophical problems" is the substance of African philosophy (120). Therefore, a field of inquiry as broad as traditional philosophy is the purview of the professional philosophers. Their methods are the traditional methods of Western philosophy. The professional philosophers see African philosophy as a developing entity that will facilitate the modernization of Africa (Serequeberhan 1991b). They expect to extend traditional Western philosophy to include the African world. Moreover, they have concluded that their academic mission is consistent with the activity and methods of Western philosophy. African philosophy, in the view of the professionals, is the work of trained, reflecting individuals. They warn that we should not confuse this real philosophy with the spontaneous activity of people who belong to a particular ethnic group.

Perhaps inadvertently, the professional philosophers developed arguments that could be used to support the assertion that philosophy did not exist in Africa before the emergence of their cadre. A professional philosopher might rebut this claim, albeit weakly, by citing the work of a scattered few formally trained individuals including Amo and perhaps Jacques Elisa Jean Captein. Still, the tendency of some of the professionals to celebrate traditional Western philosophical paradigms and practices has earned them criticism. Owomoyela ([1987] 1991) posited that in some instances when the professionals take a critical aim at ethnophilosophy, the real object of their displeasure is not always clear. Indeed, their quarrel may be with African culture itself. Certainly, the professionals have insisted that a written literature is essential to the existence of a philosophy. This is an affront to the powerful and rich oral tradition in Africa.

Initially, perhaps, the professionals rode the horse of conventional Western philosophy in a high and reckless fashion. However, criticism has caused them to strike a more guarded profile. Owomoyela ([1987] 1991) criticized Hountondji's (1983) statement, "the chief requirement of science is writing . . ." (99). Similarly he criticized Wiredu (1984) for proclaiming that "if a culture is both nonscientific and nonliterate, then in some important respects it may be backward in a rather deep sense" (151). Later, Wiredu (1991) conceded that "writing cannot be a precondition for philosophical thinking" (94).

The professional philosophers addressed African philosophy from a rather stark approach. The strong form of their thesis downplays the place of traditional African knowledge and wisdom in the philosophical enterprise. At the same time it celebrates traditional Western philosophical methods, seeing African philosophy as a latter-day branch of the European philosophical tree. Therefore, I have placed professional philosophy in a rather extreme uncritical and nonliberalizing position on the continua of figure 1. The professionals bring a new level of formal training to the philosophical enterprise in Africa. Their criticisms of the ethnophilosophers were uncompromising and incisive. However, they have failed at this early stage to extend their efforts to a thorough critical analysis of the methodology of the Western schools in which they were trained. Similarly, they tend to disdain notions that African sensibilities or the perspective of the oppressed would influence their scholarly efforts. The professionals strive to bring Western philosophical discourse to Africa. They have not modified method, perspective, or content.

The coziness of the professional philosophers with Western philosophy has caused considerable discomfort even among those who agree with their rejection of ethnophilosophy. This discomfort led Oruka ([1983] 1991) to articulate a new approach to the field. The wisdom and knowledge of certain wise individuals within ethnic groups and communities are the focus of this approach. Serequeberhan (1991b) called it *philosophical sagacity*. Oruka stated that to be considered wise, one must be steeped in the knowledge and traditions of one's ethnic group. In addition, the sage must evidence a level of thoughtfulness and reflection on the inconsistencies and problematic facets of the knowledge base he or she commands. Oruka called for a liberalization of philosophical method. He directed philosophers to set up structured dialogues with sages and record their ideas, reflections, and responses to challenges.

Serequeberhan (1991b) described sagacity as a middle ground between professional philosophers and ethnophilosophers. Whether they actually reach that middle ground is an open question. Keita (1991) argued that philosophical sagacity is dangerously close to ethnophilosophy in orientation and content. Ultimately, Keita maintained, a people's belief system originates in the thinking of a few. Over time these beliefs gain momentum and garner general acceptance. Therefore, sagacity is simply engaging in ethnophilosophy with individuals as the focal point.

Methodologically, Keita sees a contradiction in the sagacity school that centers on the issue of writing. In contrast to the professional school, Oruka's approach insists that philosophical knowledge and criticism existed before writing. Keita raises a sticky but certainly not damning point. Oruka described methods in philosophical sagacity that *require* demonstrating, in writing, through the interview with the sage, that a philosophical process exists. It seems that this methodological requirement might be an extension of the interaction between positivism and racism in the European mind. Obviously, people in Africa have produced and experienced their sages for eons. If European epistemology makes the demonstration of these encounters a convoluted enterprise, the problem is Europe's. The price paid by sagacity for peace with European methods seems high in Keita's estimation.

The sagacity approach contends, quite strongly, that traditional African wisdom contributes to philosophical knowledge. Additionally, they have modified the method of Western philosophy, to a limited extent, by the formal structured interview with the sage. Hence in figure 1 it occupies a quadrant representing a somewhat liberal methodological posture and a positive evaluation of knowledge obtained through African sensibilities. The critical and philosophical enterprise can emerge from a planned survey of the thinking of the sage. In this respect, sagacity arrives at a small measure of compromise between the ethnophilosophers and professionals. Ultimately, the value of traditional wisdom is retained in sagacity. Specifically, the focus of the philosopher becomes the internal critical analysis by an individual who lives within African culture.

The fourth approach, *nationalist-ideological philosophy*, is staunch in its criticism of ethnophilosophy. In fact, any philosophy that accepts or seeks some compromise with the "civilizing mission" of Europe is dismissed summarily by this school. The works of those whose visions shaped the anticolonial liberation struggles form the basis of philosophical discourse among the nationalist-ideological philosophers. Therefore, the writings of Seku Touré, Frantz Fanon, Kwame Nkrumah, and Amilcar Cabral constitute the central focus in this orientation.

The stark pronouncement of Wamba-dia-Wamba (1991) is an apt summary. He argued that it is necessary to examine "African philosophers in relation to the theoretical requirements of the self-organization of the African masses for the social transformation of the dominated societies" (236). Wamba-dia-Wamba identifies a condition of "scission" within African people. The colonial condition has set African people against one another and against their own cultural historical foundation. In the nationalist-ideological framework, the healing of scissions becomes the ultimate work of African philosophy. Wamba-dia-Wamba does not see this goal as inconsistent with the goals of philosophy as practiced "in many places" (224).

The gauntlet raised by the nationalist-ideological approach elicits discomfort in many quarters. This approach jostles those philosophers who wish to practice their philosophy unmindful of the material and economic conditions of masses of African people. It is equally disquieting to those who wish to ignore the reflections of individuals who fought against the colonial forces ultimately responsible for those conditions. Certainly, the nationalist-ideological school issues a strong call to see philosophical wisdom and knowledge as the outgrowth of indigenous African cultural activities. However, the criticisms of method seem to center around the fact that methods of philosophers are often applied for their own sake without the purpose of healing cleavages in the human condition. A series of fusions becomes the ultimate end of this approach. The efforts of African intellectuals, past and present, will be fused with the philosophy embedded in the anticolonial struggle of the masses of African people. For this school, the failure to unite the intellectual philosophy with the efforts of the masses will result in a sterile if not oppressive philosophical product. Thus, nationalist-ideological philosophy represents a circumscribed challenge to the method and focus of philosophical enterprise practiced in Africa. I have placed nationalist-ideological philosophy in figure 1 in a position representing the valuing of traditional African philosophical knowledge and a moderate liberalization of traditional philosophical methods.

African philosophy and black psychology

There are instructive commonalities between the search for an approach to the discipline among continental African philosophers and the search for a paradigm among the diasporic African psychologists. Figure 1 is useful in examining these. Clearly, a professional class has emerged in African philosophy and black psychology. In both instances these individuals are steeped in the methodological practices of their discipline and skeptical of or unconcerned with "traditional wisdom" gained through African (or African-American) sensibilities. Additionally, among the psychologists there are two schools that function with a moderate degree of tacit acknowledgment that significant psychological knowledge exists outside of the Western body of information. These are the deconstructionistic and the reconstructionistic approaches. However, adherents of these schools differ slightly in their position toward the utility of Western methods. The reconstructionists are slightly more critical of conventional methods.

Further, within African philosophy, three approaches, sagacity, ethnophilosophy, and nationalist-ideological philosophy, have tended to liberalize—some might say violate—traditional methods in philosophy. Simultaneously, these schools value, to varying extents, philosophical knowledge generated in Africa. Among the psychologists only the constructionistic approach tends to be hypercritical of the methodology of psychology and to value psychological knowledge and insights gleaned from traditional African sources.

Perhaps the manner in which the schools within the disciplines interact with one another is as significant as their location in the quadrants in figure 1. The African philosophers are a contentious lot. Their literature, from the perspective of the outsider, is teeming with frank and candid exchanges between members of the different schools. Consequently, they reconsider, modify, and refine their positions continually and quite readily. Sadly, we cannot say the same for the psychologists. Regardless of their school of thought, black psychologists have tended to carve out tiny areas of expertise, and to mine these ad nauseum. They almost dare anyone to defy their princely status. Internal critical analyses among black psychologists are shamefully rare. There are two very notable exceptions to this practice. The first is the series of empirical conferences organized over the past twenty-five years by Boykin, Franklin, and Yates (1979). These small closed meetings have involved the presentation of empirical research and critical commentary. Second, several recent issues of the *Journal of Black Psychology* under the editorial guidance of Kathleen Burlew have opened the forum for critical dialogue. One issue permitted a very frank and broad critical exchange between a group of constructionistic (see Kambon and Hopkins 1993), reconstructionistic (Sellers 1993; Helms 1993; Parham 1993; Taylor 1993), and professional psychologists (Penn, Gaines, and Phillips 1993). The topic was related to racial identity, but more remarkable was the frank exchange of critical statements.

But by and large the psychological camps have remained insular, electing to function in their own private spheres. On one extreme, the "professionals" persist in squeezing sometimes impoverished data from the limited traditional paradigms. Where paltry claims of relevance to the experiences of African people cannot be made, they insist on the "right" to engage in this activity in the name of academic freedom or individual professional growth. On the other extreme, constructionistic psychologists tend to make pronouncements about the nature of African psychology. Remarkably, many of these are based in the work of the ethnophilosophers. As we have seen, much of this work has been criticized harshly by continental African philosophers.

The lack of critical dialogue among black psychologists places us in a difficult position when considering the study of the impact of racism on the African mind. We will opt for an eclectic posture at this juncture. Reginald Jones (1991) included papers from all three of the critical schools in his collection of works on black psychology. Our strategy will be an inclusive one. We will cite the important works of less critical professional psychologists as well as conventional research. Additionally, each approach within the area of black psychology will make a contribution to the present analysis of Manichean psychology.

The situation is similar when we consider the work of the African philosophers. For the black psychologist, the observations of the ethnophilosophers remain intriguing. Psychologists are not particularly interested in the question of the relationship of ethnophilosophy to "true philosophy." In some instances, the careful observation of the folkways of the people will provide us with valuable insight. Critical analysis and interpretation of material, a strong suit of the professional philosophers, will be extremely important in our study. The sagacity school reminds us of the importance of traditional African wisdom. Finally, the nationalist-ideological philosophical approach makes it clear that all of our academic endeavors must have as their goal the healing of the oppressed.

At this point, then, this epistemological position begins to take form. We would be ill advised to close off any approach to obtaining or evaluating information about the nature of white supremacy as a system. Similarly, it is unwise to be epistemologically myopic in our examination of racism's history and effects and in our studies of the nature of African cultural resistance and personality. There are instances when traditional Western methods will yield informative material. However, there is also the information obtained by those whose African sensibilities remained sharp, sometimes despite training in Western methods. If we fail to value knowledge and wisdom offered by these individuals, we run the risk at best of blindness and at worst of ancestral treason (Richards 1990). Continental African philosophers and the African psychologists in the American diaspora are of many voices. However, we can hear a common theme. The system of white supremacy that has disrupted the fabric of African life is both vicious and complex. At present, the voices of the professionals, like Bayton and Hountondji, need not be ignored to hear Nobles, the constructionist, or Wamba-dia-Wamba, the nationalist. In the wake of the imposition of the Manichean order, many facets of cleavage and realms of destruction and fission exist among African people. The only reasonable course of action is to approach the study of racism from a broad epistemological perspective.

stening to the physician and the historian

Hicks (1988) traced a rich vein of research on black communities in the United States dating from Du Bois's *The Philadelphia Negro* (1899) and landmark studies at Atlanta University conducted between 1898 and 1910. Other major sociological studies were conducted under the auspices of the American Youth Commission of the American Council on Education and the Carnegie Foundation. Hicks notes that these were published as major books during the 1940s and that only after the widespread, fiery eruption of the cities in the 1960s were studies of this size taken up again. In the tradition of these studies, the National Research Council undertook in 1985 a major study of the status of black America. It culminated in *A Common Destiny* (Jaynes and Williams 1989). A bevy of social scientists that the National Research Council charged to present "data," not to recommend avenues for change in social policy, put together the weighty volume.

When Gordon and Meroe (1991) reviewed *A Common Destiny*, they raised a paradigmatic and perhaps epistemological objection. They pointed out that the "information is reported in the 'objective' almost sterile tradition of the 'scientific' community which leaves the treatment of one of the nation's most recalcitrant problems void of passion" (25). Later in that review, Gordon and Meroe identify with a position that is not far removed from that of the nationalist-ideological philosophers. They posit that "within the social sciences, objectivity is a misleading assertion . . . knowledge should be an emancipating force" (25).

The growth of knowledge in the branches of psychology concerned with nonbiological, intrapsychic, and social psychological determinants of behavior (the "softer" branches) has been slow (Meehl 1978; Koch 1981). Still, there have been advances, and young people continue to pursue careers in this relatively new science. Rosenzweig

79

(1984) estimated that there are 300,000 psychologists in the world and that 100,000 of these work in the United States. Research activities and data acquisition have gone on at a furious pace. Techniques for analyzing data have become increasingly sophisticated in a mathematical sense. Simultaneously, the computer software that makes it possible for the novice researcher to execute these modes of analysis is commercially available. Consequently, though one might concede that the field is too young to offer clear-cut, viable solutions to the problems that fester from centuries of white supremacy, it is not too much to expect that the description of these problems that psychological research generates would be moderately rich and authentic.

Sadly, from the viewpoint of the oppressed, the victims of Manichean reality, even when data are collected in a sympathetic fashion, they are but a pale and wispy pretender to reality. The empirical evidence of the social sciences is not the ultimate reality of the oppressed. A Common Destiny tells us that 43 percent of black children lived below the poverty line in 1986 (25) and that the life expectancy of black people continues to lag behind that of whites. Always, we should remain mindful that quantifications like these are not what the oppressed experience. Theirs is a life much more thoroughly preempted than these simple percentages found in the economic or epidemiological data would suggest. The chair in which one sits, the width of the aisle of the grocery store where one shops, the breadth of the smile (or depth of the frown) one's parent wears as payday approaches and passes, and the sounds that pierce the night air as one goes to sleep are all manifestations of the ultimate reality of the oppressed.

Certainly, Gordon and Meroe raise a fundamental concern about the manner in which Western academic social scientists come to know the experiences of African Americans. The data related to the effects of racism found in traditional psychological and social science journals seem to be devoid of the soul of the matter. Without passion, such data may serve as an adjunct to our efforts to come to know racism, but they cannot become the centerpiece of our thinking. We will see that Du Bois and Fanon understood this. But first, why do these data appear so ghostly?

The philosopher Anyanwu (1983) criticized the application of Western empiricism and positivism in the study of African culture. His criticisms are consistent with Gordon and Meroe's reactions to A Common Destiny. Anyanwu raised very serious epistemological concerns that provide insight into the source of the gray visage that empiricism of social science presents and calls the reality of the oppressed.

Anyanwu (1983) argued that "factual consciousness" is an outgrowth of the Western "objective" scientific method. Factual consciousness is the product of carefully controlled methods and procedures that make facts publicly identifiable. "Factual consciousness is based, more or less on head counting, on the enumeration of particular isolated facts" (55). Elsewhere, Anyanwu warned, "A person may look for simplicity in the artificial situation of mathematics, but in the context of human life, that is, life as it is experienced and lived, that simplicity does not exist" (8).

Anyanwu reminds us that knowledge and facts are not synonymous. Facts lead to interpretations and observations. These are grounded in theories and ultimately in culture. Interpretations of facts give rise to knowledge. There is no quarrel from Anyanwu that factual consciousness has served the West well, especially in the natural sciences. However, when applied to the study of African cultures, factual consciousness is limited. Echoing Gordon and Meroe, Anyanwu sees Western scientists busily gathering facts but getting only a limited sense of the real conditions they are examining.

Rational or factual consciousness contrasts with Anyanwu's view of African epistemology. Because African epistemology does not separate subject and object, personal experience is primary over the rational. "The truth of this experience is lived and felt, not merely thought of" (Anyanwu 1983, 87). Personal consciousness, then, is the capacity to experience the world and remain part of it. It eschews the process of objectifying what one perceives. Consciousness is experiential. One knows that there is an immutable connection between the world that one senses and one's self. African epistemology, then, can never reduce experience to mere quantifications or other objective indices. From an African perspective, this numerical abridgement of experience is far too radical and wholly inappropriate.

The data, be they presented through the lens of descriptive or of inferential statistics, have their place. We will not deny empirical facts when researchers have discovered them through a valid series of steps. But racism is experienced by African people in a personal mode. The Manichean order is more than material facts. Following Anyanwu's observations, we need cultural, historical, and philosophical statements on reality to analyze the impact of racism. We will have to go beyond the standard measures of the discipline of psychology and strive to "see the individual in the light of the whole and try to

81

understand the individual in terms of the ultimate principles governing him" (54). Obviously, we have to derive the knowledge that we
gain about racism, at least in part, from the manner of experiencing
that characterizes African people.

Du Bois, the historian, knew the place of empirical evidence, but
he never forgot the role of personal experience. He gathered evidence
by interviewing five thousand people for his landmark sociological
study *The Philadelphia Negro* (1899). Thirty-six years later, in his
essential study *Black Reconstruction in America 1860–1880* (Du Bois
1935), in the chapter on the founding of the public school system, we
find a careful, painstaking analysis of the legislative record and the
economic expenditures of the southern states. He pored through the
data related to the number of primary and secondary school pupils
in each state. Certainly, Du Bois knew the methods of his and related
disciplines. He understood how to present the factual evidence.

However, in his essay "Of the Meaning of Progress," found in
Souls of Black Folk (1903), Du Bois provided insight gained from
highly personal experience, insight that defies quantification. To show
us the fabric of life in the rural black belt, he tells us the tale of Josie.
Nothing born of factual consciousness could paint a picture so vivid.
He provides not only an unforgettable portrait of the woman, but
also a lucid image of the people of the region and the conditions under
which they lived. Du Bois brings her to life with her "certain fineness,
the shadow of an unconscious moral heroism that would willingly
give all of life to make life broader and deeper and fuller for her and
hers" (57). Thanks to his transcending of the factual, we are able to
see Josie and the Manichean order of her day more clearly.

It is this epistemological flexibility that allows Du Bois to give us
a profound and provocative insight in "The Founding of the Public
Schools." Du Bois argues that it was principally the agitation and
hunger for knowledge of the newly liberated black labor force that
resulted in the establishment of a public school system in the defeated
South. Why did white laborers not agitate incessantly for legislation
that would have led to a public school system in the southern states
before the Civil War? Clearly, at every turn, black laborers did. Du
Bois notes that because of the close-range view the black labor force
had of wealthy slaveholders and their low-lived ways, they knew that
wealth without education was crippled (641). He quotes Booker T.
Washington to underscore the fact that a hunger for education raged
in the black community during reconstruction. But more than the
quotations and the figures, one knows that Du Bois's insight comes

because he had experienced the people of that period. The personal consciousness of Du Bois was not made subservient to factual consciousness; hence his formidable intellect was not restrained by the methodological dictates of the discipline.

Bulhan (1985) reminds us that Frantz Fanon was a physician by training and a psychiatrist by specialization. He had a strong penchant for research. Fanon participated in clinical research on electroconvulsive therapy (shock treatment) and on milieu therapy in mental hospitals. Milieu therapy involves changing the environment to facilitate other forms of treatment, including psychopharmacology. Further, "The So-called Dependency Complex of Colonized Peoples," a chapter in Fanon's *Black Skin White Masks*, is a deconstructionistic treatise directed at a psychoanalytic study of the Malagasy people. He shows that Mannoni, a liberal researcher of his day, committed a fatal methodological error. By failing to understand the impact of colonialism on the personality of the Malagasy people, Mannoni commits the classic error of mistaking effect for cause (Bulhan 1985, 94). Clearly, Fanon published both conceptual analyses of research and empirical studies of his own (see Bulhan 1985, 289, 290).

But Fanon brings more than a mere factual consciousness to his analysis of the psychological impact of racism and colonialism. Ironically, "The Fact of Blackness" in *Black Skin White Masks* is not depicted through factual consciousness. "I was battered down by tom-toms, cannibalism, intellectual deficiency, fetishism, racial defects, slave-ships and above all else, above all 'sho' good eatin'" (112). The excursion Fanon takes into the psychological impact of white supremacy in this chapter is poetic, rich, and, most important, highly personal in nature. As a researcher and psychiatrist, Fanon could have relied on material from clinical interviews and therapy sessions. At the time he was writing "The Fact of Blackness," his peers in the field would have deemed an analysis of dreams, presented from the psychoanalytic perspective good, solid psychological science. However, he had come to know racism in Martinique and Paris. He had gained that knowledge wholly and personally. Therefore, he cited his experience and that of his "brother." He cites poets, philosophers, novelists, and playwrights, so that the "fact" can be established in terms beyond those sterile dimensions that dominate the discourse of empirical psychiatric and psychological studies of racism.

In many ways, Fanon and Du Bois anticipated the epistemological efforts of Molefi Asante (1990), who argued for an approach to research that is "holistic and integrative" and for an epistemology that

83

is participatory and committed. Additionally, Anyanwu (1983) and Walters (1990) expressed the sentiment that more than just one phase of the intellect should be involved in the process of gathering knowledge. Both argued that scholars obtain "direct acquaintance," in Walters's words, when seeking knowledge of black people (16).

Indeed, we might be accused of heresy in the court of scientific conduct for praising Du Bois and Fanon. Both men allowed subjectivity and personal commitment to enter into their analyses. The myth that the level of development in science is determined by its adherence to objectivity has been exploded from within. Repeatedly, African thinkers, including Asante, Walters, and Anyanwu, as well as non-Africans, including Koch (1981) and Staats (1981), have questioned seriously the position that objectivity characterizes and fuels the progress of the behavioral sciences. The best we can hope for is that the scientists know and make explicit the experiences and subjective elements that are central to the analysis.

To that end, I am writing as an African man born in America, which is to say a man steeped from the cradle and most likely until the grave in a racist environment. Some portions of the experiences that are part of me are a direct function of the fact that I have lived in that racist environment. As I grow in my awareness of the nature of my environment, I am comfortable knowing that the manner in which I view data will be influenced by my experiences. Many of these are infinitely more real to me than any behavioral or physiological change I have observed in my laboratory or any reliability coefficient I have computed for a psychological questionnaire I may give a group of students. I know I will not be able to quantify these experiences. Now, I willingly and knowingly allow them to color my analyses, with the hope that they will breathe life into my thoughts.

Finally, the matter of ideology cannot and should not be avoided here. In line with the nationalist-ideological philosophers, I see research on black people as having as its necessity the commitment to the destruction of forces aligned against us. Walters (1990) called for the development of a "black action research program" directed toward social system changes. Bulhan (1985) stressed the need to study matters from the perspective of the oppressed with a commitment to the eradication of oppression. I align myself with these positions. The neutral and uncommitted young social scientist of African descent is a pitiful and indeed traitorous character. It is disheartening, in the face of the current crises, to listen to young African behavioral scientists speak glibly of the mode of statistical analysis they employed or the levels of experimental control they exercised and then be struck speechless or moved to indignation if asked how their research might facilitate the "reconstruction of the race" (Williams 1974). We strive to know the effects of racism with the purpose of stomping out every last vestige of it.

* * * * * * * * *

Du Bois and Fanon will continue to light fires in the minds of my own students and in generations of African scholars to come. This will occur because these men knew their disciplines well and they were creative in their participation in traditional enterprises. In addition, they allowed themselves the latitude to come to know the world as African men existing in a reality of white supremacy, and they never deprecated that knowledge base. Finally, they were committed and participatory, fusing their scholarly activities with the construction of agendas for the liberation of African people. This commitment made their life's work timeless and rich.

To study the impact of Manichean psychology solely through the paradigms and perspectives of Western science would be like gouging out the receptors of all the bodily senses but one to simplify the input to the brain. A good deal of evidence forthcoming from Western experimental psychology will be presented in this volume. But this will not be the only source of evidence, nor will it be interpreted necessarily from a Western perspective. This study focuses on the processes involved as white supremacy is imposed on African people, a people who come to know the world in a holistic and participatory fashion. It would be immoral to conduct a study of that system in the purely objectified and "factual" manner prescribed by the descendants of those who originally imposed it.

References

Akbar, N. 1979. African Roots of Black Personality. In *Reflections on Black Psychology*, W. D. Smith et al. Washington, D.C.: University of America Press.

———. 1985. Nile Valley Origins of the Science of the Mind. In *Nile Valley Civilizations*, ed. I. Van Sertima. New York: LTD.

Anyanwu, K. C. 1983. *The African Experience in the American Marketplace.* Smithtown, N.Y.: Exposition Press.

———. 1983. The African World-view and Theory of Knowledge.

Armistead, W. 1969. *A Tribute to the Negro Being a Vindication of the Moral, Intellectual and Religious Capabilities of the Coloured Portion of Mankind with*

Particular Reference to the African Race. 1848. Reprinted, Miami: Mnemosyne.

Asante, M. K. 1990. *Kemet Afrocentricity and Knowledge.* Trenton, N.J.: African World Press.

Banks, W. C. 1976. White Preference in Blacks: A Paradigm in Search of a Phenomenon. *Psychological Bulletin* 83: 1179–86.

———. 1982. Deconstructive Falsification: Foundations of Critical Method in Black Psychology. In *Minority Mental Health*, ed. E. Jones and S. Korchin, 59–71. New York: Praeger.

———. 1992. The Theoretical and Methodological Crisis of the Afrocentric Conception. *The Journal of Negro Education* 61: 262–72.

Banks, W. C., Ward, W. E., McQuarter, G. V., and DeBritto, A. M. 1991. Are Blacks External: On the Status of Locus of Control in Black Populations. In *Black Psychology,* 3d ed., ed. R. L. Jones, 181–92. Berkeley: Cobb and Henry.

Bayton, J. A. 1987. Thank You Howard for the Experience. *New Directions: The Howard University Magazine* 14: 6–9.

Boykin, A. W. 1977. Experimental Psychology from a Black Perspective: Issues and Examples. *Journal of Black Psychology* 3: 29–49.

———. 1991. Black Psychology and Experimental Psychology: A Functional Confluence. In *Black Psychology,* 3d ed., ed. R. L. Jones, 481–508. Berkeley: Cobb and Henry.

Boykin, A. W., Franklin, A. J., and Yates, J. F., eds. 1979. *Research Directions in Black Psychology.* New York: Russell Sage.

Bulhan, H. A. 1985. *Frantz Fanon and the Psychology of Oppression.* New York: Plenum.

Campbell, A. L., Rorie, K., Dennis, G., Wood, D., Combs, S., Hearn, L., Davis, H., Brown, A., and Weir, R. 1996. Neuropsychological Assessment of African Americans: Conceptual and Methodological Considerations. In *Handbook of Tests and Measurements for Black Populations*, ed. R. L. Jones, 75–84. Berkeley: Cobb and Henry.

Clark, (X) C., McGee, D. P., Nobles, W. W., and Weems, L. 1975. Voodoo or I.Q.: An Introduction to African Psychology. *Journal of Black Psychology* 1: 9–19.

Clarke, J. H. 1990. African-American Historians and the Reclaiming of African History. In *African Culture: The Rhythms of Unity*, ed. M. Asante and K. W. Asante, 157–71. Trenton, N.J.: African World Press.

———. 1991. *Notes for an African World Revolution: Africans at the Crossroads.* Trenton, N.J.: African World Press.

Crider, A. B., Gethals, G. R., Kavanaugh, R. D., and Solomon, P. R. 1993. *Psychology,* 4th ed. New York: HarperCollins.

Diop, C. A. 1974. *The African Origin of Civilization: Myth or Reality.* Westport, Conn.: Lawrence Hill and Company.

Du Bois, W. E. B. 1899. *The Philadelphia Negro: A Social Study.* Philadelphia: University of Pennsylvania.

———. 1903. *The Souls of Black Folk: Essays and Sketches.* Chicago: A. C. McClurg.

———. 1935. *Black Reconstruction in America, 1860–1880.* New York: Harcourt Brace.

———. 1973. *The Education of Black People: Ten Critiques, 1906–1960.* Edited by H. Aptheker. New York: Monthly Review Press.

Fanon, F. 1967. *Black Skin White Masks.* New York: Grove Press.

Gordon, E. W., and Meroe. 1991. A Common Destinies Continuing Dilemmas. *Psychological Sciences* 2: 23–29.

Guthrie, R. 1976. *Even the Rat Was White: A Historical View of Psychology.* New York: Harper and Row.

Harrell, J. P., Morris, C. E., and Rasayon, N. K. B. 1996. Physiological Measures in Studies of Black Populations. In *Handbook of Tests and Measurements for Black Populations, Vol. II,* ed. R. Jones, 59–74. Hampton, Va.: Cobb and Henry.

Helms, J. E. 1993. More Psychologists Discover the Wheel: A Reaction to Views by Penn et al. "On the Desirability of Own-group Preference." *Journal of Black Psychology* 19: 322–26.

Hicks, L. H. 1988. Black Studies in Psychology: Past and Present. In *The Eleventh Conference on Empirical Research in Black Psychology,* ed A. Harrison, 28–31. Rockville, Md.: National Institutes of Mental Health.

Hilliard, A. G. III. 1986. The Cultural Unity of Black Africa: The Domains of Patriarchy and of Matriarchy in Classical Antiquity. In *Great African Thinkers, Vol. I, Cheikh Anta Diop,* eds. I. Van Sertima and L. Williams, 102–09. New Brunswick, N.J.: Transaction Books.

Hilliard, A. G. 1995. *The Maroon within Us: Selected Essays on African-American Community Socialization.* Baltimore: Black Classics.

Holloway, J. E. 1990. Origins of African-American Culture. In *Africanisms in American Culture,* ed. J. E. Holloway. Bloomington: Indiana University Press.

Hountondji, P. 1983. *African Philosophy: Myth or Reality?* Bloomington: Indiana University Press.

Hountondji, P. J. 1991. African Philosophy: Myth and Reality. In *African Philosophy: The Essential Readings,* ed. T. Serequeberhan. New York: Paragon House.

Jahn, J. 1967. *Muntu.* New York: Grove Press.

Jaynes, D. G., and Williams, R. M. 1989. *A Common Destiny: Blacks and American Society.* Washington, D.C.: National Academy Press.

Jefferson, T. 1964. *Notes on the State of Virginia.* 1861. Reprint, New York: Harper and Row.

Jones, R. L. 1991. *Black Psychology,* 3d ed. Berkeley: Cobb and Henry.

Kambon, K. K. K., and Hopkins, R. 1993. An African-centered Analysis of Penn et al.'s Critique of the Own-race Preference Assumption Underlying Africentric Models of Personality. *Journal of Black Psychology* 19: 342–49.

Keita, L. 1991. Contemporary African Philosophy: The Search for Method. In *African Philosophy: The Essential Readings,* ed. T. Serequeberhan, 111–31. New York: Paragon House.

Kent, G. 1972. *Blackness and the Adventure of Western Culture.* Chicago: Third World Press.

Koch, S. 1981. The Nature and Limits of Psychological Knowledge. Lessons of a Century qua "Science." *American Psychologist* 36: 257–69.

Maultsby, P. K. 1990. Africanisms in African-American Music. In *Africanism in American Culture*, ed. I. E. Holloway, 185–210. Bloomington: Indiana University Press.

Mbiti, J. 1970. *African Religions and Philosophies*. New York: Anchor.

Meehl, P. E. 1978. Theoretical Risks and Tabular Asterisks: Sir Karl, Sir Ronald and the Slow Progress of Soft Psychology. *Journal of Consulting and Clinical Psychology* 46: 806–34.

Nichols, E. J. 1976. *The Philosophical Aspects of Cultural Differences*. Unpublished manuscript, Washington, D.C.

Nobles, W. W. 1986. *African Psychology: Toward its Reclamation, Reascension and Revitalization*. Oakland, Calif.: Black Family Institute.

———. 1991. African Philosophy: Foundations for Black Psychology. In *Black Psychology*, 3d ed., ed. R. L. Jones. Berkeley: Cobb and Henry.

Onyewueni, I. 1991. Is There an African Philosophy? 1976. *Journal of African Studies* 3: 513–28. Reprinted in *African Philosophy: The Essential Readings*, ed. T. Serequeberhan, 29–46. New York: Paragon House.

Oruka, H. O. 1991. Sagacity in African Philosophy. *International Philosophical Quarterly* 23: 383–93. 1983. Reprinted in *African Philosophy: The Essential Readings*, ed. T. Serequeberhan. New York: Paragon House.

Owomoyela, O. 1991. Africa and the Imperative of Philosophy: A Skeptical Consideration. *African Studies Review* 30. 1987. Reprinted in *African Philosophy: The Essential Readings*, ed. T. Serequeberhan, 156–86. New York: Paragon House.

Parham, T. A. 1993. Own-group Preferences as a Function of Self-affirmation. *Journal of Black Psychology* 19: 336–41.

Penn, M. L., Gaines, S. O., and Phillips, L. 1993. On the Desirability of Own-group Preference. *Journal of Black Psychology* 19: 303–21.

Plumpp, S. 1972. *Black Rituals*. Chicago: Third World Press.

Richards, D. 1990. The Implications of African-American Spirituality. In *African Culture: The Rhythms of Unity*, eds. M. Asante and K. W. Asante, 207–31. Trenton, N.J.: African World Press.

Robinson, C. 1985. *Black Marxism: The History of the Radical Black Tradition*. London: Zed Press.

Rosenzweig, M. R. 1984. U.S. Psychology and World Psychology. *American Psychology* 39: 877–84.

Sellers, R. M. 1993. A Call to Arms for Researchers Studying Racial Identity. *Journal of Black Psychology* 19: 327–32.

Serequeberhan, T. 1991a. *African Philosophy: The Essential Readings*. New York: Paragon House.

———. 1991b. African Philosophy: The Point in Question. In *African Philosophy: The Essential Readings*, ed. T. Serequeberhan, 3–28. New York: Paragon House.

Staats, A. W. 1981. Paradigmatic Behaviorism, Unified Theory, Unified Theory Construction Methods and the Zeitgeist of Separation. *American Psychologist* 36: 239–56.

Stuckey, S. 1987. *Slave Culture: Nationalist Theory and the Foundations of Black America*. New York: Oxford.

Taylor, J. 1993. Reaction to Penn et al.'s "On the Desirability of Own-group Preference." *Journal of Black Psychology* 19: 333–35.

Tempels, P. 1969. *Bantu Philosophy*. Paris: Présence Africaine.

Turner, C. H. 1891. Morphology of the Avian Brain. *Journal of Comparative Neurology*.

———. 1901. Will the Education of the Negro Solve the Race Problem? In *Negro Literature or a Cyclopedia of Thought on the Topics Relating to the American Negro by One Hundred of America's Greatest Negroes*, ed. D. W. Culp, 162–66. Toronto: J. L. Nichols and Company.

Van Sertima, I. 1983. *Blacks in Science: Ancient and Modern*. New Brunswick, N.J.: Transaction Books.

Walters, R. 1990. Action Research and the Black Paradigm. *Howard University Journal of Philosophy* 1: 1–21.

Wamba-dia-Wamba. 1991. Philosophy in Africa: Challenges of the African Philosopher. In *African Philosophy: The Essential Readings*, ed. T. Serequeberhan, 211–46. New York: Paragon House.

Ward, W. E., Banks, W. C., and Wilson, S. 1991. Delayed Gratification in Blacks. In *Black Psychology*, 3d ed., ed. R. L. Jones. Berkeley: Cobb and Henry.

Whitehurst, K. E. 1934. A Statistical Investigation of Desire: With Special Reference to Sex and College. Unpublished master's thesis. Howard University.

Wilcox, R. 1971. *The Psychological Consequences of Being a Black American*. New York: John Wiley.

Williams, C. 1974. *The Destruction of Black Civilization: Great Issues of a Race from 4500 B.C. to 2000 A.D.* Chicago: Third World Press.

Williams, R. L. 1974. A History of the Association of Black Psychologists: Early Formation and Development. *Journal of Black Psychology* 1: 9–29.

———. (n.d.) The BITCH-100: A Cultural Specific Test. Williams and Associates, Inc., 6374 Delmar Blvd., St. Louis, MO 63130.

Williams, R. L., and Mitchell, H. 1991. The Testing Game. In *Black Psychology*, 3d ed., ed. R. L. Jones, 193–205. Berkeley: Cobb and Henry.

Wiredu, K. 1984. How Not to Compare African Thought to Western Thought. In *African Philosophy: An Introduction*, ed. R. A. Wright, 149–62. Lanham, Md.: University Press of America.

———. 1991. On Defining African Philosophy. In *African Philosophy: The Essential Readings*, ed. T. Serequeberhan, 87–110. New York: Paragon House.

Wright, B. 1975. *The Psychopathic Racial Personality*. Chicago: Third World Press.

Zimbardo, P. G. 1992. *Psychology and Life*. 13th ed. New York: HarperCollins.

CHAPTER THREE

Environmental Stimuli and Manichean Thinking

Occasionally I am seized by an overwhelming suspicion. If psychologists had the vision and sensitivities of poets, the field, certainly the "softer" branches of it, might advance much more rapidly. So strong is this suspicion that in lighter moments, I have communicated my conjecture to students. What if the late poet Sterling Brown, when an undergraduate at Williams College, had opted to switch his major to psychology? I believe that his publications, even as a psychologist, would have intrigued me. I suspect they would have been more lyrical and interesting than the very staid and sterile offerings we find in most journals in the behavioral sciences. What is more important, his insights would have significantly enriched psychologists' understanding of the fabric of black life in the United States. I am becoming convinced that good poets see people and the conditions around them not only differently, but also more clearly than good psychologists.

Psychologists, if they are eclectic enough when they examine the behavioral equation, consider three sets of events: (1) stimulus events emanating from the environment, (2) cognitive processing and other "brain-driven" events that occur in the organism, and (3) the responses themselves. Good poets discuss these three domains also. They just seem to capture the human spirit more fully when they go about their work. Let us stay with Sterling Brown as an example.

Consider his poem "Strong Men" (1980). Brown depicted significant racist events on the "stimulus" side of the equation of black life in the Western hemisphere. He told us what was done. "They dragged you from homeland/ . . . They broke you in like oxen/ . . . They made your women breeders,/ . . . They cooped you in their kitchens/ . . . . They bought off some of your leaders/. . . ." Then he showed how those who were enslaved fashioned a resilient African folk culture. Brown depicts how this slave culture shaped the behavior of African people under oppression. In psychological language he is telling us of the "organism and response" elements in the equation. "You sang: Keep a-inchin' along/ . . . Walk togedder, chillen,/ . . . Ain't no hammah/ In dis lan',/ Strikes lak mine, bebby/ . . . Me an' muh baby gonna shine."

In his poems, Brown considered the *stimulus events,* the role of culture in the *cognitive processing* of these events, as well as the *responses* of black people. The lesson he imparted to the behavioral scientist who may tend to focus on one term in the equation to the exclusion of the others is that racism sets in motion a dynamic process. From time to time, the oppressor must replace or refurbish particular practices, laws, and institutions that have supported racism. This occurs largely, though not entirely, in response to the nature of the resistance African people mobilize as they encounter racism.

The focus of this chapter is the stimulus side of the psychological equation. We are concerned with the joists and pillars that support modern racism. Their function is to ensure that a Manichean mind evolves in African people. The assumption is that these supporting structures are not static, evenly spaced, or easily located. And mindful of Brown's "Strong Men," we will identify the sources and support systems of racism and remain sensitive to the manner in which the resistance of the oppressed has ensured that this supporting structure changes continually.

On any given day during the time when Sterling Brown wrote "Strong Men," black people might have faced racism in its individual, institutional, and cultural forms. Often brutish, physical, and overtly racist interpersonal encroachments were the most obvious. Crass practices including the insulting and demeaning use of racial epithets were socially acceptable. The goal was to reinforce white supremacy by instilling a sense of fear and terror in the oppressed. White racists endeavored to position this profound sense of fear at or very close to the conscious level of mental processing. In more recent times, individual racism has become less in vogue socially. The fear and terror associated with it, terror once thought to be central to the maintenance of white supremacy, is all but absent. Indeed, the level of interpersonal racism, in James Bayton's words, tends to "wax and wane" over time. However, it is apparent that individual racism is superfluous to the existence of white supremacy.

Brown gave a glimpse of the longer view. That is, though the dialectical process that exists between oppression and resistance is protracted, "strong men git stronger." My argument in this work is the one advanced by others (Woodson 1933; Wright 1975; Akbar 1974; Hilliard 1995). The critical battle within the psychosocial reality of racism is, and has been from the beginning, the battle for the mind. When individual racism ran rampant in this society, a strong people got stronger because they resisted oppression, even in the face of death. In some cases they were on guard against the institutional and cultural forms of racism. On other occasions, they may not have been concerned with its seemingly less immediate manifestations (see Cruse 1987). As the individual forms of racism receded, white supremacy would ensure its continued existence by means other than fear. Other institutional sources would step forward to preserve racism. The stimuli emanating from these sources order the thinking of African people along Manichean lines. The challenge to the tradition of resistance is to expose these more subtle forces. In this fashion, the momentum against racism can continue. In this chapter, I will discuss four major overlapping sources of information that lead to Manichean cognition. Again, African people have mobilized resistance to every encroachment. I will include a historical perspective on each source to highlight the impact resistance has had on the current form.

~urces of input: An overview

Perhaps ironically, one pivotal nurturer of racist thinking is the real-life, day-to-day living circumstances of the oppressed. These stand in stark contrast to the corresponding conditions of those who are not the principal targets of racial oppression. I will show how the disparity between these two sets of conditions actually comes to support the development of racist thinking among the oppressed. In modern societies, those who control social institutions impose the standards by which the members of a society measure "real" worth and value. Quite often the physical and psychological conditions of the oppressed, when measured by these standards, are deficient. These conditions are often quite tangible, even when they are not material. In most instances, the difference in status between the oppressed and those in a dominant position is quite apparent. What is more important, the conditions themselves are embedded in a context that virtually requires one to view the deficiency or disparity as the fault, ultimately, of the oppressed. That is, the conditions are stripped of the proper explanatory context, which would allow the oppressed to identify oppression as the source of the disparities. The missing context is largely informational. In the next section, I will discuss the process by which social forces cloak this very important context material.

In the United States, perhaps the most sophisticated and advanced bastion of white supremacy, people of African descent have mounted an impressive resistance to the decline in their material living conditions. However, the economic and political forces have been overwhelming. In this technologically developed society, the perception of these degraded living conditions among African Americans remains a primary source of Manichean cognition.

Popular culture is a second source of stimuli that bring about a Manichean mind. In the United States, for the better part of a century, films, music, radio, television, and the press have projected and reflected racist material. In some instances, African people have cognitively synthesized this racist material into stereotypical, racist mental images and concepts that become the basis of a European-American perspective on reality. At the very least, the materials generated in the popular culture inhibit the development of self-affirming, constructive, and critical thinking by people of African descent. On the other hand, the record is clear that African people have organized protests and resistance to this oppressive influence, and consequently the content of the material has been modified over the years. For each genre, the metamorphosis of the cultural content is worthy of continued study. Individuals derive their image of black culture and black people from this content. However, a detailed analysis lies far beyond the scope of the present discussion. We will make only general remarks about the process of change.

Additionally, the creative genius of African people has had a remarkable impact on both popular and classical, or more enduring, culture in the United States. (Carl Jung [1930], the noted personality theorist, scolded white people in America for permitting African people to influence so profoundly the cultural fabric of North America.) As the United States grew, an unmistakable presence of black artists and thinkers emerged in several creative outlets in popular culture. Whites initiated a concerted effort to control the products of this genius. They did this to preserve certain elements of racist mythology, as well as for economic gain. In fact, whites attempted to resist and demean the cultural contributions of African people at virtually every turn. Part of that thrust was to fit the image of these contributions into a Manichean framework. That framework claims that black people could create only base and primitive cultural products. I will highlight elements of this complex economic and cultural history. However, the concern for this study is the effects the resulting products have had on the cognitive schemata of the oppressed.

The third source of Manichean cognition is the formal educational system. We must consider the content and ideology of the curriculum. Ultimately, educational experiences shape the perspective one takes on the events, situations, and ideas that people face as part of living. That is, education, or better, the ideological thrust of education, helps shape the mental lens through which we will analyze and interpret the events in the world around us. Of particular concern is that the ideology promoted by the education we receive will shape the inferences we make about the disparities between the worlds of the oppressed and those of the powerful.

Education in its role as a supporting structure of racism is especially significant. It operates subtly. Less blatant forms of racist input are requisite in modern "civil" societies. Dr. King spoke of a vision of the long arc of the "moral universe" that he perceived to be bending toward justice. Borrowing from his vision, we can say that racism as a process has a long arc that bends toward subtlety. Racist stimuli emanating from the formal educational structures in society are especially important because their impact tends to persist. This impact is devastating even as crude interpersonal manifestations of racism tend to fade.

Finally, religion as a source of racist information is too central to the lives of black people to evade discussion. When Arabs and, later, Europeans launched grand programs of exploitation in Africa, they *reintroduced* Islam and Christianity on new terms. Neither religion was new to Africa. Finch (1991), in *Echoes of the Old Dark Land*, shows how ancient African spiritual beliefs colored and texturized early Christianity. Early African influences on Islam are undeniable (ben-Jochannan 1970). However, a practice or cultural product that exists within a society at one historical epoch may have radically different implications later. For example, African people knew of and used alcohol and other psychoactive substances before the arrival of foreign abusers. With the coming of massive exploitation from the outside, the significance of alcohol and drug use changed (see Bulhan 1985). Similarly, when those who intended to extract economic profit from Africa carried in their bags a Bible or Koran, the implications of embracing these scriptures changed. The religions were no longer cross-cultural options. They became part of cultural hegemony.

Presently, practices within Christianity and Islam can provide racism with sustenance and support. If divine inspiration is involved in religious expression, then human, that is, cultural, elements are also part of these holy practices. It is in the cultural shadings and nuances of these religions that input or information leading to Manichean thinking resides. It is well known and accepted that African people have used both religions for healing and reform. It is nothing new for black people to modify European products toward constructive ends. Evidence suggests that Samori Ture's brilliant metalsmiths modified and improved European rifles for use in battles against colonial powers (Lewis 1987). Religion, like those tempered rifles, will serve both constructive and destructive ends in the black community.

The excursion in this chapter, then, meanders through four domains in search of the sources of information that will lead one to develop racist mental structures. The first domain is reality, or physical conditions. The second is that reality created in popular culture through the creative processes and construing of other humans. The third realm embodies the institutions that emerge as society formally trains its young people. The final source is religious practice. Information residing within these domains can converge and fester in the minds of people of African descent. It will provide the building blocks for a racist mental edifice.

Disparities in real conditions

A man climbs aboard a bus in the inner city, mumbling disjointed, incomprehensible phrases. He stumbles and falls, brushing against an elderly lady. The driver growls, "Hey buddy, straighten up or I'll throw you out." Now, the same sequence of events could have taken place next to a surgical outpatient clinic in an upscale neighborhood. In this instance, the same driver might have said, "Steady there, sir, are you all right?" The lesson in this example is one learned certainly in abnormal psychology classes, if it was missed in the basic psychology course. Simply put, the context in which behaviors occur influences the judgments we make about the behavior of others.

Two decades ago, a researcher (Rosenhan 1973, 1975) convinced eight colleagues and friends to help him conduct a simple but rather intriguing study. Each person gained admission to a psychiatric hospital, using a plan Rosenhan devised. They did this by reporting bizarre symptoms. However, after being admitted, they all behaved normally. Even though psychiatrists, nurses, and ward attendants observed no symptoms, the length of stay in the hospital for these pseudopatients ranged from seven to fifty-two days. The hospitals released all but one of these individuals with a diagnosis of schizophrenia in remission. The remaining diagnosis was manic-depressive psychosis. This outcome suggested that even if the staff did not judge normal behaviors exhibited on the hospital ward as symptoms of mental disorder, these normal behaviors could not offset the extreme diagnosis of psychosis, which was based on the self-report of hallucinations. To be sure, this study generated a firestorm of criticism (Farber 1975; Spitzer 1975). Nevertheless, the pseudopatients' initial reports of symptoms, along with the subsequent diagnostic label given to them in the hospital, evidently constituted crucial and pivotal information. This information formed a context that influenced the judgments of the attending staff. Day after day of normal behavior did not erase the diagnostic label: The contextual information was simply too powerful.

In a similar fashion, the world created by white supremacy assaults the senses of African people with events and conditions. These circumstances cause one to engage in value judgments, evaluations, and attributions of causes. In this respect, like the case of the pseudopatients, these circumstances, too, demand a "diagnosis." However, the institutions of white supremacy craftily obscure certain portions of the contexts in which these events and conditions are embedded. Most people fail to identify the network of root causal forces that have brought these conditions into being. Robbed of an understanding of the network of causes, that is, of the full context surrounding these circumstances, African people will make fundamental errors in attributing causes. They will draw faulty conclusions and interpretations related to circumstances that surround the lives of many black people. These interpretations facilitate the development of mental structures that accommodate and reinforce white supremacy.

I will refer a number of times in this section to the painstaking volume by Harold Cruse (1987), *Plural but Equal*. Cruse's study leads one to conclude that the contexts surrounding the economic conditions in the black community in the United States are shielded from the general population. Cruse affirmed the presence of formidable business acumen and spirit among African Americans during the early part of this century and declared that the demise of this spirit resulted, in part, from the civil rights agenda that black people and their allies adopted and several very important judgments made by the Supreme Court.

When does perceiving disparities between the conditions in which many blacks and most whites find themselves influence the cognition of the individual? What processes take place when this occurs? To address these questions, the behavioral scientist must address concerns on several levels. First, one must know the objective stimuli available to the senses, that is, the circumstances themselves. More important than those objective conditions, as we have noted, is the informational context that influences the individual's perception of these events. Finally, the behavioral scientist must examine the interpretations, causal attributions, and judgments the oppressed make as they view events and conditions. We will investigate three examples.

Economic realities and their extensions

Africans living in the Western hemisphere or on the African continent come to know that money is more at home in the pockets of white people than in the pockets of black people. They learn this before leaving childhood. Of course, they will recognize the exceptions. They may see athletes, entertainers, some in the criminal subculture, and the exceptional business person accumulate wealth. Class stratification exists in most societies. But even before they reach the teenage years, they quite likely will see significant transgenerational wealth resting with whites more than with blacks. The birthright of many black people is economic uncertainty or even poverty. This condition is one that the remaining complement must scrupulously avoid. Haiti, the poorest country in the Western hemisphere, is black. Forty-four percent of children of African descent who lived in the richest country in the Western hemisphere in 1985 lived in poverty (Jaynes and

Williams 1989, 279). The objective manifestations of the economic disparities are evident in every phase of life. To see them, one need only look in the homes, schools, marketplaces, and even the churches. Before leaving childhood, it is much more than likely that the African will have a notion of the economic realities of white supremacy.

Obviously, in a society that inordinately values money, there is a risk of devaluing those who do not have it. The danger, of course, is to conclude that those without capital lack the energy or the intellectual ability to acquire it. In the United States, there is a tendency for the white population to forget the pivotal role uncompensated black labor played in the building of the economy (see E. Williams 1964; Du Bois 1935). Instead, the society tends to conclude that the poverty of people of African descent is caused, simply, by an unwillingness to work hard and save money. Historically, African Americans have labored within a capitalistic opportunity structure that was much more closed than open. Their economic status is more a function of this structure than of their failure to strive (see Allen 1969). Most people in the United States are not aware of the abiding entrepreneurial spirit that black people have displayed in this country (Cruse 1987). Thriving commercial centers once existed in black communities across the land. These momentous efforts fly in the face of the purported inherent laziness of African people.

If one intends to make fair causal attributions and judgments about the economic plight of black people, historical information is an essential part of the context. Regarding conditions in the United States, if one knows that vibrant entrepreneurial spirit and willingness to work once existed in these blighted communities, then one draws more informed conclusions. Knowing that a similar work ethic and business spirit exist all over the African world shifts one's focus away from the failings and lethargy that will always exist within segments of poor communities. The focus becomes the actions of the social structure that have discouraged a once energetic, vibrant, and dedicated workforce.

However, there is an additional detrimental impact of these economic disparities. In the African world, including African communities in the United States, people find it difficult to raise the capital to construct vital information-disseminating institutions. The development of these communication and educational entities depends, in part, on money. Still, their function goes far beyond the acquisition of wealth for the proprietors and owners. The lack of personal and community capital spawns deficits in the local informational infrastructure. Thus, there is a persistent dearth of crucial contextual information. The role of this information would be to reduce the negative impact of perceiving disparities. The therapeutic potential of institutions, including viable, autonomous press and educational institutions, is quite formidable. They have the power to nurture and undergird African people cognitively in an environment of white supremacy by helping the oppressed comprehend the context from which the economic disparities arise. These institutions have the capacity to provide historical information and critical analyses of current situations. Economic disparities are responsible, in part, for the failure of such institutions to thrive and execute this function. The cycle is most vicious.

For example, when I leave my office at Howard University, I often see young African boys involved in a football scrimmage in the middle of the street. If I drive to the more distant suburbs, past the Beltway (the interstate highway that surrounds the city), I find communities where fewer boys look like my son. There I see large, grassy areas where the sons of white men play. Recall the situation described earlier of the reactions to the man who fell getting on the bus. Here, too, we will make a judgment and interpretation of some kind. The economic disparity that exists between these communities does more than ensure that there will be no spacious playground for black children around Howard University. These disparities do more than increase the likelihood that there are ample grassy meadows for white children in certain suburbs. The power of this disparity extends beyond its capacity to elicit an attribution of cause from the perceiver. There is a third function of the economic disparity. It decreases the likelihood that information from viable institutions that will help us avoid a horrendous attributional error will ever touch my mind and the minds of most black people. Without this information, we will attribute quite wrongly, I insist, the poverty of these young brothers to the lack of initiative of their forebears. Therefore, we will view these conditions through the prism of Manichean cognition.

In fact, the weakening of black-controlled institutions, both informational and purely commercial establishments, can serve to reinforce white supremacy in quite another way. One can easily misinterpret the failure of African people to maintain these institutions, while the institutions of others appear to be flourishing, as further evidence of the inferior competence of the race. This is the most paradoxical of circumstances. The agitation for integration and constitutional changes, what Cruse (1987) called "noneconomic liberalism," was the hallmark of the civil rights agenda. This movement came to a triumphant climax with the 1954 *Brown v. Board of Education* decision. According to Cruse, the trajectory of this movement becomes quite evident when we explore the factors that led to the split between Du Bois and the National Association for the Advancement of Colored People in 1934. The civil rights agenda envisioned African people as a group that deserved to be "attended properly" by the nation (Du Bois's words, see Cruse 1987, 91). Du Bois favored an activist agenda that involved economic cooperation and development within the black community. The side effect of the former strategy was to weaken black-controlled institutions. The thrust of the latter was to nurture black institutions. The irony is that the civil rights movement, whose purpose was to mitigate the effects of white supremacy, would become its unwitting ally. That is, black institutions became weaker with the limited desegregation of the society. These crippled or virtually absent institutions would become fodder for the development of a racist mentality.

Black control over political institutions has increased significantly during the last half of this century. Ironically, this has taken place as black control over information-disseminating institutions in the United States has declined. In the United States and indeed, all over the African world, whites no longer control each and every rein of government. On the continent of Africa and in the Caribbean, independence movements resulted in black control over the instruments of government. Similarly, in the United States, black people celebrated the rise of many black elected officials, including the mayors of major cities and, recently, a senator and a state governor.

We have to raise if not wave the caution flag here. James Baldwin (1985) eloquently and succinctly articulated the reason that he failed to leap for joy at the sight of black mayors in the cities of the United States. "It is a concession masking the face of power, which remains White. The presence of these beleaguered Black men—some of whom, after all, putting it brutally, may or may not be for sale—threatens the power of the Republic far less than would their absence" (26–27). Certainly, both in the West and on the continent of Africa, black political officials inherited faltering economic infrastructures (Chinweizu 1987). For the most part, city officials here and presidents there were left to preside over worsening conditions. It is appropriate to view the failure to better these circumstances within that context.

This does not make their failure excusable. Indeed, correcting these ills, as Chinweizu (1987) noted, may have resulted in the kind of sacrifice and effort that in the short term people in a materialistic society would find difficult to accept. In the long run, these sacrifices and efforts would have produced results that seriously jeopardize white supremacy. The situation demanded that people be willing to do without certain products and comforts until they were able to strengthen their own institutions and achieve self-sufficiency. This proved too bitter a pill for most black political leaders to take or to ask their constituencies to swallow.

Ultimately, that black elected officials preside over an increase in the magnitude of the economic disparities between the black and white world supports racism. It buttresses the Manichean notion that proper government must be white. Both in the diaspora and on the continent, apparently black politicians orchestrate the economic demise of their own societies. How then, could this "progress" made within the political arena represent a challenge to white supremacy or prove therapeutic, ultimately, for a Manichean mind?

Disparities in development

Rodney (1972) authored an extensive study of the relationship between African and European societies. He proposed that the level of a particular society's development encompasses but is not limited to the economic sphere. Development, according to Rodney, is the capacity of a society to "regulate both internal and external relationships" (10). As societies develop, the relationships among products, people, and institutions change. With development, people carry out the activities that advance culture and sustain the life of the members of the society in a less harried fashion. In Chancellor Williams's words, the people are left with "time to think" (1974, 56). They are able to enhance the quality of their lives.

Rodney maintained adamantly that under normal circumstances development is a universal process. The forms that development takes differ from culture to culture. Certainly C. Williams (1974) would agree. However, the concept of underdevelopment becomes meaningful when we consider two conditions. First, some societies are relatively less developed than others. Second, in modern times, exploitation of one society by another often leads to differences in the level of development that we observe.

The concepts of development and underdevelopment may seem somewhat remote to the discussion of Manichean cognition. However, each harbors important consequences for the development of mental content. Each member of the society perceives certain manifestations of the abstract notion of development. People come to know if they are dependent on others for their own food and clothing. Similarly, the adult members of a society will know of their dependency on external agents for socializing functions and services, including schools and hospitals (see Rodney 1972, 25). No forces and no manner of cloaking will be able to hide indefinitely the sources outside of one's community that control these functions.

However, there are instances when members of one's group control these institutions inefficiently. This lack of efficiency becomes evident through a process of comparison. People compare their own conditions with media images or popular lore about how things should be or how things are elsewhere. In essence, the perception of the developmental status of one's community centers around the sensing of a general level of autonomy and efficiency. It is along these dimensions that members of a community judge their institutions and their ability to execute certain life-sustaining functions.

Chinweizu (1987) described a "cargo cult" mentality that is important to consider in a discussion of development. According to him, cargo cults emerged during the colonial period. Members would engage in a set of unproductive and alienating rituals that included raising and lowering European flags and participating in military formations and parades. In exchange, they expected to receive food, clothing, tobacco, and other products. These were brought forth quite magically from the fuselages of planes and the holds of ships. Cult members attributed a godlike status to those who mysteriously produced these goods. Equally tragic was the planting of the insidious thought that only Europeans possessed the competence to produce these items. For countless centuries, the forebears of the cult members had met their own needs quite effectively.

Very young children in urban areas in the United States envision retail stores as the sole and ultimate source of food and clothing. Viewing retail stores as the source of necessities poses no threat to the regions of cognition that the Manichean order tends to influence. Mistaking retail stores for the origin of goods remains innocuous as long as a child sees clerks and proprietors of her or his race in these outlets. Arguably, it is likely that children and, for that matter, most adults rarely consider or comprehend the intricacies related to the production of goods and services.

Black businesses provide only a fraction of the goods and services black people consume. Indeed, about one-third of 1 percent of all business receipts generated in the U.S. economy go to black businesses (Jaynes and Williams 1989). This figure is not part of the consciousness of most people of African descent. But it is likely that a form of this information finds its way into the minds of young people. Usually it does so in a very general way, stripped of an explanatory context. People know to whom they give their money, and in a sense they know who produces the resources they buy.

In addition, recall that it is around third and fourth grade in the United States that social studies classes begin. In these classes children learn of the very productive farm lands of the Midwest and California. They are told of the movement of agricultural products to supermarkets. Land and farm ownership by blacks has fallen precipitously. Billingsley (1992) noted that in 1890 over 90 percent of black families in the United States lived in the rural south and worked as farmers. By 1980, 90 percent of families had migrated to urban areas. This was due in part to the loss of agricultural employment.

There is a real risk that a dim notion of the underdeveloped state of the black community begins to form in the minds of urban African-American children. They learn that it is white people who produce the food and move it to stores. The Manichean mind is reinforced if this notion grows into an assumption that others produce food, clothing, cars, and electronic equipment for African people to consume. The mind festers when one begins to conclude that this consumer status exists simply because African people are unproductive. These beliefs need not be verbalized or verbalizable. Whether it is a question of food, shelter, or clothing, African people in the United States and in too many other corners of this world play the role of colonized consumers and wait for others to deliver the cargo.

The fact is, increasing numbers of non-African Americans own the retail outlets in black communities where black people buy most of their life-sustaining products. Whites and Asians own many of the grocery stores where one buys food and the pharmacies where one secures medicine. This becomes obvious as one moves through black communities all over the United States. As we have noted, this was certainly not always the case. Indeed, even with underdevelopment, black resistance and persistence ensure that there will be black-owned retail outlets. But these, on the whole, for complex economic as well as psychological reasons, are often smaller and more expensive than their white counterparts.

Underdevelopment is reflected in the health care systems and in the health status of the oppressed. The health status of black people in the United States suffers because of a number of factors. One factor is the quality of care available (Jaynes and Williams 1989). The disparity between the system available to attend the health needs of most white people in this country and the system that African Americans use is great. Hospitals and clinics that serve African people, especially those in the inner cities, are often deluged with patients. Even when modern equipment is available, delays are long and taxing to those who are already suffering.

Heart disease and cancer, the leading causes of death in the United States, are far more prevalent in blacks above the age of thirty-five than in whites (Krieger et al. 1993). Homicide is the leading cause of death in black men thirty-four years of age and younger. In 1990, many Americans recoiled when they learned that a black man living in Harlem was less likely to reach sixty-five years of age than a man living in Bangladesh (see LuSane 1991). Indeed, death hangs like a pall over many black communities. This omnipresent shroud of death, be it from homicide, heart disease, cancer, or, more recently, AIDS, looms large. An overtaxed and underdeveloped health care system represents at most a minor annoyance to the threat of death. Bulhan (1985) was absolutely correct. The yield of the Manichean order for the oppressed is premature death. The health care system in the community of the racially oppressed is rarely sufficiently developed to mitigate this reality. Exhausted physicians in bustling clinics and packed emergency rooms resemble medical units one might find on a battlefield in a declared war.

Black people tend not to trust or make use of the system as it is constituted. Perhaps this is the clearest indication that African Americans perceive the disparities between health care systems. Black people tend to be reluctant to use services or they use them only when diseases are quite severe. To some extent, the failure to employ the system stems from the perception that the institutions available to them are not of sufficient quality to ameliorate existing states of disease.

With health care systems then, again, we find the oppressed cognitively processing a state of underdevelopment in the black community. Of course, the society provides little contextual information explaining the causes of this underdevelopment. Sometimes black

105

people will tacitly accept these conditions; at other times they may openly challenge them. In either case, the perception remains that not even the institutions that safeguard life itself are efficient in African-American communities. The Manichean attribution is that it is the lack of competence of African people that is the sole and root cause of this condition. What a splendid fertilizer this perception provides for a belief in fundamental black incompetence.

Disparities in Ambience

A word about ambience is a fitting conclusion to this section. One who observes the objective conditions of black and white existence will sense fundamental, somewhat intangible differences in the quality of the settings. Bulhan (1985) pointed out this category of disparities when he defined the Manichean order (141). Certainly, the tone of voice the policeman uses, the luster on the brass arch over an entrance to a business, and the amount of litter allowed to blow about in the street differ between the environs of the black and white worlds. In major U.S. cities, the gutted buildings, ominous alleyways, broken windows and bottles, advertisements for mind-numbing alcohol, abandoned cars, and shattered bus shelters seem to increase in frequency as one moves deeper into the bowels of the black community. These provide the backdrop for the development of a mindset that equates the Caucasian world with all things good and worthy and the African world with utter depravity.

Summary

Desperate economic conditions; ineffective political, educational, and health care institutions; and a persistent negative ambience exist too often in the communities of African people. These are part of the information that impinges on the senses of the inhabitants. Eventually, perceiving the general disparities between the ecology of whites and African people can be mentally crippling. One can avoid the negative effects if parents, teachers, or writers provide the proper historical and political context surrounding these disparities. In the absence of this context, these perceptions alone derail efforts to nurture and foster minds free of Manichean cognition. Sadly, all can readily perceive the disparities we have mentioned. For the most part, primary socializing agents do not provide African minds the information that would allow them to critically analyze the forces that have created these conditions.

In the next two sections, we will discuss how forces in the society sabotage two potentially liberating crucibles of contextual information. The formal education system and popular culture have a remarkable therapeutic potential. Information from these sources might lead African people to develop a critical consciousness that would be capable of deciphering and decoding the causal chain of events lurking behind the ostensible disparities between the lives and environments of blacks and whites. However, African people do not acquire a therapeutic knowledge base from these sources. In many instances, black people consume a popular culture and a propagandistic education that tend to fuel the development of Manichean cognition. The ideas and images contained in both are often damaging. We will come to see that popular culture and formal education all too often reinforce the misdirecting of the minds of African people.

Popular culture

The nature of mental images

The mental image is the brain's representation of a perceptual event. The image is one of the brain's tools for symbolizing and representing a particular aspect of our experience. We derive images from encounters with the external as well as the internal sensory environment. That is, we can derive a mental image of a picture we have seen or a song we have heard. Also, we can have a mental image of our sense of the loss of balance that we may experience if we have an attack of vertigo. Imagery bears some similarity to language, another important symbolic process. Certainly, humans use both language and images in thinking. When educators and psychologists think about cognition, they tend to emphasize forms that are mediated by language, including linguistic reasoning and verbal comprehension. However, one's capacity to recognize a face or a familiar grouping of notes from a song depends on imagery processes. Likewise, the capacity to picture a diamond shape in one's mind and then rotate that shape one half-turn depends on the use of mental images.

Another similarity between language and imagery is related to semantics or meaning. As is the case with verbal symbols, that is, words, an image can be linked to a referent—the event, state, person, or place from which the image was derived. In the study of semantics, which examines the manner in which language takes on meaning, the word referent is the *denotative* meaning. Additionally, images, like words, will contain a kind of meaning that is subjective and highly evaluative: That is, both images and words elicit sets of emotional and attitudinal responses. The subjective facet of meaning is commonly designated *connotative*. The word "snake" refers to a legless reptile denotatively. It will have a variety of connotative meanings depending on one's personal history with snakes and, perhaps, beliefs in religious mythology. Similarly, in our research laboratory we find that most people can generate a mental image of the setting sun, or at least they report to us that they can. Hence, the image seems to have some significant denotative elements. However, the response to this image varies considerably from wonder and amazement to casual disinterest. The connotative meaning seems to depend on a host of personality factors and a variety of other factors related to individual history. This is the highly personal nature of connotative meaning.

However, there are instances where the symbolic activity involving words differs from that involving images. Certain aspects of language are public in nature and to a large extent can be examined directly in an empirical fashion. Images are perceptual events and are not wholly or sometimes even partially reducible to verbal statements. That is, the mental image may or may not be verbally mediated. For example, I can describe in words the image I have of a vicious attack on U.S. citizens by Alabama state authorities on March 7, 1965. This assault on civil rights marchers occurred at the Edmund Pettus Bridge in Selma, Alabama. I have derived this particular image from film footage I have seen over and over again. Because I constructed this image from a filmed sequence, I could probably reduce it to words. Language seems to manage both the connotative and denotative elements of my image of the horrible event. By contrast, I was fortunate enough to see Avery Brooks's portrayal of Paul Robeson on the stage. I have tried to communicate to friends the magnitude and dimensions of the image this event left in my mind. Each time, I feel the words have come up short. Further, consider this image of an internal sensory event. My mind has a clear image of the proprioceptive event that was part of the cracking of my right ankle during a high school football practice. Phrases like "unrelenting, dull pain" and "dull snapping sound" do little justice to this image. I hesitate to use them. Indeed, there are times that verbal statements simply cannot capture the very rich content and dimensions of images. The verbal statements may fail both the denotative and connotative meaning of the image.

In the past, we humans garnered a good portion of our mental images from encounters with the real world. These were supplemented by images provided in cultural activities including folklore, myths, song, and dance. However, as societies became more complex, this second source of images encroached on those we were extracting from reality. In essence, cultural activities represent the intricate, variegated world that other human beings create or construe. In modern times, we can divide the construed environmental space into the worlds of formal education and popular culture. We will address the images that come forth from popular culture first.

The primary manifestation of popular culture is the mass media, including the recording industry, radio, television, and film. These media use both kinds of symbolic processes: images and words. Often, they artificially fuse the word with a nonverbal perceptual experience; this will often heighten the impact of the experience. Obviously, the purpose of the soundtrack in a radio or filmed drama is to enhance the impact of a particular event. Again, thinking employs both words and images. Therefore, it is conceivable that records, radio, television, and films might provide a context for understanding the disparities in the conditions between whites and blacks. Sadly, for the most part, this is not and has not been the case. Images and information coming from the popular culture have tended to reinforce the development of a Manichean mind-set. This story is not simple, however. Several examples from the experience in the United States are worthy of consideration. The United States produces one of the more influential and variegated popular cultures in the world.

Dates and Barlow (1990b) provided a comprehensive analysis of the portrayal of black people by the mass media in the United States. They entitled their book *Split Image: African Americans in the Mass Media*. They took a historically conscious approach to this material. Their observations provide important insights into the popular culture. In their introduction, Dates and Barlow (1990a) argued that the ultimate yield of the negative image of African people in the various media has been to cement the superordinate/subordinate power relationship, whites over blacks. They traced these efforts to the literary tradition that existed during slavery. They placed their analysis in a dialectical framework, as did most of the contributors to this important volume. Within this framework, there rages an ongoing struggle for control over the image of people of African descent, who, with their allies, meet attempts at negative or less than authentic portrayals with varying forms of resistance. Subsequently, the purveyor of negative images introduces stylistic and sometimes minor substantive changes in the distorted portrayal. Again, resistance to these surfaces. The process continues. I have used much of the material in *Split Image* as the basis for a brief discussion of the products of several branches of the media. Individuals obtain the bulk of their mental images of African people from these sources. They are, perhaps, the most influential manifestation of the popular culture.

Recording industry

In a haunting and incisive exchange with a trusted member of her band, playwright August Wilson's Ma Rainey confides, "As soon as they get my voice down on them recording machines, then it's just like if I'd be some whore and they roll over and put their pants on. Ain't got no use for me then" (1985, 79). This line frames the intricate exigencies, the pitfalls, and the payoffs that constitute the history of African Americans in the recording industry. To be fair, the medium has given the material created by artists of African descent worldwide exposure. Virtually every corner of the globe knows of blues, jazz, and gospel, as well as rhythm and blues, rock and roll, and hip hop music. Simultaneously, as Barlow (1990a) pointed out, their efforts often enriched, to an inordinate extent, generations of white businessmen. These men largely managed the major record companies. In some instances, they pressured artists to modify their music to "conform to racist stereotypes" (Barlow 1990a, 26).

In other cases, business interests demanded that the musicians dilute their product to bring it into line with European aesthetics, musical conventions, and standards of respectability. Hence, in the recording industry the battle of images has been waged on at least two fronts: First, there has been a struggle for authentic expression of art against the dilution or altering of these forms. This is basically a struggle centered around the cultural aesthetic. The second struggle has been ideological. The creators of music have had to take a position on the extent to which they would saturate their product with Manichean images. Further, they have had to decide if their music would criticize racist and oppressive images at large in the society itself.

One avenue black people used to move records in the direction of cultural authenticity and nonracist ideology was to control the production, promotion, and distribution of records. Certainly, the most celebrated instance of black control over the production of records is the Motown corporation. However, George (1988) and Barlow (1990a) have discussed other historical instances of black ownership of record labels. For example, the Black Swan label, founded by W. C. Handy in 1921, prided itself on the exclusive involvement of black people in each and every level of its operation. It was equally proud of the diversity of the artistic expression to which it gave voice. Therefore, the existence of the label alone, theoretically, served to counter Manichean thinking in the competence and cultural historical regions.

Further, by providing a wide spectrum of black expression, Black Swan endeavored to underscore the richness of black culture and militated against the development of stereotypes of black music. However, the managers of Black Swan were walking a thin and shifting tightrope. Efforts to show the variability of black expression set in motion currents against the pure folk traditions of African-American music. The thrust became a shift in the direction of favoring a more "highbrow" product (George 1988). The trajectory away from demeaning stereotypes, wittingly or unwittingly, was accompanied by the deprecation of cultural products that were deeply rooted in folk traditions. Regarding the war against white supremacy, what black people gained on one front, they lost on the other. The Black Swan label showed that African people need not depend on white people to produce their records. The independent efforts reinforced a strong sense of black competence and efficacy. Still, the executives at Black Swan attempted to prove the racist stereotype false by promoting participation in European or Europeanized expressions on record. They risked abandoning authentic artistic renderings and, to an extent, supported cultural racism.

Garofalo (1990) drew an instructive contrast between the material produced and the business practices of two black-owned record companies in the second half of the century. The companies were the heralded Motown and (eventually black-owned) Stax records. Those who managed Motown were concerned with reaching a white audience. They wanted their product to "cross over" into this lucrative market, so they developed a "glossy" product, replete with multitrack dubbing, horns, and strings, which became the hallmark of their records. Stax executives, on the other hand, directed their product to the fans of rhythm and blues. There was less redubbing of the music. All the musicians worked together in session to create the recordings. If

111

the sound they produced crossed over to white audiences, it did so "on its own terms" (95).

Again, black record companies were born of a striving to control the product of black creative efforts. These companies, too, wrestled with the problem of authenticity. They might produce a diluted or altered record product for two reasons. The first would be part of the process of resistance to racism. Self-conscious attempts to establish the capability of Africans to produce variegated musical forms could have shattered racist stereotypes. However, this effort risked alienating companies or the artists themselves from their own African musical and cultural traditions. The second reason was purely monetary. The lure of greater profits available from crossing over to large white audiences has led some black companies to produce records that were less authentic expressions of black culture.

So what is wrong with the undiluted form of African music? One objection was that whites perceived black music and, for that matter, black dance as earthy and sexual. The open celebration and reflection of life that tended to characterize early blues, jazz, and rhythm-and-blues music indeed was at odds with the sexually ambivalent European tradition. The manner in which procreation is viewed in African and in European culture has been at odds for centuries. These discordant views were exemplified in the musical forms. The existence of this state of affairs between two cultures is of small consequence when power is equally distributed between them. It is simply a difference in world view. But this mismatch of views was played out in the context of white supremacy. Cultural racism resulted. True to the Manichean order, authentic forms of African music were deprecated as primitive and sexual. White culture viewed them as an expression of the African's lower state of human development.

With respect to the ideological issue raised by music, titles of some of the earliest recordings by African Americans reflect an acquiescence to racist stereotypes. Barlow (1990a) discussed George W. Johnson's late-nineteenth-century cylinder recording for Thomas Edison's company. The title was "Whistling Coon." Soon after, the complicated, richly talented, and perhaps tragic Bert Williams during his first recording session in 1901 committed to cylinder "The Phrenologist Coon" (see Charters 1970). From the beginning, black performers delivered the recordings with the demeanor that reflected the constraining stereotypes of the day. The black entertainer was to be demure, obliging, and ingratiating. Producers restricted the content of the material to the ephemeral, self-deprecating, silly, and obsequious. They addressed matters of the heart in a "sanitized" fashion. Often they avoided material that reflected or critically analyzed life in the apartheid United States. It would have been dangerous indeed in the early days of the recording industry for performers to sing regularly of oppression. Tragically, America would pound this lesson into the great, multitalented vocalist Paul Robeson.

To some extent, the trajectory away from presenting serious themes in black music in the United States persisted in recordings, though minstrel-like presentations went out of vogue. As a concession of sorts from those in power, the performers were allowed to abandon the sanitized presentation of love themes. They liberalized these across the decades of the century. Sexual material became more explicit. Currently, the focus on interpersonal, male-female problems and sexual themes dominates recorded material. Some modern hip hop artists complain that record companies encourage them to focus on sexual themes and exclude political commentary. These sexual themes are often fraught with material that is degrading to women and blatantly sexist (Dyson 1996). Thus the apparently unconventional and belligerent rap artists often become patsies. They fail to go beyond simple descriptions of violent interpersonal conditions in black communities. When these descriptions are sexist, simplistic, or sensationalistic, they deepen the wedges and divisions that exist between black people. Thus, even the rap artist becomes a pawn in the game of white supremacy. The trajectory away from socially critical material continues even with the hip hop generation.

Still, the exceptions in every generation have been notable. There is a tradition of rejecting stereotypes and presenting deeply critical material in black records. Acklyn Lynch (1993) shows how the musical artists of the 1940s were able to construct meaningful work under oppressive conditions. This authentic creative pulse may grow faint at times but is likely to persist. Each generation produces its cadre of uncorruptible black musicians. Foreshadowing present modes of expression, Gill Scott Heron and the Last Poets provided insightful critiques of white supremacy and the conditions that it creates. An endless array of hip hop artists have continued the critical tradition, including Grand Master Flash, Arrested Development, Digable Planets, Public Enemy, KRS1, Sister Souljah, and Common Sense. The powerful works of these artists, as well as those of continental Africans and West Indians, including Bob Marley, Harry Belafonte, and Mariam Makeba, remind us of the potential of the recording industry. It is an instrument that might at some time in the future come to preempt rather than support the development of Manichean thought.

Motion pictures

Humans have the unique capacity to concoct a story, communicate it to others, and in so doing influence the thoughts and feelings of their audience. The film industry has refined this universal process of storytelling to a staggering extent. Several features of the film medium and the settings in which movies are shown add to their awesome power. The motion picture screen is much larger than life. The movement of the camera controls the visual field, often magnifying very small, carefully selected events. Technicians combine sight and sound in an uncanny fashion. They fuse the musical score, dialogue, and sound effects with visual events that they have edited in painstaking fashion. The film and the viewer meet in a dark, almost surreal room in the theater. The viewers' palms overflow with highly palatable, nonnutritious semiedibles. The open mouth comes to symbolize a wide-open mind. The story pours forth and in.

The power of a story told on film is nowhere more apparent than in the history of the impact of motion pictures on the minds of North Americans. Has any medium in history been as profitable for businesspeople as the film industry? Hollywood, the town and the concept, is, ultimately, as much a product of the power of the film medium itself as it is an outgrowth of the formidable capitalistic dynamic in the United States.

Bogle (1974, 11) recounted that historical moment at the White House when President Wilson privately screened the 1915 film *Birth of a Nation*. Wilson was reported to have exclaimed, "It's like writing history with lightning!" Surely, eighty years of technological innovations have sharpened the lightning bolts. The power of films will only increase as the technology of filmmaking becomes increasingly more sophisticated.

From the beginning, when images on film moved haltingly and silently for brief periods, African people were present. Again, Bogle's memory is important: "In the beginning there was an Uncle Tom" (1974, 1). His reference was to the 1903 film *Uncle Tom's Cabin*. Cripps (1990) noted that two films celebrating the efforts of black soldiers were produced before the turn of the century. Clearly, the portrayal of the African in film reaches back to the beginning of film history. Often, filmmakers presented African people peripherally in the movies. Occasionally, however, they moved to the center of the frame. Perhaps because of the power of film, the impact of these portrayals on the development of racist cognitive processes has been profound.

One fact should be established. Though they were servant to a powerful order of white supremacy, white filmmakers were not able to portray people of African descent in any fashion their biases dictated. Organized protests of negative portrayals, the subtle dignity of the women and men who were paid to act out demeaning and one-dimensional roles, the need for national unity and brotherhood during war efforts, and the efforts of independent black filmmakers all influenced the portrayals of Africans. The journey toward authenticity in the portrayal of Africans on film continues to this day.

There are four avenues along which film may direct and reinforce the development of a Manichean mind. These are characters, ideology, framing, and symbols. I will discuss each presently. Perhaps the most salient influence emanates from the attributes of the characters. Elements of physiology, personality, and action are important when analyzing the impact of characters. Bogle (1974) was especially helpful by delineating five character types, indeed stereotypes, that are ubiquitous in the history of blacks in films. In earlier days, films portrayed these characters in such a blatant, unapologetic fashion that one might attribute the major portion of the negative impact of these films to the stereotypic characters. Enter Bogle's big five. There are the loyal *Tom* and the generally worthless but sometimes humorous *Coon*. The cantankerous, nurturing *Mammy* stands in stark contrast to the sexually depraved, brutal *Buck*. Finally, Bogle described the tragic *mulatto*—tragic because of this character's valiant but doomed effort to ascend the throne of whiteness.

Each character in its own fashion supported the inculcation of a racist mentality in African people. Surely each reflected the racist mentality of the filmmakers. As table 2 proposes, the region of Manichean cognition that each influences varies. Additionally, organized resistance and the general ebb and flow of historical events have modified the depiction of each type. For example, the Tom of the turn of the century becomes the Tonto-like, loyal black sidekick seen in the *Lethal Weapon* films and *Top Gun*. Likewise, the buck from *Birth of a Nation* is transformed into Celie's incestuous father in *The Color Purple*. Indeed the mindless junkies make excellent, if pitiful, coon characters. Chris Rock's ill-reformed crack addict in *New Jack City*

TABLE 2. Defining Themes and Regions of Cognitive Impact of Five Film Stereotypes

Character	Primary/Secondary Impact	Theme
Tom	Efficacy competence/ Cultural historical	Loyal to the death
Mammy	Cultural historical/Body image	Nurturing and succoring white culture
Coon	Efficacy competence/Body image	Intellectually out of step with the times
Mulatto	Body image/Efficacy competence	Halo effects: tragic white beauty leading to goodness
Buck	Body image/Cultural historical	Black as biological

is an excellent example of the modern coon. Marlon Wayons reprises the coon in the movie *Senseless*. It is useful to consider how modern films transform each of these types.

The Tom undermines, first, the African's perception of competence and, second, cultural and historical awareness. In the final analysis, no matter how able Tom may be, he pledges his unflagging loyalty to the agenda of the master. Turner (1994) argued convincingly that neither the earlier nor the modern Tom reflects the essence of Uncle Tom in Harriet Stowe's novel. The original Uncle Tom, though loyal to the master, did not betray those who planned to escape enslavement. Eventually he accepted the fate of being sold because he believed it would benefit his family. The modern Tom, too, can be insightful and courageous. Still, his failure is his inability to carve out his own vision. Therefore, regardless of his high level of "refinement" or training, Tom is never truly competent. He remains wooden and robotic, unable to forge a path that is truly his. True to the original Uncle Tom, he entertains a limited number of options in negotiating life's challenges. These are the options of which his master approves.

Like Tom, Mammy suffers from a peculiar alienation of loyalty. Whoopi Goldberg has given us the modern Mammy in *Clara's Heart* and in *The Long Walk Home*. A ubiquitous nurturing quality distinguishes the Mammy from the modern Tom. Gender differences aside, this is Mammy's distinguishing feature. Often she is mentally more capable, more insightful, and more sensitive than either her employers or charges. Mammy suckles, cajoles, and scolds the hardheaded, often brattish white fledglings. Her function in life is to ready these neophytes for participation in the high culture to which they are heir and from which Mammy, so sadly, is excluded.

Women play an essential role in maintaining and embellishing culture. Even in the last decade of this century, they see children through the process of early childhood education. Therefore, the Mammy figure sometimes becomes a virtual linchpin for the continuance of white supremacy. Indeed, Mammy may be much more a constructed image than a historical reality. Turner (1994) argued that few black women wielded the kind of power on plantations that many films attribute to Mammy. Certainly, Tom has his protective function. But Mammy, at least figuratively, assumes two destructive roles in one fell swoop. She tends to the everyday needs of the next generation of white supremacists, and at the same time she reminds African people that their place, their culture, and their history are less important. That is, by the time Mammy gets home, if indeed the screen portrayal allows her a home at all, she is tired and her feet hurt. She has nothing left to give to her own family. This form of alienation of both loyalty and labor sends the signal to the black community that the culture worthy of nurturing and preserving lies on the other side of the tracks. How insidious the Mammy.

Tom undermines the African mind's development of a sense of competence because he fails to advance an authentic, autonomous agenda and world view. The coon, however, undermines the sense of competence because he lacks the capacity to ascribe knowingly to any agenda at all. Early coons, with their malapropisms, as well as latter-day victimized addicts and grade school pushouts are of limited intellectual resources. They give comfort to white society by assuring it that Africans, those of this ilk anyway, are quite incapable of generating a plan that would expose, let alone destroy the fabric of white supremacy. To add insult to this profound injury, the coon influences the body-image facet of Manichean cognition. Often he is blessed with richly dark skin, a strong, broad nose, and full lips. At the same time he emits exaggerated facial expressions including bug-eyed and droopy-lipped poses. The coon poses as a Eurocentric caricature of African features. Subtly and sometimes not so subtly, an association is forged between selected caricatures of African physical features and incompetence. Thus, with the construction of this false association between physiology and mental competence, the damage that coon inflicts is often twofold.

Even today's audiences, and this includes audiences of African descent, are not particularly comfortable with films that feature ebony-skinned leading ladies. This is especially true when the hair of these ladies, in the words of Gwendolyn Brooks, "has not looked the hot comb in the teeth." This is the legacy of the "tragic mulatto." Happily and significantly, *Tap*, a movie starring Gregory Hines, contravened this convention. The regal Suzzanne Douglas performed with style and grace as the leading lady. (*Tap* is significant because it cast the late Sammy Davis Jr. in a rich and dignified role, one befitting his truly awesome, multifaceted talent.) Ms. Douglas also starred in Matty Rich's *Inkwell*. More recently, Julia Dash's *Daughters of the Dust* brought to the screen some of the most impressive pictures of African women ever seen in the genre. Spike Lee's interesting *School Daze* attempted a head-on confrontation with the tragic mulatto legacy. Lee managed in *Crooklyn* to provide some of the best portraits of Alfre Woodard yet seen on screen. These provide a strong critique of the tragic mulatto image. Still, the use of the mulatto or lighter-skinned actress as the sole or ultimate image of African beauty persists, as shown tragically in *Cooley High, Coming to America*, and countless other films. The mulatto character is among the most potent weapons white supremacy has to inculcate negative body image in Africans.

As discussed earlier, this facet of the Manichean order is especially devastating to black women. Never to be denied, however, women of astounding screen presence, including Alfre Woodard, Beah Richards, and Cecily Tyson, have presented dignified African beauty in films throughout their careers. Happily, Beah Richards revealed to the hip hop generation of movie goers her towering dignity in *Beloved*. Still, the movies tend to skew the presentation of the spectrum of black physical beauty. This misrepresentation is especially true for women. The legacy of the tragic mulatto is that women whose physical traits approach the lighter and more Europeanized regions of the continuum will be cast in leading roles.

Buck has escaped the color coding that has dogged African women on the screen. Filmmakers cast men with the physical characteristics of Ron Oneal to Wesley Snipes in the new, tamed version of the role of Buck. Buck's attacks on the body image of African people are from a different direction. Buck sees his body as desirable and beautiful, but he views it with the eyes of a psychologically troubled European. That is, he sees himself as Thomas Jefferson ([1861] 1964) saw him two centuries ago. Jefferson claimed that the black male was "more ardent after their female" (134) than were "normal" (white male) humans. Buck views himself in sexual terms or, as Fanon (1967) put it, "The Negro is the genital" (180). Buck has climbed out of one Manichean pit, where he would see his skin as too black, his hair as in need of a straightener, and his nose and lips as too broad. Tragically, he fell over backward into an abyss in which his body is reduced to being an efficient sex machine. Now he becomes capable of and obsessed with the sexual conquest of thousands of women. Too often the buck pulls numb audiences into this pit with him. Of course, the consequences of propagating this image are dire for relationships between black men and women.

These false, generally one-dimensional portrayals of characters are but one of the avenues through which films will support the intentions of white supremacy. A second avenue is the ideological posture that the movie assumes. The nub of this ideological issue is whether the film will acknowledge and challenge racist oppression or on what terms it will advance that oppression.

Two recent film adaptations illustrate this ideological question. These examples show how the ideological posture of the film may affect the audience's vision of struggle against racism. An individual forms this vision out of the personal memory of culture and history and the sense of black efficacy and competence. Ideological shifts are often subtle. Still, they tend to influence these two regions of Manichean thought. The movie version of Charles Fuller's theater drama *A Soldier's Play* involved several significant alterations that are ideological in nature. In the film, entitled *A Soldier's Story,* the final dramatic scene gives us the upwardly mobile Captain Davenport confronting the resolute and courageous, if very dangerous, Corporal Peterson. He delivers a meaningless "love all God's children" lecture to Peterson, who stands mute, quite out of character. Shortly thereafter, the film shows the entire unit of black troops marching in a parade of glory—off to fight fascism abroad. In Fuller's (1981) original stage version, the audience is left to contemplate the extreme option Peterson takes to solve the dilemma posed as the treacherous and self-despising Sergeant Waters acts out his psychopathology. To be sure, in the play Davenport has his dignity. Still, there is no attempt to diminish the magnitude of Peterson's character, who opts for the less bourgeois and less palatable solution to a moral dilemma. Similarly, there is no glorious parade at the end of the play. Instead, Davenport, as narrator, tells us that the entire company of black soldiers is wiped out in its first encounter with the enemy. Futility looms large on the stage while flag-waving patriotism is paraded in the movie.

Similarly, the filmed adaptation of Earnest Gaines's gripping novel *A Gathering of Old Men* (1983) received some serious ideological manipulations. In both the novel and the film, older black men in rural Louisiana take up arms in a battle with a cruel system of white supremacy. They vow to block the arrest of the most dignified, fiercely proud older black man in their community. They know that the arrest will be both morally and legally unjust. A shoot-out between these men and several local whites is a central part of the climax in the novel. During this violent engagement, Gaines, through dialogue, uncovers forces that transform Big Charlie, a major but cryptic character in the novel. He changes from crouching, servile field hand into a resolute, towering, and imposing African man. The movie version refused to give the old black men the option to pull the trigger. The filmmakers seemed to have lacked the courage to allow a violent confrontation between black people and white supremacy. It is largely for this reason that the film did not work and the novel did. In the end, the ideological position assumed by the movie equivocates on the question of the need for African people to defend themselves against state-supported and fascist violence.

The impact of a film's ideology is significant. Accommodationist ideologies can be damaging to the African viewer's sense of history and culture and concept of efficacy. Films will encourage compromises with unworthy authorities and a destructive social system. Certainly this is the case in *Gathering*. The danger here is that people will identify with the protagonist who makes this compromise. White supremacy, then, is supported by movies whose ideological postures accommodate it or apologize for it.

Obviously, there is room for variability in the liberation strategies promoted by movies. Moviemakers can depict any number of ideologies on a continuum. They will range from integrationist to nationalistic. All may fashion a challenge to the dehumanizing facets of white supremacy. However, ideological perspectives that tend to rationalize racist oppression or belittle the efforts of the oppressed to thoroughly crush any and all manifestations of racism are common in film. Equally common would be those perspectives denying that racism exists at all. Both approaches harbor damaging consequences for the developing African mind.

The focal point of the film is the third venue by which a film may support or challenge Manichean cognition. Cripps (1990) would advise us to determine where the black character is situated in the frame.

Often, the race films of the 1930s and 1940s focused entirely on black life. In this respect the work of Oscar Micheaux is significant for portraying a broad spectrum of black life (see hooks 1992, chap. 8). More recently, Spike Lee's work has not only dwelled on black life, it has "self-consciously reached for a black audience" (Cripps 1990, 166). He has reopened the concept of black life as the central component and focus of films. We should not minimize Lee's impact. He has contributed a host of films that are directed to black audiences including the epic *Malcolm X, Crooklyn, Do the Right Thing, Mo' Better Blues, Get on the Bus,* and *He Got Game.* He facilitated the production of the subtly complex and interesting movie *Drop Squad* and the hard-hitting *Tales from the Hood.* These films show black life as interesting, complicated, and worthy of viewing.

Unless one is willing to make a film about drugs and violence, Hollywood seems to discourage putting black people's lives in the middle of the frame (George 1994). Filmmakers who wish to put black people center-frame struggle economically. Julia Dash spent ten years filming *Daughters of the Dust,* a film Toni Cade Bambara rightly noted black women had been waiting a lifetime to see. Haile Gerima's *Sankofa* shows slavery through the eyes of the enslaved. Apart from the beauty of the film, its uncompromising ideological posture and its framing of Africans at the center of the drama make it an achievement. The good slave master or the good master's spouse seemed to find their way into many films about the enslavement period. Both were absent in Gerima's film. Hollywood wanted no parts of *Sankofa,* and the early promotion of the film was done largely through word of mouth in the black community. Similarly, even the efforts of box office star Danny Glover could not give Charles Burnett's fascinating *To Sleep with Anger* the exposure it deserved. Obviously, films that place African people in the middle of the frame will not be blockbusters. However, they constitute an authentic critique of Hollywood's habit of peripheralizing black people in film.

Some films persist in their attempts to palliate the discomfort that they anticipate white audiences will feel if a movie treats primarily black themes. This they do by inserting white characters and modes of expression. Judd Nelson, playing a somewhat psychopathic white cop, has virtually no function in *New Jack City.* The narrative in the Civil War movie *Glory* is extremely confused. The film fails to decide which story to tell. One story is of black soldiers struggling with the age-old dilemma of whether to fight a battle whose victory guarantees

121

them nothing. The other story is of the ubiquitous noble white officer, wrestling with and overcoming his own racial prejudice. In trying to squeeze both stories into the frame, both suffer irreparably.

Pandering to white audiences by inserting white themes, characters, and even modes of expression does much more than change the payrolls of movies. There is a damaging subtext in this exercise. It reads that stories about African people are important only if whites are present. To alter a story or even one's lexicon or style of expression solely to please a white perceiver is potentially dangerous. It suggests, perhaps subtly, that black people reach true human expression only if we speak of issues involving white people and do it in a fashion they comprehend. Both these themes constitute support for deprecating the culture of African people. Both are tantamount to cultural racism.

Symbols in film refer to the manner in which the filmmaker links inanimate objects and attributes to concepts and values, including the manner in which those who construct the film pair music, colors, religious artifacts, and a host of cultural products with the full range of social interactions that take place. For example, hip hop music often plays when violent scenes are shown. Conversely, European classical music backs tender or sentimental moments. In the primitive days of film, audiences came to know that the "good guy" would invariably wear lighter-colored clothing.

Spike Lee, in Mo' Better Blues, self-consciously broke from the film tradition of associating African-American classical music (jazz) with rainy, dank, and dreary scenes. He uses the full-color spectrum as the pictorial backdrop for his study of the lives of women and men whose lives center around this music. Patricia Turner (1994) raised an objection on the symbolic level to the 1986 film Crossroads, about a Mississippi blues man and a young white music student. Ultimately, to save the bluesman's soul from the devil, the young white musician must demonstrate his prowess on the guitar. He plays Mozart and rescues the old bluesman from the depths of hell. Thus, even in a movie that celebrates the blues, European music becomes the mechanism and the symbol for salvation.

The symbols in films, when used correctly, operate in a subtle, nonobtrusive fashion. It is precisely for this reason that critics and scholars should examine them for their potentially racist and culturally hegemonic content. These symbols operate on the periphery of our perceptions. In many cases we will not focus on what the character said or did. Rather we must study what music played or what color she or he wore when certain actions occurred. The racist information may be nested in obscure associations. However, it is unwise to assume that these symbols are harmless.

Clearly, a film becomes a source of Manichean thought through the characters it portrays, the ideological posture it assumes, the extent to which it courageously frames African people in an unselfconscious authentic manner, and the symbols it uses and associates with good and evil. Additionally, films reinforce racist cognition even when Africans are absent altogether. In these instances, an endless parade of white characters, themes, ideologies, and perspectives rains down on the audience. For each Buck there are several cerebral but sexy James Bond types, alluring but able. When the coon is safely in the closet, the scientist or slightly eccentric genius of the white race bumbles across the screen. This reminds the world where true intellectual competence lies. Exclusive, soft focuses on Caucasian ideals of beauty season otherwise innocuous films. Themes that glorify the murder of Third World people by an efficient American military machine or by a white superhero are common in the current film offerings. Plenty is available in movies to reinforce racist cognition even when African life and people are not the subjects of the story.

And African people in the United States go to the movies—movies of all kinds. Black people buy an inordinate number of the movie tickets sold in the United States. The struggle to stop this very powerful medium from filling the African mind with Manichean notions will soon be a hundred years' war. It is encouraging indeed to see fresh troops in the person of young and talented black filmmakers such as Julia Dash, Spike Lee, Robert Townsend, and John Singleton, who are joining the battle to create authentic portrayals of black life that will serve to counter the negative impact of other films. Hopefully, with time, they will extinguish an appetite or tolerance in the African public for characters, ideologies, and framing that support any facet of Manichean cognition.

Radio

Inevitably, in its early years radio became a primary showcase for the products of the record companies. Hence, the forces that caused recording artists to shape their product to be in line with existing aesthetics, conventions, ideologies, and stereotypes influenced radio programming. Records played on radio were consistent with the dictates and the growth of white supremacy. In many instances, stations refused to play black artists (Barlow 1990b). Other times, the black music that stations would play was only of the most mundane and unoffensive sort. Much of commercial radio directed toward the black communities played material that constituted little threat to any of the major facets of Manichean thought. Today, of course, the coon songs of old have faded from the airways. Still, rarely do the records we hear on most radio programs focus on serious themes. Lyrics obsessed with sex, love, and betrayal tend to dominate the airtime.

But radio is not and certainly has not always been solely an outlet for the recording industry. Radio comedies and drama, as well as news and public affairs programming, have seasoned the landscape of radio broadcasting. These alternatives to music formats have aired from the dawn of commercial broadcasts in the early 1920s through the golden age of radio in the 1930s and 1940s. In comedies and drama, racially stereotypic programming was the order of the day and, in fact, dominated for a time. *Amos 'n Andy, Pick and Pat*, and *Two Black Crows* were popular early radio comedies. They brought the kind of material that would foster notions in a nation of listeners that African people were, for the most part, coons and clowns— totally incapable of efficacious functioning in modern society. In the mode of the minstrels, these programs depicted black people as humorous in their inability to comprehend the ways of white folks. As was certainly true in the case of Burt Williams, the power and magnitude of an individual performer may have redeemed and humanized a moment or two of an individual program. But usually, the potentially mentally destructive thrust of these programs raged unabated.

However, there was resistance in radioland. These efforts to resist demeaning programming remind us, as they do in the case of the recording industry, what this medium could become. Barlow (1990b) recounted the histories of several excellent black documentaries and dramas. These programs not only took exception to existing racial stereotypes, they challenged the framework within which the public was discussing the problems of race. One such program was *New World A-Coming*. This half-hour program, which premiered in 1944, tackled issues that are topical even today, including apartheid in southern Africa, racism in the entertainment industry, housing discrimination, and black music in America. Episodes attacked stereotypes and misconceptions candidly. The best and brightest talent in the black community, including Paul Robeson and Canady Lee, contributed to these outstanding broadcasts.

Because television is a dominant force, it is not likely that we will see a general rebirth of critical documentary and public affairs radio. However, the middle 1990s has witnessed a growth in the syndication of radio programs with "talk" formats around the United States. The right wing has used these masterfully to propagate its message against big government and poor people. Seasoned black talk-show hosts with a progressive antiracist agenda are reaching growing audiences in a number of markets. Their messages may counter some of the negative input that might be coming from records and other media outlets. The Association of Black Psychologists honored one veteran host, Bob Law of New York City, at its annual meeting in 1990. The association recognized Law for the profound impact his shows have had on the thinking of many people of African descent.

Black-owned stations struggle to remain commercially viable. They are experimenting with a variety of musical formats ranging from jazz to pop. In the shuffle, progressive information radio seems to be taking a back seat (see Barlow 1990b) and the legacy of the outstanding if limited documentaries and dramas seems to be lost. The talk format may reverse this trend.

In summary, in radio as in other media, there is a tradition of resistance that black people must reclaim, and there are errors of the past to be avoided. There is a strong tendency for commercially successful black stations to strive to cross over to white audiences. In so doing, these stations are likely to dilute the forms of black music they play and avoid information or drama that challenges racism in uncompromising tones. In black radio, efforts to maintain commercial viability and authenticity continue.

Television

From a psychological perspective, we must consider television an extremely powerful socializing force in the United States and worldwide. Certainly, television is partially responsible for the decline of radio dramas and documentaries. Radio programming could generate persuasive images related to efficacy and competence, as well as observations on the value of African culture and history. Television has the same power as radio and brings with it the added visual dimension. Therefore, television has the power to refute or support Manichean notions of physical beauty (body image). This, radio could only approximate with verbal descriptions. The verdict on television is not kind. In general, in its rather short history, television has provided a reliable source of material that would both generate and support racist thinking. Like the film industry, it does so by the manner in which it includes black images and its tendency to exclude black people in its programming.

Dates (1990a) traced the earliest presence of Africans on U.S. television to comedy (*The Beulah Show*, 1950–53; *Amos 'n Andy*, 1951–53) and the variety programs (*The Billy Daniels Show*, 1952; *The Nat King Cole Show*, 1956–57). *Beulah* depicted the loyal servant, mammy-like stereotype, while the laughable, incompetent coons often surfaced in *Amos 'n Andy*. The variety programs showcased artists who had gained wide popularity and did so in a nonthreatening fashion. However, for both comedy and variety shows, the runs were short.

Dramas where the story line actually revolved around black characters did not emerge until the 1960s. These were influenced by the rich story lines inherent in the civil rights movements of the 1950s and 1960s and the black consciousness movement of the 1960s. However, to this day, television has yet to generate a sustained presentation of a serious, central, "strong and multidimensional" black hero in a dramatic series (Dates 1990a, 261). In fact, Dates (1990a) could list only thirteen dramatic series revolving around a black character in the forty-year history of television. Not one of these remained on the air for more than two years. He could identify nearly twice as many comedy shows. At least ten of these lasted for five seasons. Clearly the tendency has been to show African people in light-hearted settings.

It is unfair and historically incorrect to assume that black people cannot use laughter and comedy to present characters and analyses that challenge Manichean concepts. Work songs (see Courlander 1963; Maultsby 1990), folk lore (Stuckey 1987), and even the work of the modern stand-up comedians (Watkins 1994) have shown that comedy can sharply criticize racist conceptualizations of Africans. However, on the whole this has not happened in the case of television comedy. Promises have often gone unfulfilled. A successful black businessperson, George Jefferson, became a modern extension of the coon in the long-running series *The Jeffersons*. Nell Carter's phenomenal talent and acerbic wit could not save her from the trappings of Mammy in *Gimme a Break*. Two shows that have featured young people of the hip hop generation have shown remarkable slides. *The Fresh Prince of Bell Air* featured some significant early shows with two strong, loving, and successful black parents. However, in the later years, the show embraced stereotypes. The young women on the show became bodies without minds. The young men emerged as more, not less, bumbling and silly with age. Similarly, Martin Lawrence, a gifted comedian, squandered the opportunity to bring the attitude and insight of the hip hop generation to his show *Martin*. Instead, the show was content to let Lawrence revel in his often loveless portrayals of the less educated, less wealthy, and less articulate members of the black community. Between these, he hurled insults at a black woman friend that rival any of those Redd Foxx hurled at Lawanda Page (Aunt Esther) on *Sanford and Son* some twenty years earlier.

Attempts by blacks to produce authentic images of themselves on television have met with mixed results. Alex Haley's series *Roots* could have been an extremely powerful challenge to the historical/cultural manifestations of racism. However, in the end the series was badly flawed, most probably through the exclusion of black directors and screenwriters (see Dates 1990a). However, powerful portrayals and messages have appeared from time to time. For example, Bill Cosby (*The Cosby Show*), Avery Brooks (*A Man Called Hawk*), Tim and Daphne Reid (*Frank's Place*), and Charles Dutton and the cast of *Roc* provided some unforgettable images. They fashioned authentic and occasionally unforgettable challenges to the one-dimensional projections of African people that litter modern television. Listervelt Middleton produced a syndicated public television series *For the People* for South Carolina Public Television. This show was made in the tradition of two important late 1960s and early 1970s shows, Ellis Haizlip's *Soul* and Tony Brown's *Black Journal*. *For the People* has provided a forum for major thinkers who have spent their lives challenging various facets of white supremacy. Frances Welsing, Na'im Akbar, Martin Bernal, Asa Hilliard, Joseph ben Jochannan, Chancelor Williams, John Henrik Clarke, Cheikh Anta Diop, Marimba Ani (Donna Richards), Wade Nobles, Sterling Stuckey, and a host of others have appeared on this program. The shows were enlightening and entertaining.

Finally, Black Entertainment Television (BET) is a relative newcomer to the burgeoning cable industry but may flex its muscles in the future. It has the potential to expand its format of music videos and sports and include programs that seriously challenge white supremacy. Already, BET has expanded to include jazz programming. Also, BET showed reruns of *Frank's Place* and *Roc* when the networks aborted these series. One looks forward to seeing more original drama and informational offerings on this network. Certainly, BET would do well to offer programming in the tradition of *New World A-Coming* and *For the People*. This powerful outlet could make a worthy contribution to the struggle against racist programming.

As is the case with film, the second source of Manichean thinking inherent in television programs emanates from the steady visual and audio drone of Caucasian images and perspectives. Television is saturated with characters and messages insisting that white people are the prototypes of competence and beauty. These characters behave in a manner that supports the notion that white culture and history are superior to all others, if there is any acknowledgment that others might actually exist.

Show after show, commercial after commercial, television reminds, cajoles, seduces, and bludgeons the black viewer into perceiving white people as competent, just, culturally superior, and aesthetically blessed. To be sure, to have a good story line, television must also show white characters as bumbling, criminal, decadent, and ugly. But these are the exceptions, and their purpose is to highlight the positive attributes of the central characters. The skilled, virtuous, and aesthetically pleasing are usually white. Ultimately, the order on television is Manichean. A steady diet of these characters and perspectives, unfettered by critical analyses, would all but ensure the growth of Manichean lines of thought.

News media

One of the hallmarks of the latter half of the twentieth century is the rapid pace with which forces and processes virtually transform the world. One branch of the popular media is dedicated to keeping its hearers informed of recent events. Given the very rapid rate of events in the postmodern world, it is even more appropriate to call this branch news.

As discussed earlier, in a Manichean reality there is a chain of events that begins with a number of forces imposing stultifying conditions on the oppressed. Subsequently, academicians and other purveyors of information in the society embroider a racist mythology or ideology whose purpose is to rationalize, legitimize, and apologize for these conditions. This mythology is replete with postulates of the inferior dispositions and capabilities of the oppressed. Toward the end of a chain of events, one finds the oppressed emitting treasonous, self-negating, and self-defeating patterns of behavior. These often become "news." Members of the media ignore the precipitating and predisposing elements in the causal chain when they report the events. Thus, news becomes additional evidence supporting the racist mythology. That is, when reporters misstate or omit the context surrounding news events, the news itself becomes a source of information that supports the developments of a Manichean mind. This is an extension of the argument advanced regarding the cognitive impact of perceiving disparities between white and black conditions in the real world. If one sees these in the decontextualized, they can support the development of racist thinking.

Africans in the United States understood at a very early juncture the importance of putting the news related to one's community in context. Dates (1990b) noted that the United States was but fifty years old when Sam Cornish and David Russworm founded the black newspaper *Freedoms Journal* to "plead our own cause" (346). The thrust, certainly, was antislavery in many of the early black papers, but the underlying issue was one of perspective. There was a need to articulate an unadulterated African vision of the events impinging on African people. Dates (1990b) seems in agreement with Robinson's (1983) assessment of the need for an authentic or radical intellectual tradition. Clearly, the political and social agendas were different for blacks and even their closest white friends. The theme would be repeated over and over again during the history of resistance to oppression in the United States. For a century and a half, a strong, diverse black press countered the rendering of the news and its context that the white media offered. Indeed the agenda of the white press differed from that of the black press. Then, and now, the white press evinced an understanding of the fabric of life in the black community that was woefully inadequate.

As the century closes, themes in the news strike at the core of the competence and efficacy component of Manichean thought. As of this writing, young African boys in the United States bicker over a full spectrum of stakes ranging from absolutely nothing, mere trinkets, to the control of turf for the sale of drugs. They readily butcher each other with exotic, high-technology weapons. In southern Africa and in other regions on the continent, death-dealing of a different sort between African men dominates the news. The press inundates us with stories of black political corruption at home and dictatorships abroad. The news depicts dire conditions in the African world in an almost monotonous fashion.

To be sure, the eager, post-Watergate, white press routinely exposes white incompetence. Energetic investigative journalists uncover scoundrels and offer their heads to the public. However, such reports are not destructive to racist mythology. The press paints white scoundrels as aberrations. Identifying them does not threaten the notion of white competence. On the contrary, finding these abnormal creatures points up the skill of the investigators.

In any case, the news media, by its decontextualized presentation of the turmoil in the black world, becomes a devastating source of racist cognition. The traditional black ally, the independent black print media, is in a weakened state. Dates (1990b) noted that several factors, including the integration of large white newspapers, have led to a decline in the caliber and influence of the once dynamic black press. Certainly, another reason for the decline in the clout of the black print medium has been the rise of television journalism. For a series of different reasons, we can expect even less from this news source.

Blacks are virtual newcomers to the television news industry. Black people participate in this medium for reasons quite distinct and different from black participation in the print medium. There is much less of an independent African tradition in television news. In fact, Thorton (1990) traced the burgeoning African-American participation in television news to the need for black reporters to cover the urban uprisings of the 1960s. White reporters could not or would not enter these areas. This is not to say that there are no independent-minded black television news reporters. Rather, the fact is that a history of independence and autonomy does not exist in this medium. Coupled with the restricted and truncated nature of television news, black reporters often find it difficult to generate a framework for presenting a proper context for reporting events in the African community.

In conclusion, in an information-oriented society, there is a thirst for news. Two main sources of this rapidly and perpetually changing information are the print and television media. However, the news itself can have a destructive cognitive effect. News from the black community presented without a proper context is often a simple description of criminal acts and of the substandard conditions in which the oppressed live. This picture lacks a proper depiction of the cryptic, causal chain of events that led to these circumstances. Television news and the white press are not inclined to provide this context. An enfeebled black press is less efficient than it once was in establishing the context for these conditions.

ducation

Du Bois (1935) concluded his momentous *Black Reconstruction* with a chapter titled "The Propaganda of History." In that chapter he argued that the scientific study of history engaged in what in today's parlance we might call a "cover-up." Du Bois claimed that historians distorted the record surrounding the causes of the Civil War and the reasons for the failure of Reconstruction. The textbooks of that day maintained black people were, on the whole, ignorant, lazy, dishonest, extravagant, and incompetent lawmakers during Reconstruction. These claims were part of the falsification of history. Later in the same chapter, Du Bois tells of withdrawing an article from the *Encyclopedia Britannica*, 14th edition. The editor praised Du Bois's article but refused to include a statement critical of the prevailing (white) historical interpretation of the role African Americans played during Reconstruction.

Du Bois (1935) echoed the issue that the "young, new school" historian Carter G. Woodson raised in his famous *The Miseducation of the Negro*. Society must grapple with the content of the educational curriculum the instant after it makes the decision to dispel ignorance. Woodson was most articulate in his argument that a falsified history was part of the foundation of an "autocolonial" system (Bulhan's term, 1985). In such a system, the oppressed reinforce their own oppression. Woodson (1933) argued that "to handicap a student by teaching him that his black face is a curse and that his struggle to change his condition is hopeless is the worst sort of lynching. It kills one's aspirations and dooms him to vagabondage and crime" (3).

Hord (1991) provided a modern analysis of the promotion of Manichean thinking through the education system. Du Bois and Woodson dealt with the open falsification and blatant overstatement by the historians of their period. The modern, integrated, even multicultural educational agenda is more insidious in its approach. Hord argued that for African students in the United States, mystification and dehumanization are the outcome of contact with the educational system. He defined mystification as "institutional efforts of the American colonizer to universalize their particularity by reproducing European-American memories and hierarchies of culture" (vii). In psychological terms, Hord argued that mystification occurs when the educational system promotes the cognitive framework European

Americans use to evaluate reality as a universal standard to be accepted by all educated humanity.

Dehumanization, according to Hord, should be viewed as an outcome. Dehumanization is a condition that occurs when the mystification process is successful and the mind of the European is introjected into the African. As black people abandon or are excluded from their own cultural memory and perspective and accept white culture, they become marginalized. As Hord wrote, "They are no longer subject but object: he/she has succumbed to dominant means of the colonizer" (vii). In the terms of the present analysis, they have been fitted with a Manichean cognitive set.

Education formally exposes the young mind to the significant words, deeds, and thoughts of others. Its tremendous power is in determining what is significant. The writers of curricula, as a function of their own education, elect to celebrate particular cultures and histories or ignore and deprecate them. They bring into sharp focus the competent actions of individuals and groups, or they veil these actions. Hord (1991) and Hilliard (1995) have correctly condemned a curriculum that leaves young black students ignorant of their own culture and history and renders them unsure of the collective capabilities of Africans to change their conditions. It also threatens their sense of personal identity.

"Enlightened" texts that the formal educational system now gives students contain, most certainly, cursory treatment of and allusions to the cultural and historical contributions of African people to the world. But the lens, the framework, and indeed the lexicon for discussing these contributions will be European. The principal focus of the entire curriculum remains the glorification of European and American history and culture. The outcome for the African mind will be essentially the same as the outcome Woodson predicted would result from the digesting of the vulgar texts of his day.

The racist educational curriculum seals off the African from the tradition of black thought discussed by Robinson (1983). This tradition, a dynamic response to oppression, would allow Africans to generate a psychological environment that can nurture the growth of minds free of white supremacy. However, most school systems use a curriculum that insists that philosophy, literature, history, science, and technology are the creation of the Europeans with a dab of participation from people of color on the periphery. This curriculum does its part to continue white supremacy. As Woodson said, it encourages behaviors from the oppressed that support persistent oppression.

Religion

Semmes (1992) discussed the impact of religion on African-American behavior and social organizations. He pointed out that for the African American community, "religion has been a force for change and human transcendence and it has also been a force for oppression and human degradation" (140). The constructive and destructive functions of religion are apparent and real. The energy and vision of the civil rights movement in the United States had its locus in the Christian church. The Islamic tradition, through the Nation of Islam and Moorish Science Temple, has extended lifelines to dispossessed and forgotten black people in U.S. prisons (see Dyson 1996 for a personalized account). To be sure, the Nation of Islam has proved moderately successful in actualizing a black nationalist agenda of self-help, institution building, and self-determination. Though both religions now have centuries-old traditions among African people, the fact is that invaders to Africa promoted Islam and Christianity. These religions and the process of assenting to their tenets can promote the development of racist thinking. This occurs as an extension of the doctrine, icons, and metacommunicative aspects of the religions.

Religious doctrines establish the status of infidels and nonbelievers. In the past, fundamental Christianity (Semmes 1992) and Islam (Lewis 1987) have relegated nonbelievers to an inferior status. People of African descent who embrace these doctrines risk falling victim to cultural racism, which occurs when they elevate their own personal status based on their rejection of African religion or ethos and acceptance of European or Arab religions. Richards (1990) suggests that these doctrines will have a second destructive effect. She argued that they alienate African people from a circle of traditional African spirituality and threaten essential links with ancestors and the unborn. For Richards then, the acceptance of these religions is part of the most destructive facet of cultural racism.

Religious rituals are, in part, culturally determined. Culture shapes and directs the nature of the icons and images that personify deities and venerated individuals. Christianity in practice is replete with

Caucasian images that represent the good, the pure, and the powerful. Though many modern theologians, churches, and temples reject these images (Felder 1989), they are still a potent source of Manichean thinking among those who embrace the religions.

Finally, the most subtle avenue that provides fodder for the development of racist thinking is metacommunicative in nature. That is, the destructive element is not the acceptance of the religious doctrine or images, it is what the acceptance of the religion communicates about the status of various people. Accepting religions that invaders promoted attributes a measure of superiority to those invaders. Some people of African descent will believe that Caucasians (Arabs or Europeans) brought light and salvation in the form of their religions to pagans and animists. The milder form of this tragic thesis is the belief that a deity selected the invaders to bring salvation to those who lived in foreign lands. In either form, the destructive metacommunication blares that those who carried the religion were chosen or superior beings. After all, they were the ones to whom God gave the divine message. This perverse and troubled metacommunication is a potential source of support for Manichean thinking.

Conclusion

It may be that racism is resilient because its supporting structure is both fluid and variegated. One can identify a common thread that links the histories of the four broad sources of racism that we have identified. That thread or theme is their exceedingly pliant nature. It is remarkable that events and processes that are so malleable can continue to exert such a profound influence. However, modern racist stimuli tend to wreak havoc in the minds of the oppressed as did earlier, cruder forms. Underestimating the impact of these modern manifestations would be an act of pure folly.

References

Akbar, N. (Luther X). 1974. Awareness: The Key to Black Mental Health. *Journal of Black Psychology* 1: 30–37.

Allen, R. L. 1969. *Black Awakening in Capitalist America: An Analytic History.* New York: Doubleday.

Baldwin, J. 1985. *The Evidence of Things Not Seen.* New York: Henry Holt.

Barlow, W. 1990a. Cashing in: 1990–1939. In *Split Image: African Americans in the Mass Media,* ed. J. L. Dates and W. Barlow, 25–55. Washington, D.C.: Howard University Press.

———. 1990b. Commercial and Noncommercial Radio. In *Split Image: African Americans in the Mass Media,* ed. J. L. Dates and W. Barlow, 175–250. Washington, D.C.: Howard University Press.

ben-Jochannan, Y. 1970. *African Origins of the Major Western Religions.* New York: Alkebu-lan Books.

Billingsley, A. 1992. *Climbing Jacob's Ladder: The Enduring Legacy of African-American Families.* New York: Simon and Schuster.

Bogle, D. 1974. *Toms, Coons, Mulattoes, Mammies and Bucks: An Interpretive History of Blacks in American Films.* New York: Bantam Books.

Brown, S. 1980. *The Collected Poems of Sterling A. Brown.* Selected by M. S. Harper. Chicago: Another Chicago Press.

Bulhan, H. A. 1985. *Frantz Fanon and the Psychology of Oppression.* New York: Plenum.

Charters, A. 1970. *Nobody: The Story of Bert Williams.* New York: Macmillan.

Chinweizu. 1987. *Decolonising the African Mind.* Lagos, Nigeria: Pero Press.

Courlander, H. 1963. *Negro Folk Music, U.S.A.* New York: Columbia University Press.

Cripps, T. 1990. Film. In *Split Image: African Americans in the Mass Media,* ed. J. L. Dates and W. Barlow, 125–72. Washington, D.C.: Howard University Press.

Cruse, H. 1987. *Plural but Equal: A Critical Study of Blacks and Minorities and America's Plural Society.* New York: William Morrow.

Dates, J. L. 1990a. Print News. In *Split Image: African Americans in the Mass Media,* ed. J. L. Dates and W. Barlow, 343–87. Washington, D.C.: Howard University Press.

———. 1990b. Commercial Television. In *Split Image: African Americans in the Mass Media,* ed. J. L. Dates and W. Barlow, 253–302. Washington, D.C.: Howard University Press.

Dates, J. L. and Barlow, W. 1990a. Introduction: A War of Images. In *Split Image: African Americans in the Mass Media,* ed. J. L. Dates and W. Barlow, 1–21. Washington, D.C.: Howard University Press.

———, eds. 1990b. *Split Image: African Americans in the Mass Media,* eds. J. L. Dates and W. Barlow, 253–302. Washington, D.C.: Howard University Press.

Du Bois, W. E. B. 1935. *Black Reconstruction in America 1860–1880.* New York: Harcourt Brace.

Dyson, M. E. 1996. *Between God and Gansta Rap: Bearing Witness to Black Culture.* New York: Oxford University Press.

Fanon, F. 1967. *Black Skin White Masks.* New York: Grove Press.

Farber, I. E. 1975. Sane and Insane: Constructions and Misconstructions. *Journal of Abnormal Psychology* 84: 589–620.

Felder, C. H. 1989. *Troubling Biblical Waters: Race, Class, and Family.* Maryknoll, N.Y.: Orbis Books.

Finch, C. S. 1991. *Echoes of the Old Darkland: Themes from the African Eden.* Decatur, Ga.: Khenti Inc.

Floyd, S. A. 1995. *The Power of Black Music: Interpreting Its History from Africa to the United States.* New York: Oxford University Press.

Fuller, C. 1981. *A Soldier's Play.* New York: Hill and Wang.

Gaines, E. J. 1983. *A Gathering of Old Men.* New York: Random House.

Garofalo, R. 1990. Crossing Over: 1939–1989. In *Split Image: African Americans in the Mass Media,* ed. J. L. Dates and W. Barlow, 57–121. Washington, D.C.: Howard University Press.

George, N. 1988. *The Death of Rhythm and Blues.* New York: E. P. Dutton.

———. 1994. *Blackface: Reflections on African Americans and the Movies.* New York: HarperCollins.

Guerrero, E. 1993. *Framing Blackness: The African-American Image in Film.* Philadelphia: Temple University Press.

Hilliard, A. 1995. *The Maroon within Us.* Baltimore: Black Classics Press.

hooks, b. 1992. *Black Looks: Race and Representation.* Boston: South End Press.

Hord, F. L. 1991. *Reconstructing Memory: Black Literary Criticism.* Chicago: Third World Press.

Jaynes, D. G., and Williams, R. M. 1989. *A Common Destiny: Blacks and American Society.* Washington, D.C.: National Academy Press.

Jefferson, T. 1964. *Notes on the State of Virginia.* 1861. Reprint, New York: Harper and Row.

Jung, C. G. 1930. Your Negro and Indian Behavior. *Forum* 83: 193–99.

Krieger, N., Rowley, D., Hermann, A. A., Avery, B., and Phillips, M. T. 1993. Racism, Sexism, and Social Class: Implications for Studies of Health, Disease, and Well-being. *American Journal of Preventive Medicine, suppl.* 6: 82–122.

Lewis, D. L. 1987. *The Race to Fashoda: European Colonialism and African Resistance in the Scramble for Africa.* New York: Weidenfeld and Nicolson.

Lusane, C. 1991. *Pipe Dream Blues: Racism and the War on Drugs.* Boston: South End Press.

Lynch, A. 1993. *Nightmare Overhanging Darkly: Essays on Black Culture and Resistance.* Chicago: Third World Press.

Maultsby, P. K. 1990. Africanisms in African-American Music. In *Africanisms in American Culture,* ed. J. E. Holloway, 185–210. Bloomington: Indiana University Press.

Richards, D. 1990. The Implications of African-American Spirituality. In *African Culture: The Rhythms of Unity,* ed. M. K. Asante and K. W. Asante, 207–31. Trenton, N.J.: African World Press.

Robinson, C. J. 1983. *Black Marxism: The Making of the Black Radical Tradition.* London: Zed Press.

Rodney, W. 1972. *How Europe Underdeveloped Africa.* Dar es Salaam: Tanzania Publishing House.

Rosenhan, D. L. 1973. On Being Sane in Insane Places. *Science* 179: 250–58.

———. 1975. The Contextual Nature of Psychiatric Diagnoses. *Journal of Abnormal Psychology* 84: 462–74.

Semmes, C. E. 1992. *Cultural Hegemony and African-American Development.* Westport, Conn.: Praeger.

Spitzer, R. L. 1975. On Pseudoscience, Logic in Remission and Psychiatric Diagnosis: A Critique of Rosenhan's "On Being Sane in Insane Places." *Journal of Abnormal Psychology* 84: 442–52.

Stuckey, S. 1987. *Slave Culture: Nationalist Theory and the Foundations of Black America.* New York: Oxford.

Thorton, L. 1990. Broadcast News. In *Split Image: African Americans in the Mass Media,* ed. J. L. Dates and W. Barlow, 388–418. Washington, D.C.: Howard University Press.

Turner, P. A. 1994. *Ceramic Uncles and Celluloid Mammies: Black Images and Their Influence on Culture.* New York: Anchor Books.

Watkins, M. 1994. *On the Real Side: Laughing, Lying, and Signifying: The Underground Tradition of African-American Humor that Transformed American Culture, from Slavery to Richard Pryor.* New York: Simon and Schuster.

Williams, C. 1974. *The Destruction of Black Civilization: Great Issues of a Race from 4500 b.c. to a.d. 2000.* Chicago: Third World Press.

Williams, E. 1964. *Capitalism and Slavery.* London: Andre Deutsch.

Wilson, A. 1985. *Ma Rainey's Black Bottom.* New York: Plume.

Woodson, C. G. 1933. *The Mis-education of the Negro.* Washington, D.C.: Associated Publishers.

Wright, B. 1975. *The Psychopathic Racial Personality.* Chicago: Third World Press.

CHAPTER FOUR

Properties of Racist Stimuli

Ore than 100 people died when two aerial walk-
ways of the Kansas City, Missouri, hotel col-
lapsed. A crowd had gathered to spend some
portion of a lazy summer evening listening to the sounds of the
house band. Spontaneously, some danced, others clapped, all
swayed more or less rhythmically to the music. Then, quite literally, the world fell from beneath their feet. Concrete and flesh
merged, and rescue crews were left to sort through the tragic
mix (see Gist and Stolz 1982).

The nation was horrified. How, with all that is known in the
field of structural engineering, could such a tragedy occur? I
posed this question to a friend of mine, an architect, and he
proffered an interesting hypothesis. He contended that the
weight of those standing on the walkway, quite probably, was
not sufficient to cause the collapse. Rather, he charged that the
rhythmic movements, the pulses of energy, placed too much
stress on the supporting framework. In psychological terms, the
causal agent was a volley of stressful events, that is, a particular
pattern of input. Not one physical event, not a summation, but
a fateful *configuration* . . . and "the walls came tumblin' down."

139

I thought of the work songs sung by African people here in the United States and on the continent. Scholars have explained that those rhythmic outpourings helped concentrate the energy of the workers while turning their minds away from the drudgery of the task at hand (see Southern 1971). Perhaps these work songs represent a perfect, intentional fusion of the physical and psychological. The gandy dancers on the railroads are an excellent example (see Courlander 1963, 95). These workers structured their songs to resonate with the lifting actions of their crowbars. They used the leverage of their bars, in concert with their songs, to align the rails. When their songs were over, the trains and their loads made smooth passage. The songs ensured that the railroad crew would expend its energy in unison. Heavy rails yielded to the persuasion of iron and muscle, coordinated by the rhythm of the songs.

Obviously, the specific patterns of events in time can have an effect that may be unanticipated and underestimated. Often, we wish to predict the impact of a set of events on an individual's behavior. If we base the prediction on the circumstances taken separately, rather than on the pattern of input that they form, we are likely to miss the mark.

This brief chapter introduces information, concepts, and principles derived from nearly a century of work in experimental psychology. It merges this information with my own speculations and suspicions. As in chapter 3, the focus is the environmental events and conditions that form the building blocks of a Manichean mind-set in people of African descent. I will fuse psychological principles and models that are not controversial with hypotheses and speculations that are an outgrowth of personal experiences. Hence the reader will find that the present chapter cuts a zigzagging path between principles and models that have received years of empirical scrutiny and quite liberal conjecture on my part. Epistemologically speaking, I will be invoking both factual and personal consciousness.

In contrast to chapter 3, the present focus shifts from the content of specific stimuli to a consideration of three more general facets of psychological input. The first relates to an interesting phenomenon that occurs when environmental information becomes repetitious. The nervous systems of organisms have evolved in such a way that if stimuli of moderate intensity and of no particular importance occur often enough, they tend to lose the influence they originally had on the organism. The first topic I treat in this chapter addresses the manner in which, wittingly or unwittingly, the social systems that deliver Manichean stimuli have solved this problem.

Second, we will take up a particular and peculiar instance of the patterning of environmental input. Stimuli occur in temporal and spatial proximity with other stimuli. In certain instances, repeated presentations of different stimuli in proximity can cause the organism to associate them with one another. A truly remarkable effect on behavioral output may result.

Finally, we will consider the ontogeny of stimulus input from a Manichean world. We will argue in favor of a model proposing that African people meet with stimuli leading to Manichean cognition in a series of waves. These are experienced in a fashion not unlike the tragic event on the Missouri balcony. Waves of input resonate with previous input from different realms and regions in the social structure. They converge along a pathway leading to a destructive Manichean cognition.

The intent of this chapter is to show that comprehending the impact of social institutions saturated with racism or with the effects of racism is not a simple process. To do so we must attend to subtle alterations in stimuli and conditions. Further, we have to examine the clustering of environmental input and not solely specific and particular events in isolation. It is often best to consider input in terms of articulated patterns of events: The configurations of these events are responsible for effects above and beyond what we might predict on the basis of an understanding of the isolated events. Still, we can state the core of the issue raised in this chapter succinctly. We commonly tend to focus exclusively on the content of information and events encountered in a racist environment. We neglect the temporal and sequential patterning of these events. When this is the case, it is likely that the investigator will seriously misunderstand and miscalculate the consequences of living in a Manichean world.

Orienting to the racist message

Human responses to environmental input

Animals, from the simplest forms to those with the most complicated nervous systems, must have some capacity to respond very rapidly to changes in the external environment. Of course, organisms differ in the extent to which and the manner in which they are able to sense changes in environmental conditions. For example, the sense of smell in humans is no match for the olfactory prowess of the average German Shepherd dog. Indeed, the common honeybee is capable of perceiving colors to which our dim eyes are quite blind (see Brown and Deffenbacher 1979; Denny and Ratner 1970).

However, responsiveness to the environment involves more than the capacity of specialized sense organs to transform physical input into neural activity (sensation). The brain integrates information into formal perceptual wholes. The manner in which organisms operate on input varies considerably from species to species. Creatures with complex nervous systems can store, anticipate, relate, and self-generate information rapidly. They execute all of these functions in a highly intricate fashion. Human organisms excel at the tasks of perceiving and integrating environmental input.

Events and situations of an infinite variety occur and reoccur in the environment. Some will facilitate life and growth, others have no particular impact at all, and still others pose an immediate threat of some kind to the organism. At the same time, some of the events within these classes will be predictable, and others will come about unexpectedly. The successful creature is able to move toward or approach stimuli that facilitate or enhance life processes, ignore those that are irrelevant, and avoid those that have detrimental effects on the organism.

Frances Graham (1984) noted that humans emit one of four kinds of responses within the first few seconds after they meet with environmental stimuli. Table 3, which I derived from Graham's more detailed discussion, provides a summary of these. It describes the responses in terms of the duration or temporal component of the response, the kinds of immediate, reflexive physiological reactions that are part of the response, and the general purpose of the response as we understand it.

Additionally, consistent with Graham's presentation, I will discuss the rate of habituation of each response. (Table 3 notes the habituation rate for each response also.) Habituation refers to a reduction in the extent or magnitude of a response because of repeated exposure to a stimulus. Psychologists distinguished habituation from two other processes that entail a reduction in responsiveness. The first is the simple adaptation of sensory organs. In this instance, sustained input to a sensory system alters its capacity to respond. A second process leading to reduced responsivity is fatigue in the efferent processes. In

ABLE 3. Temporal, Physiological, and Psychological Properties of Initial Responses to Environmental Stimuli

ponse	Duration	Physiological Components	Purpose	Habituation Rate
ansient nulus ection	Short (msec)	Heart Rate (HR) increase or decrease	Register change in stimulus level	Slow
rtle	Short (msec)	HR increase Pupil dilation immediately	Bring organism to full alert	Rapid
ienting	Long (seconds)	HR decrease Pupil dilation Reduced blood flow to limbs, increased blood flow to head	Prepare for stimulus intake/ attention	Rapid
fensive	Long (seconds)	HR increase Reduced blood flow to head, increased blood flow to limbs	Prepare for "fight or flight"	Slow

Adapted from Graham 1984.

some instances this occurs when prolonged activity has exhausted the systems that mediate the response to the environmental event. In these cases the sensory input processes are intact, and the absence of a response is due to a failure in the *output* side of the behavioral process.

Researchers demonstrate dishabituation to differentiate habituation from adaptation and fatigue in effector processes. Dishabituation involves eliciting a response in the habituated system by changing the quality of a stimulus. For example, you may find that the tenth time a phone rings your concentration on an article that you are reading is not disrupted. However, the first time it rang it was quite bothersome. It is likely that habituation is occurring. However, I may replace the ring with a tone or a buzzer that is no louder or softer than the initial ringing. If the buzzer disrupts your reading, I have demonstrated dishabituation.

Habituation and dishabituation refer to processes that take place as organisms integrate and operate on input. That is, these processes are not occurring at the level of sensory and effector systems. A glass of orange juice tastes bitter after you have eaten a candy bar. Sensory adaptation and not habituation causes the orange juice to lack sweetness. If an infant fails to lift its head the fifty-fifth time an interesting sounding set of chimes rings, effector fatigue, not habituation, has taken place. There is a good chance the baby's neck muscles are tired. Thus, habituation refers to a process that takes place deep within those systems where the brain processes stimuli. It has less to do with the branches of the nervous system where input arrives or the output realms where behaviors are ultimately effected.

Humans show two responses to stimulation that are of extremely short duration. They occur within milliseconds and are of minor interest to our discussion. The first is the startle response. Stimuli that are sudden and intense cause startle responses characterized by dilation of the pupils and an increase in heart rate. The startle response habituates very rapidly. Often, when a stimulus that initially elicited a startle response occurs the second time, there will be no startle response at all. The startle response brings the organism to full alert very rapidly. Its function is to prepare the organism for emergency situations.

The other response of short duration, the transient stimulus detection response, is more difficult to conceptualize and demonstrate. Psychologists measure this response in terms of milliseconds. It occurs when we experience stimuli of moderate intensity and involves an immediate, momentary increase or decrease in heart rate. It seems to reflect the registration of a change in the level of environmental input to the information processing system. Generally, it is a prelude to a more deliberate analysis of environmental stimulation. The transient stimulus detection response habituates slowly.

In contrast to these short-term responses, the orienting response lasts for a somewhat longer period. Pavlov, the Russian physiologist, called this response a "what is it" reflex (see Lynn 1966). Its function is to prepare creatures for a closer inspection of incoming stimuli. Physiological changes associated with the orienting reflex include slowing of the heart rate and increases in the blood flow to the cerebral regions and decreases in blood flow to the limbs.

The orienting reflex is not synonymous with attention or sustained information processing. Rather, orienting prepares the individual for attention or vigilance. When our environments present us with novel stimuli or events of some known significance, orienting is elicited. If the stimulus reappears once orienting has occurred, there is no need to prepare the nervous system in the same manner to process the significant event that is impinging on the organism. The nervous system has answered the "what is it" question already. Therefore, the orienting response habituates rapidly. When the brain generates a "match" for the stimulus, there is no longer a need for the kinds of cognitive and physiological adjustments associated with orienting.

Since an understanding of orienting is crucial to the present discussion, an example may be helpful. I was sitting in a waiting room adjacent to the garage where mechanics were fixing the brakes on my car. Without warning, for no longer than two or three seconds, the lights in the room dimmed noticeably. I looked up from the page of the newspaper I was reading and listened intently. I heard nothing unusual. Those around me sat impassively. They too were reading magazines or newspapers or were staring vacantly into space. Perhaps all of us were preoccupied with the bill we would receive when the technicians finished repairing our cars. Was I the only one who noticed that the lights had dimmed? Was I the only one who cared? I went back to my sports page. A few minutes later, the lights dimmed again. I paused in my reading and resisted the impulse to look around at the others in the room. By the third time the lights dimmed, several moments later, I took only passing notice and the change in illumination hardly interrupted my reading.

Glean three points from this example. The first relates to the impact the stimulus had on my cognitive and behavioral states. The dimming of the lights was out of the ordinary, but it was not threatening. It caused me to attend to the external environment somewhat more assiduously. I studied the faces around me, searching them for signs of alarm. I sought an explanation for the phenomenon, listening for the sound of a powerful engine whose starting may have siphoned off voltage needed by the lights. However, nothing about the stimulus or the context in which it was embedded suggested that I was in danger or that the event was of any importance at all. I had been alerted, certainly I was distracted momentarily, but the dimming of the lights did not alarm me.

The second point to keep in mind is that my own physiological responses to the stimulus did not intrude on my consciousness. That is, my heart did not pound, I felt no sweating on my palms, and the splenius muscles in the back of my neck did not tighten. The dimming of the lights was a moderate change in the environmental conditions. Additionally, in terms of neural chronometry, the rapid rate with which human nervous systems are able to respond, the stimulus onset was reasonably gradual. No physiological cues alerted me to danger as would have been the case had a sudden or radical change in stimulation elicited a startle response. Indeed, our own very rapidly occurring physiological reactions can alert us to danger long before we are able to appraise all elements of the situation we are in (Parkinson and Manstead 1992). However, in this situation, no physiological responses of this kind were present.

Finally, the moderate change in luminescence did not signal the immediate occurrence of another significant event. There were no subsequent explosions, alarms, or public address announcements. In fact, nothing of significance followed these events. To this day, I have no idea what caused them. It is understandable, then, that with each successive occurrence, the magnitude of my response to the dimming decreased. My orienting habituated rapidly. I would expect, according to theory, that had the lights become noticeably brighter instead of dimmer while I continued to wait, dishabituation would have taken place. I would have been distracted once again.

The defensive response is the second of the responses of longer duration. This response to stimulation is preparatory for the *flight or fight* responses that occur in emergency situations. The defensive response is associated with an increase in heart rate and a shunting of blood away from the intestines to the large skeletal muscles. The defensive response occurs when humans (or animals) encounter potentially dangerous or threatening stimuli or stimuli of high intensity. This response habituates slowly. If the goal of the orienting response is to prepare the organism for closer contact with the environment, defensive responses seem to function to ready the organism for rejecting environmental input or for maneuvers that will mitigate the impact of incoming stimuli.

Consider in the previous example an instance that we have already belabored. What would we expect to occur if a loud buzzer had gone off intermittently while I waited for the technicians to finish my brake job? This is tantamount to asking what the consequences of a defensive response would have been. Putting aside the very real possibility that the noise may have elicited a startle response, other sequelae are quite likely to follow a defensive response. First, my heart rate is likely to have increased and other physiological changes would have heightened my sense of annoyance. Second, it is probable that I would have either inquired as to the source of the noise or left the room if its intermittent interruptions persisted. Finally, each time the dreaded buzzer sounded, it is likely my reading would have been disturbed.

Habituation to this stimulus would have been much slower than the habituation to the dimming lights.

All four of these responses fit into the sequences of thoughts and behaviors that are part of normal human social interactions. However, they do so in a highly complicated fashion. In the laboratory, carefully controlled studies have demonstrated that these reactions take place. In the normal walk of our existence, matters are not so simple. Indeed, we attend to events that startle and disturb us, just as we attend to those that initially elicit orienting. However, it is likely that we process in a singular fashion the information we inspect and integrate following the elicitation of an orienting response. We treat this input differently from material whose sustained processing follows a startle or defensive response. The defensive response occurs because an entity or event threatens the physical or psychological integrity of the organism. It is more likely that an intense and negative mood state is likely to follow defensive or startle responses. Certainly we are likely to view more cautiously and perhaps more critically the input that we process subsequent to defensive and startle reactions. The mood that follows an orienting response is less likely to be intense and negative. It is plausible that we inspect the input in a more casual fashion subsequent to orienting. In short, the properties of stimuli that determine their initial impact are very significant and influence subsequent information processing activities. In this vein, the initial reactions of the nervous system to stimuli that might support the development of Manichean schema are of particular importance.

Racist stimuli and orienting

I will argue that people of African descent, in many instances, orient to mentally toxic stimuli. These stimuli are psychologically poisonous in that they have the potential to instill or reinforce Manichean thinking. Certainly, there are two very crucial questions nested within this argument. The first is, Why do African people fail to show a defensive or startle response to these stimuli? Shrill and vulgar racist stimuli and information should elicit defensive responses. The second is, Why are these responses so resistant to habituation? Individuals will habituate to repetitious and time-worn input. Redundancy alone then should ensure that we allocate very little attention to input that for centuries has promoted thinking patterns consistent with white supremacy. In either instance, that is, if defensive responding or habituation takes place, the potentially detrimental input would fail to have the toxic effect. We will find it too revolting or utterly boring. Perhaps it would simply go unnoticed. Unfortunately, the information that leads to the development of racist thinking in the modern Manichean world is often times not revolting, far from boring, and still remains quite noticeable.

In chapter 3 we located the sources of input leading to Manichean thinking in the popular culture, the real disparities between the conditions of African and white people, the formal educational system, and religion. A vast amount of the information from all of these sources has acquired elements of *subtlety* and *novelty*. The novel and subtle aspects of these stimuli profoundly affect our initial reactions to them.

As the toxic elements of stimuli become more subtle, it is less likely that the stimuli will elicit startle or defensive responses. In the United States, for the past forty years the movement toward subtler forms of racism has been unmistakable. The trajectory has been in the direction of less virulent and strident forms of input that lead to a Manichean mind-set. This metamorphosis was to be expected as the legal status of racial apartheid eroded (Harding 1975; Cruse 1987). Admittedly, this movement toward subtler input stalls occasionally along the way. Sporadically, some of the old-guard, crass instances of individually racist behavior surface. From time to time we read or hear lightly warmed-over, grossly offensive racist ideas from the past (Rushton 1994). But for the most part in the United States, we experience manifestations of blatant cultural racism from the educational system less frequently than earlier in the century. The popular media also are now less likely to advance nakedly stupid or bestial images of African people.

However, we find an interesting variation on the theme of increasing subtlety in the case of decontextualized disparities. Here, we process information from the environment that characterizes the differences between black and white living conditions. Although the actual disparities between the economic and developmental conditions of African people and those of European descent are anything but subtle, we may tend to process them in a nondefensive and uncritical manner for two related reasons. First, the modern environment allows for exceptions to what appears to be the rule. Hence the presence of wealthy as well as high-status black people provides some assurance that one might avoid the "wretched" fate. Second, the hand of the perpetrating system that structures these disparities remains cleverly hidden. This is the essential function of the decontextualization process. In fact, the exceptions, that is, blacks who are affluent or hold high office, provide support for the mistaken attribution that degraded conditions are entirely the fault of the victims of oppression. "They succeeded; why can't you?" Decontextualization has become more sophisticated, and in this respect the disparities are an increasingly insidious source of racist thinking.

Some of the most interesting movements toward subtlety can be located in the cultural racism that saturates the educational establishment. In the United States, the enlightened curriculum of the last two decades of this century boasts of cleansing many of the Manichean concepts that littered previous offerings. A special issue of the *Journal of Negro Education* (Summer 1992) described some of these changes, which include textbooks that offer more generous helpings of illustrations and narratives in which people of African descent are central figures. However, a closer look often reveals the inadequacy of the modifications.

Consider this example taken from introductory psychology textbooks. As an undergraduate, I read Kimble and Garmezy's (1968) *Principles of General Psychology*. On page 547, they adapted and published an old estimate of the IQs of some of the world's geniuses. Of course, all of these geniuses were white men. In this last decade of the century, few texts would be so presumptuous and vulgar.

Twenty-five years later I was glancing through the thirteenth edition of Zimbardo's (1992) very remarkable textbook *Psychology*. The illustrations on page 60 and on page 653 are subtly dangerous. The first illustration is a time line of events in human evolution. The illustration depicts the Australopithecines in dark brown color as are *Homo habilis* and *Homo erectus*. Golger's law holds that mammals living closer to the equator will have darker coats. The darker coverings serve a protective function against the sun's radiation. However, at the point where *Homo erectus* emerges, the author inserts the phrase "out of Africa" on the time line. This asserts correctly that a number of the later hominids, especially *Homo erectus*, left Africa. However, as Finch (1991) pointed out, the majority of the hominids remained in Africa. Still, on Zimbardo's time line immediately following the out-of-Africa notation, the *lightened*, upright *Homo sapiens* appears. The subtle suggestion is that *Homo sapiens* evolved outside Africa. Hence, the melanin content in the skin of the first of *Homo sapiens* was reduced significantly. Of course, the substance of the message is still clear. The first real human had to be white.

The second illustration in Zimbardo (1992) is of a man of African descent, holding what appears to be traditional spears and perhaps a bow. His hair is in dreadlocks. Initially, the picture seems to sound a clarion for remembering the diversity of human cultural expression when we study human behavior. In fact, an individual of African descent wearing dreads and traditional African dress is not unusual in Washington, D.C. Certainly, it would not be as unusual in my neighborhood as a grown man wearing plaid kilts. However, the caption to the picture assures us that what is perceived as schizophrenia in one culture is perfectly normal in another: a true statement that in this context amounts to cultural racism by subtle innuendo. Thus, there is a remarkable element of subtlety in both of these illustrations in this very progressive basic psychology textbook. One tends not to be alarmed by the noxious content.

We should attend to a second crucial facet of some of the modern input that reinforces Manichean schema—the novelty of the information. Usually, information has become more subtle, but almost invariably it has the capacity to change in form but not in substance. This is true of the educational system with its constant revision of methods and material. It is true to an extent of disparities in the environment where the root causes of the conditions of the oppressed become more and more clouded. The most ironic of situations looms presently where the global disparities between the Northern and Southern hemispheres are lamented loudly by the very colonial powers that helped create them. The changes in these conditions ensure that the element of novelty is maintained. Thus, orienting to these stimuli persists. The brain finds that there is no match for these conditions in one's memory. A "what is it reflex" occurs. Habituation takes place only if the same stimulus occurs repeatedly.

The manner in which novelty ensures that habituation will not occur is especially interesting in the case of input that leads to the development of Manichean body image. The Caucasian models that movies, television, and magazines display as representations of beauty have certain common physical characteristics. However, the models themselves change. The faces on the popular magazines at supermarket checkout counters vary from month to month. Screen idols, like Messiahs, are short-lived. Hence black children and adults continue to orient to new white models of beauty because the various sources present a novel entity as the standard-bearer of the Manichean idea of beauty. The process facilitates orienting, paying attention, and eventually buying cosmetics and hair products as part of an effort to emulate these exemplars. It is the ability to change these models that causes the persistence of orienting rather than habituating to them.

To summarize, popular culture, formal education, and everyday events and circumstances met with in one's normal walk of life provide input that we do not perceive as alarming. Still, this input to our senses is far from innocuous. African people casually and uncritically inspect and process information from the environment that endangers the development of healthy cognitive schema. Initially, these stimuli tend to elicit orienting responses because of their subtle nature. These responses tend not to habituate because changes in facets of the input permit it to maintain novel elements.

Classical conditioning and the racist environment

Typically, psychologists distinguish between two basic forms of learning: operant or instrumental and classical or respondent conditioning. In very general terms, operant conditioning entails presenting a stimulus (reinforcement or punishment) after an organism emits a voluntary behavior. Reinforcing stimuli, by definition, increase the likelihood that the behavior will occur again. Punishment decreases this probability. Clinical and educational psychologists developed innovative applications of operant conditioning principles during the third quarter of this century (Karoly 1980). Behavior modifiers systematically reinforced the utterances of autistic children. These technicians were able to shape these vocalizations into understandable, if simplistic, verbal statements (Sherman and Baer 1969). Others used operant technologies to control disruptive outbursts in the classroom, eating behavior and obesity, as well as marital disputes. During the high point of the applications of operant techniques, the proponents proposed using them to modify the behaviors of individuals living within restricted social settings, including group homes and mental institutions (Bandura 1969).

In operant conditioning, the presentation of the stimulus is contingent on the individual's emitting a particular response. Certainly, operant conditioning principles operate in the human environment under natural conditions. However, the original formulations of operant principles in the human social context (see Skinner 1948) overstated the extent to which external stimuli control behavior. They underestimated the roles played by cognitive processes in particular and personality variables and traits in general. The field of personality psychology fell, for a time, under the influence of those who argued that behavior is solely a function of input from the external environment (see Mischel 1968). However, personality psychologists have been backpedaling from these strong stimulus-response formulations for the past twenty-five years (Bem and Allen 1974; Kenrick and Funder 1988).

However, the manner in which classical conditioning operates in the human social environment is less apparent. In addition, therapeutic applications of the principles of classical conditioning, though very impressive (see Paul 1969a, b), have assumed a lower profile than operant applications. Still, I will argue that in certain instances we enhance our understanding of the impact of environmental stimuli on the Manichean mind-set by viewing certain instances within the framework of classical conditioning.

The processes involved in classical conditioning are straightforward. A neutral event or stimulus occurs in very close temporal proximity to an event that elicits an unlearned, often reflexive response in an organism. The neutral event is usually present shortly before and during the presentation of the eliciting event. If the neutral and eliciting event occur together repeatedly, eventually the neutral event will come to bring about a response that is very similar to the behavior elicited by the original stimulus.

Table 4 illustrates this process and provides terminology for the various components of classical conditioning. The original eliciting

TABLE 4. **Therapeutic Applications of Examples of Classical Conditioning**

unconditioned stimulus (UCS)	————————	unconditioned response
conditioned stimulus (after pairings with UCS)	————————	conditioned response
	* * * * * *	
painful electric shock	————————	reduced penile blood flow
child's picture (after pairings with shock)	————————	reduced penile blood flow
	* * * * * *	
Antabuse® and alcohol	————————	vomiting
alcohol alone (after pairings)	————————	vomiting

event is called an unconditioned stimulus. It causes an unconditioned or unlearned response. Learning theorists labeled the originally neutral stimulus (neutral regarding the response in question) a conditioned stimulus. After repeated pairings with the unconditioned stimulus, this stimulus has the capacity to elicit a conditioned or learned response from the organism.

The examples in table 4 are of therapeutic applications of the principles of classical conditioning and show how conceptually close operant and classical conditioning actually are. A painful stimulus like an electric shock can serve as an unconditioned stimulus for decreases in blood flow in the penis. These decreases are interpreted as objective indices of reduced sexual arousal. The increases in blood flow in the penis associated with sexual arousal largely disappear when a man encounters a painful event. Clinicians based one therapeutic application of classical conditioning on an accepted theory that the parasympathetic branch of the autonomic nervous system mediates sexual arousal. This approach maintains that sympathetic nervous system arousal will block sexual arousal. For example, when one experiences pain or anxiety, sexual arousal would decline (see Sternbach 1966). That this antagonistic model of sexual arousal is controversial today is not of direct consequence to this illustration (Geer and Head 1990). In the treatment of a pedophile, for example, a therapist might present a picture of a young child just before the painful shock. Essentially, the therapist expects that after a number of pairings of the two stimuli, the pictures will come to elicit no sexual arousal at all. Hopefully, after treatment, children in the real world will not occasion sexual arousal in this troubled person.

A more complicated but widespread application of classical conditioning is the use of Antabuse® drug therapy to facilitate the detoxification of alcoholics. Antabuse is a drug that causes severe vomiting if one drinks alcohol while the drug is in the system. If alcoholics are taking Antabuse, ingesting alcohol in any form will cause them to vomit. The intent of therapy is for alcohol alone to begin to elicit a sense of revulsion. This will occur, theoretically, after several occasions of drinking while taking Antabuse. Table 4 illustrates this application of classical conditioning in the lower panel. In a discussion of classical conditioning, Houston (1990) described police officers as conditioned stimuli for fear reactions in black people. Houston argued that some officers engage in abusive behavior, and this action constitutes an unconditioned stimulus for fear. Eventually, the uniform and officers themselves begin to elicit fearful emotions.

In contrast to operant conditioning, classical conditioning influences involuntary responses. Often it is associated with reflexive behaviors that the autonomic nervous system controls. Accordingly, researchers have found it easy to demonstrate classically conditioned changes in salivation, heart rate, blood flow, and galvanic skin responses. Autonomic nervous system fibers are major mediators of the activity in the organs that control these responses. Other organs that the autonomic nervous system sends fibers to besides the heart, salivary glands, arteries, and sweat glands are the lungs, kidneys, pupils of the eyes, intestines, and genitals. The actions of organs that are mediated by this branch of the nervous system make up an important part of the physiological substrate of our emotional experiences. That is, when we become angry or frightened and when we experience joy and contentment, physiological changes occur. We may feel our hearts pounding, our stomachs turning or fluttering, and sweat building up on our palms when we experience strong emotions.

Among those who study human emotions, a one-hundred-year-old controversy persists. It concerns the order of occurrence and the direction of the causal influence of the physiological and subjective components of emotions. William James (1890) held that physiological changes precede and determine the nature of our subjective experiencing of strong emotions. Walter Cannon (1927) maintained that humans experience the physiological changes and the emotions simultaneously. Richard Lazarus (1984), a cognitive theorist, argued that cognitive—and therefore subjective—events determine the physiological changes.

Here is not the place to attempt to resolve the older forms of this protracted controversy. More modern phrasings of the issue are available, and the interested reader can find evidence supporting each position (see Zajonc 1984; Lazarus 1984; Bornstein 1992). The crux of the issue is that classical conditioning can exercise a pronounced impact on physiological responses that are under the control of the autonomic nervous system. These physiological events are very much part of our emotional responses to the world around us.

Again, consider several examples. The neighbors behind my house once owned an unruly Doberman pinscher. This dog engaged in a practice that for me was very nerve-wracking. He would growl and bare his teeth when I approached our back fence. Then he would commence to jump and throw his body against the flimsy fence. He seemed undecided whether the best course of action was to vault the barrier or knock it down. I feel a flutter in my heart and must confess to experiencing a tinge of fear whenever I encroach on the portion of the yard the raging canine must have considered part of his territory. This happens to me even though I know that the dog is no longer alive. Obviously, the area of my yard close to the weak fence has become a conditioned stimulus for my fear reaction.

In fact, examples of the impact of classical conditioning on emotional responses are more common than one might think. The scent of the perfume, cologne, or body oil worn by one's first love will for some time elicit a fleeting twinge of an emotional response in the absence of the loved one. Obviously, the conditioned emotional response may be positive or negative, depending on the outcome of this encounter. Television advertisements often use a form of higher-order conditioning. Here they employ a previously conditioned stimulus as an unconditioned stimulus. Several steps are involved in this process. In one application, they capitalize on two unique aspects of being young. One, young people, certainly in modern times, tend to follow and consume popular music. Two, life in the latter years of high school and during college is spiced with exhilarating if unpredictable social encounters and events. Some people spend a good portion of their adult lives trying to recapture the flavor of these years. For most of us, this is a truly unforgettable period of our lives. Songs that were popular during these charged years become conditioned stimuli for intense emotions later in life. Years later, merchants tell advertising executives the age group to which they wish to market a particular product. The advertisers then carefully select music popular at the time this targeted group was experiencing early adulthood. They play this music in the background as we see the product. The intent is that the product will begin to elicit strong emotional responses. Clearly, the role of classical conditioning in our daily lives can be considerable.

In a Manichean world, stimuli are arranged in such a way that African people and, sometimes by extension, cultural products of African people become conditioned stimuli for negative emotional experiences. We find the most obvious examples of this in the world of entertainment. It is most common in the manner in which films use symbols. Filmmakers often pair particularly vile, violent, or evil events with the physical characteristics or the creative works of African people. We discussed this when the matter of symbols in films was presented in chapter 3. Other examples abound. Disney's *Jungle Book* features the conniving orangutan, King Louie. Louie's speech and scat singing are delivered in a fashion saturated with elements of African-American style. (That a white singer, Mel Torme, did the voice is more a matter of the economics of racism than a contradiction of this example.)

The comedian-turned-actor Steve Martin portrays a dishonest preacher in the movie *Leap of Faith*. He performs his antics with a black gospel choir in the background. Quite clearly, Martin patterned many of his mannerisms after the styles associated with black preachers. The film version of *Little Shop of Horrors* gave the grotesque, carnivorous plant the voice of Levi Stubbs of the Four Tops. The villain Darth Vader in the original *Star Wars* dressed according to Manichean symbolism (long black garments). His voice was that of veteran black actor James Earl Jones. Often in film, tender moments are backed musically with string renditions of European concert (classical) music. Hip hop music is frequently scored behind crime and the activities of villains. Examples of such pairings abound. The effect is to begin to associate blackness with these less than desirable human characteristics, traits, and actions.

We experience the more insidious instance of racist classical conditioning of emotional responses in our contacts with the real world. The source of the stimuli lies in the disparities between the conditions of the oppressed and privileged communities. In the reality of the oppressed, the threshold for interpersonal violence is often quite low. Bloody, violent death is not uncommon and, sadly, often occurs in the very young. In the United States, the cancerous impact of racism is eroding African cultural structures that once had a buffering influence. Intragroup violence is becoming increasingly common. The faces and the forms of groups of young African boys who are onlookers often appear in close temporal and spatial contiguity with violence. These individuals were usually not the perpetrators. Gradually, these young men are becoming conditioned stimuli for the negative emotions that violent, premature death elicits.

On a broader scale, Fanon (1968) described very aptly what the real-world, unconditioned stimuli in a Manichean environment are. "The settler's town is a well-fed town, an easygoing town; its belly is always full of good things ... the Negro village, the medina, the reservation, is a place of ill fame, peopled by men of evil repute" (39). The physical realities of the worlds of the oppressed and those who benefit from oppression are lyrically described in detail in these pages of Fanon. Bulhan (1985) cited them in his exploration of Manichean psychology. This reality is rife with unconditional stimuli for negative emotions. The risk and the tragedy are that the *people* living in this "world cut in two" (Fanon 1968, 38) become conditioned stimuli for the emotional responses the unconditioned stimuli, quite appropriately, elicit. Accordingly, innovative and energetic black children go about their play. In their games with jump ropes and basketballs, they often challenge the limits of psychomotor speed and accuracy. They play touch football on sidewalks and between cars in the neighborhoods of the oppressed. Unknowingly, however, they risk becoming conditioned stimuli for negative emotions that the sight of the economic decay and blight that surrounds them elicits. Conversely, and with equally tragic consequences for the oppressed, gray-suited white men conduct business in front of sparkling office towers. They enjoy the prospect of becoming conditioned stimuli for the awe that these architectural marvels that frame their profiles inspire.

The issue is best summed up in these terms. We must consider not only the environmental stimuli as we size up the power of one's environment to elicit emotional responses. We have to examine the temporal and spatial contiguity of sets of stimuli. African people are likely to become associated with the negative conditions and circumstances reserved for them by the facts of oppression. This is an inevitable extension of the Manichean world in which they live. Caucasians become associated with developed and privileged outcomes and conditions. The impact of this process is on the core, reflexive, physiological components of our emotional responses. In this fashion, stimulus contiguity forms one of the well-cut paths to the development of a Manichean mind.

Resonating racist input: A developmental perspective

In *Black Skin White Masks*, Fanon (1967) described the psychological toxicity of the world he knew from the 1940s through the early 1950s. This world differed in many respects from the one faced by a plurality of African children that parents strive to socialize in the last years of this century. Fanon could say, with some assurance, that "a normal Negro child, having grown up within a normal family, will become abnormal on the slightest contact with the white world" (143). He meant that on his island of Martinique, black people could live an existence that was relatively insulated against some of the destructive myths that prevailed in France about African people. If this was true of Martinique in the 1940s, it is doubtful that it is the case in the

United States today. If this kind of isolation existed in certain all-black rural places in the United States before the 1950s, as Asante (1993) argued, it is probably fading rapidly in the Caribbean today.

Most children of African descent, during the first five years of life, have had plenty of contact with stimuli that will cause them to veer toward developing a Manichean mind. Those nurtured in all-black settings are not exempt. Contact occurs long before they formally experience "Europe" in the form of the state-sanctioned or state-supported educational system. By the first grade of elementary school, they have experienced several waves of toxic stimuli. I will argue that this early input can prepare the way for Manichean thinking long before they meet their first white person.

Developmental psychobiologists (see Shatz 1992) tell us that the human brain is in the process of organizing itself anatomically during early childhood. Neurons are still fingering forth to form their final pathways. Early experiences play an important role as this "final" wiring of the system is taking place. In addition, the important myelin sheaths that will speed up neural processing are still being developed after birth. Ironically, then, even before the brain has finished sculpting its fully developed hardware, dangerous stimuli from a racist world have found ports of entry. The world wastes no time introducing the young, developing mind to input that reflects the racist nature of the society.

Sadly, parents can often be the first carriers of the stimuli out of which we construct racist ideas and notions. Those parents who have failed to screen Manichean input can do little more than transmit their biases and racist propositions to their children. Sometimes they do so indirectly. They consume products of the popular culture that may have a negative influence on the child. There may be damaging content in the television programs parents watch or in the magazines they buy. Other times parents are much more direct in their influence. Far too commonly, parents and other caregivers utter negative references to color.

For example, on my bus ride home I watch a playful toddler lose her balance as she tries to walk in the cluttered aisle. Even adults stumble as the bus rocks and rolls along. "LaTanya, you better sit your black behind down," warns the mother impatiently. I feel an urge to caution the mother about pairing her harsh, negative tone with the reference to the child's color. I would tell her of the likelihood that the descriptor of her color may come to elicit negative emotions. LaTanya's young mind might come to associate her color with the unpleasant tone of mother's voice and the sanction against her behavior. I have sense enough to suppress my urge, however. This is not the proper setting for my treatise, and I am sure the mother would give me the same instruction she gave young LaTanya.

Obviously, when parents use racist epithets, make disparaging comments about African people, and show color, feature, or hair preferences, they transmit input that may lead to Manichean thinking. Arguably, many of the parental behaviors that reflect racist cognition are too fleeting and subtle for very young children to process. Still, the purpose here is to establish that the first wave of input that the child is likely to construe along Manichean lines enters the phenomenological field at this very early juncture. It is beside the point that some portion of this information may be too ephemeral for the young child to process. I would agree that an empirical test that could determine the extent to which this input affects the child is not an uninteresting question.

The world violently confronts the African child quickly with a second wave of stimuli that resonates with those the parents and other caregivers usually unwittingly provide. Fanon, in *Black Skin White Masks* (1967), discussed the impact an excursion to motion picture houses had on him and his contemporaries when they reached their early teens. In modern times, images from an oppressive popular culture invade the home. One need not even open the door. Long before they enter school, children watch television and see the pictures on the magazines that litter the house. They learn the lyrics to mind-numbing songs that trivialize or ignore the social and political plight of the listeners in favor of an obsession with sexual conquests. Further, young children may venture into the outside world very briefly as they attend church with the family. Unfortunately, there these preschool children may see pictures of white people representing God, angels, and holiness. The young person meets all of these classes of stimuli just out of infancy. Too often they will remain a part of people's reality for the rest of their lives.

Children come to evaluate conditions around them in line with evaluations that the adults in their lives make. They also contrast these conditions with other realities to which they are exposed. It is altogether likely that African children become dimly conscious fairly early of disparities between their environs and the world depicted on their televisions. It is likely that classically conditioned, negative associations between impoverished ecological conditions and people of African descent form at this time. Similarly, these conditioned associations between Caucasians and pristine surroundings may also occur initially at this juncture.

Of course, there is a legion of middle-class black children whose worlds may approximate those they find in the popular media. Their problem becomes finding a way to distance themselves from the masses of black people who fail to meet the standards society imposes. In the case of both middle-class children and their less wealthy cousins, if caregivers do not provide some causal explanations of these negative associations, the young people will integrate them, however primitively, in a fashion that supports racist thinking. Adults must provide a context for understanding these disparities, which of course entails having parents and other caregivers discussing the nature of racial oppression with the child at this very early age. If this discussion does not take place, the disparities will begin their insidious work. Thus, the third wave of Manichean input has arrived.

As we have argued, under circumstances that are the norm in the United States, the state-sponsored education system projects a barrage of racist messages. This occurs in many other settings where African people live, and it starts at the earliest levels of training. These messages join with, amplify, and reinforce the previous waves of toxic stimuli. Often they become the voice of intellectual authority. They outline the rationale for ubiquitous disparities between the environments of the privileged and the oppressed that a young person encounters. Of course this rationale centers on the failings of the oppressed. Additionally, the educational curriculum favors the art and culture of Europe, so it reinforces the growing Manichean aesthetic preferences.

Eurocentric educational information is the cradle of cultural racism. This body of thought settles and seals off the lingering questions that one may have about the legitimacy of white superiority. The educational system sends its input in pulses that become more subtle and destructive as the child grows older. Even with gestures toward multicultural education, the child learns of Africa as a continent on the periphery of the European continent. Africa remains a place where unfortunate and regrettable events occur. Animals and people die there. Strange and horrible diseases originate there. The child learns that in this respect his or her community and Africa have very much in common. Slavery? "[A]n ugly chapter, but remember, Africans helped enslave their own people" (King 1992).

At least in the United States, the African child, as she or he grows, witnesses the failure of peers in this toxic educational environment.

The impact for survivors is complicated. On the one hand, they may become increasingly suspicious of the inherent competence of their failing African-American peers. On the other hand, they may try to erase any link or connection with those falling by the wayside. Tragically, what teachers recite about African people in the classroom and what happens to the plurality of African children in the educational system are in synchrony and harmony.

Finally, by adolescence, individuals have direct encounters with more of the social institutions of the society. In addition, they become increasingly aware of the status of the conditions in which humans live. Many will observe repeatedly the disparities between the lives of the majority of people of European and those of African descent. This very crucial information, emanating from their immediate neighborhoods and local municipal environments, as well as that derived from national and world news, strikes a softened target. Noxious parental input, early continued contact with the media and entertainment from popular culture, vague early experiences with disparities between black and white environments, and the subtle but toxic message of the state-sponsored educational systems have already arrived in a series of resonating waves. In each instance, a second volley of stimuli intensifies the impact of the previous source. Consider, then, not the single source of input, but the sequential arrival of waves of stimuli. The African mind contends with these in the modern Manichean environment.

Final characterization of stimulus information

In summary, the input that will lead an African mind to construe the world along Manichean lines has several conceptually salient features. Obviously, over time, certain forms of input have become more subtle. Additionally, in many instances, these subtle stimuli are not static but tend to retain their novelty by changing form but not substance. Thus, African people persist in orienting to this input and often process it without assuming a particularly critical or defensive cognitive posture.

In some instances, events tend to occur in close temporal contiguity with one another. Classically conditioned emotional responses may be elicited in these instances. For example, we may come to associate neutral events, including the physical presence of African people, with events or circumstances that are the outgrowth of oppression. We will understand the emotional impact of stimuli in this instance by studying how they are paired with other stimuli.

Finally, developmentally, input can be seen as arriving in a series of waves from different realms of the social environment. Each wave delivers information that potentiates the impact of previous waves of input. These converge and combine, impinging on the individual from all sides and from various levels of the social environment.

So often have I heard young and even older adults of African descent insist that they have never experienced racism. Usually, these were unusually economically fortunate individuals. Others argue that they experienced racism for the first time when an event involving interpersonal insult or meanness occurred in their lives. The purpose of this chapter was to point up the absolute and utter absurdity of such statements. African people meet with racism often simply as mildly noxious information that can foster the development of a Manichean mind. Sometimes the input will be subtle, and at times its impact is due to a contiguous relationship with other events. Volleys and waves of events will saturate a racist environment, and in many cases, the oppressed will not be fully aware of what is hitting them. Part of the destructive impact is not a function of the content of the input. Investigators do well to study these other facets so that they will avoid underestimating their impact.

References

Asante, M. K. 1993. Racism, Consciousness and Afrocentricity. In *Lure and Loathing: Essays on Race, Identity, and the Ambivalence of Assimilation*, ed. G. Early, 127–43. New York: Penguin Press.

Bandura, A. 1969. *Principles of Behavior Modification*. New York: Holt Rinehart and Winston.

Bem, D. J., and Allen, A. 1974. On Predicting Some of the People Some of the Time: The Search for Cross-situational Consistencies in Behavior. *Psychological Review* 81: 506–20.

Bornstein, R. F. 1992. Inhibitory Effects of Awareness on Affective Responding: Implications for the Affect-cognition Relationship. In *Emotion*, ed. M. S. Clark, 235–55. Newbury Park, Calif.: Sage.

Brown, E. L., and Deffenbacher, K. 1979. *Perception and the Senses*. New York: Oxford University Press.

Bulhan, H. A. 1985. *Frantz Fanon and the Psychology of Oppression*. New York: Plenum.

Cannon, W. B. 1927. The James-Lange Theory of Emotion: A Critical Examination and an Alternative Theory. *American Journal of Psychology* 39: 106–24.

Courlander, H. 1963. *Negro Folk Music, U.S.A.* New York: Columbia University Press.

Cruse, H. 1987. *Plural but Equal: A Critical Study of Blacks and Minorities and America's Plural Society.* New York: William Morrow.

Denny, M. R., and Ratner, S. C. 1970. *Comparative Psychology: Research in Animal Behavior.* Homewood, Ill.: Dorsey Press.

Fanon, F. 1968. *The Wretched of the Earth.* New York: Grove Press.

Finch, C. S. 1991. *Echoes of the Old Darkland: Themes from the African Eden.* Decatur, Ga.: Khenti Inc.

Geer, J. H., and Head, S. 1990. The Sexual Response System. In *Principles of Psychophysiology: Physical, Social and Inferential Elements,* ed. J. T. Cacioppo and L. G. Tassinary, 599–630. New York: Cambridge University Press.

Gist, R., and Stolz, S. B. 1982. Mental Health Promotion and the Media: Community Response to the Kansas City Hotel Disaster. *American Psychologist* 37: 1136–39.

Graham, F. K. 1984. An Affair of the Heart. In *Psychophysiological Perspectives,* ed. M.G.H. Coles, J. R. Jennings, and J. A. Stern, 171–87. New York: Van Nostrand Reinhold.

Harding, V. 1975. The Black Wedge in America: Struggle, crisis, and hope, 1955–1975. *Black Scholar* 7: 28–46.

Houston, L. N. 1990. *Psychological Principles and the Black Experience.* Lanham, Md.: University Press of America.

James, W. 1890. *The Principles of Psychology.* Vol. 2. New York: Holt.

Karoly, P. 1980. Operant Methods. In *Helping People Change,* 2d ed., ed. F. H. Kanfer and A. P. Goldstein, 210–47. New York: Pergamon Press.

Kenrick, D. T., and Funder, D. C. 1988. Profiting from Controversy: Lessons from the Person-situation Controversy. *American Psychologist* 43: 23–34.

Kimble, G. A., and Garmezy, N. 1968. *Principles of General Psychology.* 3d ed. New York: Ronald Press.

King, J. E. 1992. Diaspora Literacy and Consciousness in the Struggle Against Miseducation in the Black Community. *Journal of Negro Education* 61: 317–40.

Lazarus, R. S. 1984. On the Primacy of Cognition. *American Psychologist* 39: 124–29.

Lynn, R. 1966. *Attention, Arousal and the Orientation Reaction.* Oxford: Pergamon Press.

Mischel, W. 1968. *Personality and Assessment.* New York: Wiley.

Parkinson, B., and Manstead, A. S. R. 1992. Appraisal as a Cause of Emotion. In *Emotion,* ed. M. S. Clark, 122–49. Newbury Park, Calif.: Sage.

Paul, G. L. 1969a. Outcome of Systematic Desensitization I: Background Procedures, and Uncontrolled Reports of Individual Treatment. In *Behavior Therapy: Appraisal and Status,* ed. C. M. Franks, 63–104. New York: McGraw-Hill.

————. 1969b. Outcome of Systematic Desensitization II: Controlled Investigations of Individual Treatment, Technique Variations, and Current Status. In *Behavior Therapy: Appraisal and Status,* ed. C. M. Franks, 105–59. New York: McGraw-Hill.

Rushton, J. P. 1994. *Race, Evolution and Behavior.* New Brunswick, N.J.: Transaction Publishers.

Shatz, C. J. 1992. The Developing Brain. *Scientific American* 267: 60–67.

Sherman, J. A., and Baer, D. M. 1969. Appraisal of Operant Therapy Techniques with Children and Adults. In *Behavior Therapy: Appraisal and Status,* ed. C. M. Franks, 192–219. New York: McGraw-Hill.

Skinner, B. F. 1948. *Walden Two.* New York: Macmillan.

Southern, E. 1971. *The Music of Black Americans: A History.* New York: W. W. Norton.

Sternbach, R. A. 1966. *Principles of Psychophysiology.* New York: Academic Press.

Zajonc, R. B. 1984. On the Primacy of Affect. *American Psychologist* 39: 117–23.

Zimbardo, P. G. 1992. *Psychology and Life.* 13th ed. New York: HarperCollins.

CHAPTER FIVE

Understanding How Humans Process Information

I
f any group of psychologists experiences moments of absolute wonder and awe, it probably would be those in the
biological branches of the field. These women and men
spend their lives fathoming the relationships between the human
brain, as a biological substance, and its functional operations.
At the physical level, the brain is unimpressive. There is nothing
aesthetically pleasing about it, and it weighs just over three
pounds. But when one ponders how it works, the brain reveals
itself as one of the most remarkable entities known. The more
one probes, the more one wonders.

Admittedly, anatomically speaking, it is remarkable that the
human brain contains 100 billion specialized cells called neurons. Also, the brain has about ten times that many glial cells,
which give it its form and nourish the neurons. Neurons have
the unique capacity to receive and conduct electrical charges
that are in the range of one hundred millivolts. They may have
up to one thousand juncture points, called synapses, with other
neurons. A formidable task is for the neurons to conduct their
electrical charges across the synapses. This they do with the aid
of chemical substances called neurotransmitters and neuromod-
ulators. The number of synapses in the brain is inestimable. A

figure of 100 trillion is not exaggerated (Hubel 1979; Fischbach 1992).

What the human brain is able to do and the manner in which it functions are nothing short of astounding. It constantly receives and integrates input from specialized receptors that are sensitive to mechanical, thermal, chemical, acoustical, and photic input (Leukel 1976). Humans process this sensory information in the familiar forms: visual, auditory, smell (olfactory), taste (gustatory), balance (vestibular), temperature, touch (tactile), and sensory input from muscles (kinesthetic). Incoming, or *afferent*, information is screened, processed, and interpreted continually. We can identify another distinct set of brain functions involving control over the mechanisms of movement and coordination of the body's skeletal muscles and the activities of certain internal organs, as well as the mechanisms of speech. These functions are referred to as the *efferent* actions of the brain. Additionally, the brain makes a virtually permanent record of our individual biography. The record, as our personal memories, gives our lives continuity and forms the currents and connections of our day-to-day existence. Finally, there is a generative aspect of the brain's activity. New entities, physical and abstract, are brought into being by the actions of the human brain. The brain oversees our chiseling tools, cultivating crops, cooking food, drawing figures, and building structures; our singing, sewing, dancing, reflecting, and musing. The brain is the architect, engineer, and sentinel over a veritably infinite range of experiences and actions. These are unique events on the stage of human existence because a brain, possessed of idiomorphic memories and singular motives, interprets the experiences and directs the actions of each highly complicated human being.

Tragically, the confines of racial oppression severely truncate the functioning of the brain. I have argued in earlier chapters that in service of the ends of white supremacy, images, ideologies, and events inundate the minds of the oppressed and cause them to belittle the African facets of their existence. The consequences for the realization of the wondrous potential of the brain are dire. No matter how much the oppressed achieve, create, and overcome, the conditions under which these accomplishments were achieved must be regarded, at best, as deterrents. It is probably more precise to call them toxins. They serve to thwart the authentic, creative unfolding of the intellect.

Indeed, it is the physiological psychologist who should be most outraged by racism. In the final analysis, racism limits the development of the most creative instrument in the universe. In our own hideous time, every day we come face to face with the spectacle of often poor, commonly young black men and boys killing one another. They use state-of-the-art weapons to extinguish the light in the brains of their peers. The bony skull, designed to protect the invaluable brain, is no defense against these weapons. Ultimately, we have to see these men and boys as individuals who processed and accepted uncritically and perhaps unwittingly the messages of white supremacy. Ironically, during the enslavement period, not a century and a half ago, people of African descent were less likely to be allies of the forces of their own destruction. Then, fiends from another part of the world did all in their power to create an environment that would reduce African people to a subhuman intellectual level. In all times, since its inception until now, racism must be known for the horrible squandering of human potential that it inevitably brings. No one should appreciate this more than those who dedicate their lives to uncovering the brain's secrets.

This chapter is the unlikely centerpiece of the present study of racism. The focus is the manner in which the brain processes information. Surprisingly, after one hundred years of formal scientific inquiry into matters of memory and human information processing, these subjects remain frontiers in psychological research. Even the nomenclature is confusing. Often it is necessary to take special care to delimit the use of particular terms. The terms have come to mean different things to different people. Therefore, I have taken some pains to define concepts carefully. I am entering the academic rooms where human information processing is the central topic. It is necessary to carry in my pocket a list of demands, or better, an agenda that serves the study of racism. Without this protocol, we risk becoming mired in the seemingly endless esoteric issues and scientific exchanges that echo in these chambers.

Accordingly, the following framework guides our cursory look at what psychologists know about certain aspects of human information processing. First we examine models that explain how human beings incorporate information into memory. We are concerned with processes that translate the events that occur in the world outside us into a relatively permanent part of our internal world. Two challenges to more established models are then described in order to provide a sense of current thinking. The focus in the first section is to derive an understanding of a complicated and pivotal series of mental activities involving the incorporation of information. Second, we outline two theories that describe the manner in which we organize permanent memories in the brain. This discussion gives more substance to our proposition that Manichean cognitive fictions govern both afferent and efferent wings of cognitive activity. The focus in the second section moves from process to structure. In the penultimate section I provide a brief introduction to an approach to thinking known as parallel distributive processing. It purports to be based on an understanding of the functioning of networks of neurons in the brain. This vein of research is hybrid in that it employs methods and findings from the fields of neuroscience, psychology, and computer sciences. Eventually it may prove useful in the study of Manichean thinking. Finally, I address the problem of the role of conscious awareness in information processing. Are we aware of all the thinking that we do, and do we think about only those things of which we are aware? The core issue to be decided in this section is whether we are influenced only by events of which we are conscious. In each of the four sections, we evaluate competing theories and empirical evidence in light of the facets of racism and the regions of the impact of racism that have been discussed in previous chapters.

Models of information storage

Multistorage models of memory

For over twenty-five years, instructors have compelled students in basic psychology classes to become familiar with a model of memory that identified three distinct storage locations in the brain. Initially Atkinson and Shiffrin (1968) presented the model. Investigators have updated it from time to time (see Craik and Watkins 1973). According to this conceptualization, we hold information initially in sensory registers. Actually, researchers suspect that each sensory system has its own memory. These registers retain the material for very short periods of time. Visual memories held in the sensory registers have been termed *iconic*, while material that is held in auditory sensory memory is designated *echoic* (Neisser 1967). Many researchers think that the duration of iconic representations is a matter of milliseconds, while we hold echoic memories for up to several seconds (see Howard 1983).

Conceptually speaking, the capacity of the sensory registers is quite large. For example, visual sensory memory can encompass all that is in one's visual field at a given instant. Imagine awakening in a room that is completely dark. You turn on a dim lamp and glance around quickly. Your visual sensory registers are able to retain briefly all items you see in that instant. Material in sensory memory is lost as new information arrives. Hence, current researchers believe that there is a continual updating of millisecond- or seconds-old material in sensory memory (Howard 1983).

According to the multistorage model, we are able to move the information in sensory storage that is not displaced and lost forward to short-term memory storage. Several versions of the model claim that humans can detect features of material in sensory storage. In the process of attending to these features, we retain information and pass it to this next distinct storage unit. Howard (1983) noted that short-term memory differs from sensory memory in several respects. First, its capacity is considered to be quite limited. Only a few "chunks" of material can be held in short-term memory at any given time. Second, in this model, short-term memory is considered capable of retaining information for longer periods of time than sensory memory. Under normal circumstances, we are able to retain inactive items in short-term memory for about eighteen seconds (Peterson and Peterson 1959). After this period, most of the inactive information in short-term memory faces one of two fates. Either we forget the material as it decays or is displaced by new material or we move the material on to the next level of storage.

However, a third difference between short-term and sensory memory is that material can be retained or kept active in short-term memory by a process called rehearsal. Two types of rehearsal have been identified (Craik and Tulving 1975; Craik and Lockhart 1972). They represent different levels of processing of information. Maintenance rehearsal occurs when one simply repeats material over and over again. Repetition is the crucial facet of the activation process. Elaborative rehearsal involves a more extensive and "deeper" level of processing of the information. Rather than just mentally reciting information repetitively, elaborative rehearsal occurs when the individual relates the new information to material that is already being retained in permanent memory. Sometimes elaborative rehearsal processes take the form of organizing material into conceptual or subjectively meaningful clusters. One might try to remember a name better by associating it with a physical characteristic of the person. Regardless of the nature of elaborative rehearsal, it increases the likelihood that the material we are retaining in the short-term memory will be incorporated into permanent memory. Simple maintenance rehearsal is not the best strategy for moving material from short-term to more permanent storage.

The manner in which people retain infrequently used phone numbers before dialing them is a classic instance of maintenance rehearsal. Take, for example, what we might do in order to place a call to a local eating establishment. First we obtain the phone number through a call to directory assistance. Then we would probably say the number over and over again, that is, practice it, right up to the time we finish touching the numbers on the phone dial. Seldom do we retain this sequence of digits beyond the time that we call the establishment. More elaborate processing is needed to pass the material on for permanent storage.

We have already alluded to the existence of long-term memory within the multistorage model. Long-term memory constitutes the brain's permanent storage area, housing material that we retain for indefinite periods of time. The capacity of long-term memory is massive, in fact, virtually limitless. Tulving (1972) distinguished between two forms of long-term memory. *Episodic memories* can take a variety of forms. They are linked to specific times and places. Two examples can serve as illustrations. In the fourth grade, my instructor required us to memorize Lincoln's Gettysburg address. A quarter of a century later, my son informed me that his teacher had told the class to memorize Claude McKay's poem, "If We Must Die." He was attending a local Pan African school in Washington, D.C., and was about the same age I was when the teacher assigned me Lincoln's address. We both carried out our tasks rather dutifully. Both assignments resulted in the encoding of episodic memories, though I think my son got the better of the bargain from a mental health and literary perspective. The memories are episodic because the temporal and spatial parameters of the information that was retained can be specified. That is, we both committed the material to memory in elementary school at a particular age and in a particular city. Obviously, we will be quite concerned with episodic memories in an examination of Manichean cognition.

Tulving (1972) called knowledge of a more general nature that allows us to use and manipulate language and its concepts *semantic memory*. The organizational structures of meaning that determine how we will construe and integrate a significant portion of the information we receive reside in semantic memory. Therefore, semantic memory is of particular importance when we examine mental development in a racist society. Indeed, the environmental disparities, the images from popular culture, and the information from the educational system that converge to engender Manichean cognitive structures in the oppressed contain some elements that we can describe verbally. Of course, this is not to say the input from these sources is purely verbal. We have argued through the course of this study that there are dimensions of stimuli from each of these sources that transcend verbal description. Still, the organization of verbal meaning categories becomes involved continually in the processing of this input. We attach labels like "ghetto" and "squalor" to conditions we see in African communities. Sometimes we mock, using terms like "ugly" or "incompetent," the distorted images of black people the popular culture provides us. Therefore, the organization of semantic memory is crucial. It should be a primary focus of a study of racist cognitive structures. We will return to a discussion of the permanent organization of meaning and memories later in this chapter.

Critical problems with the traditional multistorage model

Disgruntled rumblings among cognitive psychologists have become a roar. Several problems with the multistorage model have caused its popularity to dwindle markedly. Similarly, if one tries to fit various facets of Manichean thinking by the oppressed into this model, several glaring problems arise. Neither the ontogeny nor the common operation of Manichean thinking seems consistent with the model. Ultimately, difficulties with the multistorage model have led to alternative theories. These theories preserve some of the previous notions, but in other respects they constitute radical departures. We will show that the modifications facilitate, to a greater extent, our understanding of the development of Manichean thinking. Before considering only two of several alternatives that are available, we will outline a few specific problems with the multistorage model.

First, the old multistorage model proposes that memories move along a "pipeline" (Broadbent 1984) from sensory to short-term to long-term memory storage. The theorists conceived these as discrete memory systems that exist physically in the brain. Cognitive psychologists are becoming more and more uneasy with this proposition. Tulving (1985) argued that it is inappropriate to develop memory classes solely on the basis of performance on memory tasks. An alternative is to conceptualize memory systems on the basis of what psychologists and neuroscientists know about the brain itself.

171

Clinical neuropsychologists learn a great deal about memory systems as they examine the capacities and capabilities of brain-damaged individuals. For example, a famous patient in Canada known to psychologists as H. M., received an operation that included the destruction of portions of a structure in the brain called the hippocampus. After surgery, H. M. evidenced a form of amnesia. In essence, he was unable to form new memories. That is, H. M. has no memory for episodes or events that he may have experienced just hours before on the same day that one might test him. However, H. M. and other patients with similar forms of amnesia will show improvement as they practice certain kinds of tasks and puzzles (see Seger 1994). They will, of course, have no memory of ever practicing! Therefore, studies of the brain and memory suggest there may be two types of memory. One system depends on hippocampal functioning, while another may function independently of this particular structure. In this instance, knowledge of the brain has informed the development of our thinking about memory systems. This amounts to using neuropsychological criteria to guide the development of a model of memory (Nilsson 1989). At this point, the field of cognitive psychology seems to be holding out little hope that discrete memory systems, as described in the traditional multistorage models, will measure up to neuropsychological criteria. On the one hand, performance on tasks presented to people in the laboratory seduces us into believing that these various memory systems are real. However, little that we have learned about brain structures supports this belief.

Second, researchers have challenged the descriptions of the processes that move material from one kind of memory to the next in the multistorage models. Early formulations held that we move the material forward from sensory memory when we allocate attention to it. The problem with this notion is that we often process and store as permanent memories unattended events. That is, we make a record of events to which we have paid little or no attention. Consider this evidence. Dichotic listening tasks provide participants different streams of information over stereo headphones. Sometimes participants are required to repeat or "shadow" the information in one channel and ignore the input from the other. Twenty years of experimental evidence is available showing that people process the information in the unattended channel, at least to some extent (Lewis 1970; Dawson and Schell 1987; see Best 1989). In one study, for example, Mackay (1973) told participants to shadow sentences that included ambiguous words (e.g., bank). Mackay presented words in the nonshadowed ear that were related to one of the meaning possibilities of the ambiguous term (e.g., money or river). Later, he gave participants a sentence recognition task. The task included the sentence the participants had shadowed previously but the ambiguous term was transformed to include a term that had the same meaning as the word that had been presented in the nonshadowed ear (e.g., financial institution). Interestingly, though they did not recall hearing the nonshadowed word "money," they tended to recognize these sentences as being the ones that Mackay had presented earlier in the shadowed ear.

Evidence from dichotic tasks is more than a psychological parlor trick. The tasks are not unlike what we experience in the real world. Every second of our waking existence is alive with stimuli. In fact, Cherry (1953) viewed the dichotic listening task as an analogy to the chatter at a cocktail party. Input rains down on us constantly. We attend to only a portion of it. In the dichotic listening studies, experimenters measure the impact of information that seems to be "going in one ear and out the other." The evidence suggests the impact is significant. Thus, we can move information forward for further processing without allocating full attention to it.

The multistorage model proposed that elaborative rehearsal is the chief mechanism responsible for moving material from short-term to long-term memory. This proposition has fared about as well as attention fared as the mechanism for moving information from sensory to short-term stores. Indeed, experiments have shown that elaborative rehearsal facilitates the memorization of some information. Still, permanent memories can result in the absence of this type of rehearsal or rehearsal of any kind. For example, we have all encountered events and information whose characteristics are so striking that we need not rehearse them to recall their details. An insult from a friend or the terrifying sight of a car accident can be called to mind even though it is difficult to identify any rehearsal process that resulted in its storage. It seems reasonable to consider elaborative rehearsal as sufficient for the formation of permanent memories. However, it is not a necessary condition for the formation of permanent memory.

Does the multistorage model provide plausible explanations of the flow of information into Manichean cognitive structures? One major problem that surfaces when we apply this model in a study of racism centers around the manner in which the model proposes that short-term memory operates. It seems unlikely that individuals would hold the lion's share of input that is potentially racist in memory through rehearsal processes. Is it conceivable that we intentionally rehearse information that will eventually be integrated in a manner that accommodates racist thinking? Holding self-deprecating and even subtly noxious information in short-term memory for extended periods of processing time increases the probability that we may identify its racist or potentially racist elements. As described in the model, short-term memory is where we can inspect facets of stimuli more extensively before we store them. In the case of elaborative rehearsal, we process them at a much deeper level than is conceivable for memories in sensory storage. Accordingly, short-term memory is a staging area where a filtering process that will ferret out racist and potentially racist elements of the incoming stimuli may exist. If short-term memory and elaborative rehearsal operate in the fashion described in the model, it is difficult to see how black people integrate into long-term storage a good portion of input that leads to Manichean thinking.

However, we should not dismiss the counter argument in favor of the multistorage model too quickly. This thesis would posit that in many people of African descent the existing cognitive structures, including semantic memory, are organized in a fashion compatible with Manichean thinking. For these individuals, rehearsing racist input, even on an elaborative level, will not be disturbing. Quite simply, they might repeat this input and construe, inspect, and elaborate it within a Manichean framework. The argument seems tenable, at least in two extreme instances. The first, as noted, involves individuals possessed of minds that are replete with Manichean structures. These individuals are capable of construing and rehearsing even blatantly racist information without being disturbed by its self-deprecating elements. I once heard a group of black professional men engage in a sexist discussion of the relative aesthetics of women from several islands in the Caribbean. One stated, and several nodded in sheep-like agreement, that on islands where the women had retained African features, "The white man failed to do his job." Thus, the women were less attractive. As a teacher, I have encountered some young people of African descent who wrestle for semesters and sometimes years with the notion that a black male instructor might teach them effectively. Often, but not always, the young people have completed secondary education in suburban, overwhelmingly white school systems. In extreme cases like these, where the structures of Manichean cognition are so deep-seated, resilient, and formidable, rehearsal processes of racist input are plausible.

The other extreme where rehearsal is possible is where racist input is subtle and ambiguous. For example, Cedric Robinson (1983) divined the subtly racist elements that reside in a particular historical question. He noted that historians have posed the question of whether or not the enslaved Africans in the United States resisted their captors (176–7). As Robinson pointed out, for decades the emphasis in studies of this period was on the efforts of white abolitionists and the adaptive behaviors of the enslaved. The question of resistance is comparable to asking if the African women raped by white men resisted the savage invasion of their bodies. As Robinson pointed out, to question if they resisted is to question their very humanity. By virtue of their humanity there was resistance. This applies to both the particular question with respect to African women and the more general question. The appropriate interrogative is to ask what form the resistance took! Now, this is a rather subtle point. I would posit that we could rehearse material related to the original question (was there resistance?) as part of our school lessons and never identify the racist assumptions that are at the core of the question itself.

It is fair to say, however, that the multistorage model conceives of the development of memories as a deliberative sequence of events. We turn our attention to elements in sensory storage to move them to short-term memory. Further, we rehearse, sometimes elaborately, material in short-term storage to move it to long-term memory. In all but the extreme occasions, deliberation, even naive deliberation on moderately subtle input, will militate against the development of a racist mentality. This is true especially as the sophistication of African people increases with respect to dealing with subtle racism.

Our concern here is not the esoteric one of the primacy of one model of memory over another. Researchers in the area of learning and memory will settle the issue eventually. The matter at hand is that white supremacy slings toxic informational arrows incessantly. We must keep our feet planted squarely on the ground walked by those on the receiving end of this harmful information. More than a small number of people of African descent will develop memories fraught with this information. They will find it difficult to mobilize authentic, critical cognitive and behavioral postures toward the conditions in which they live. Only in rare instances will active elaborative rehearsal be involved in the production of this mind-set. Elaborative rehearsal is most likely to take place when the source of the toxic material is the formal educational system. I have tried to depict the range of convenience of the concept of rehearsal in a racist context in figure 2. The figure is three-dimensional and captures the relationship between subtlety and degree of saturation of Manichean cognitive structures. It depicts, simultaneously, the relationship of these factors to the utility of the concept of rehearsal. As subtlety and Manichean saturation increase, rehearsal is more likely to operate.

In summary, we rehearse the numbers to local carryout establishments from which we purchase a meal from time to time. Similarly, when learning the lines and spaces of the treble clef or the twelve cranial nerves, rehearsing a mnemonic is sometimes quite helpful. I even recall trying to rehearse a set of reasons for the complex rela-

FIGURE 2.   Graph in three-dimensional space of the suitability of maintenance rehearsal concept. The application is to the storage of racist input. Suitability in terms of applicability (z-axis) varies as a function of blatancy versus subtlety of the input (y-axis) and the extent of saturation of cognitive schema with Manichean concepts (x-axis).

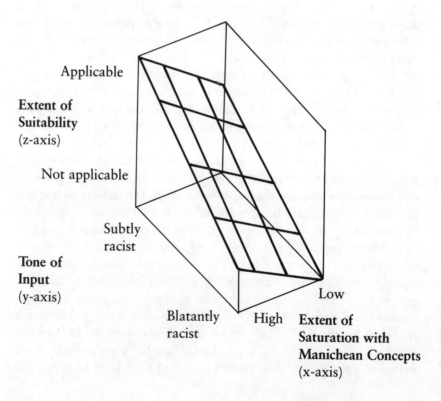

tionship between W. E. B. Du Bois and Booker T. Washington. I gleaned these reasons from David Lewis's (1993) excellent discussion of the matter. But apart from circumscribed information and episodes of this kind, there is input of a different quality. Input, stored as permanent memories, affects the manner in which one evaluates the struggling black businesses in her or his neighborhood (competence), the facial features of a new entertainer of African descent (body image), or the rituals practiced in the Akan religion (cultural-historical). These crucial memories were not formed, by and large, with the aid of rehearsal. For this failure in applicability, I join others in criticizing the traditional multistorage model in general and the rehearsal feature in particular.

Two alternatives to traditional models of memory

The Maltese cross. Broadbent (1984) presented a model of memory that retains certain elements of the traditional multistorage approach, but in other respects makes significant departures. The model is not revolutionary in its thrust, but it is a robust effort to modify a number of features of the multistage model. Broadbent does not envision information as moving serially from briefer to longer-term memory locations. Rather, he postulates that there are four separate facets of processing that interact with a central processing system. The model is referred to as the Maltese cross because all of the processing units interact with a core executive processor (see figure 3). For the most part, he concluded that these processing units exist on the basis of performance on memory tasks. Hence, at the outset we acknowledge that this otherwise intriguing model may meet the neuropsychological criteria no better than the multistorage model. As a critique of the earlier model, then, it is best thought of as an exercise in partial reform.

In the model, the *long-term associative store* is similar in many respects to long-term memory described in the multistorage model. The long-term associative store houses many forms of episodic memory. In this respect it is identical to long-term memory as discussed previously. Broadbent opted to describe the structure or arrangement of items in long-term memory somewhat differently from the manner in which long-term memory storage is conventionally described. We will discuss this departure from the conventional views of long-term memory in the subsequent section.

FIGURE 3. Broadbent's Maltese Cross

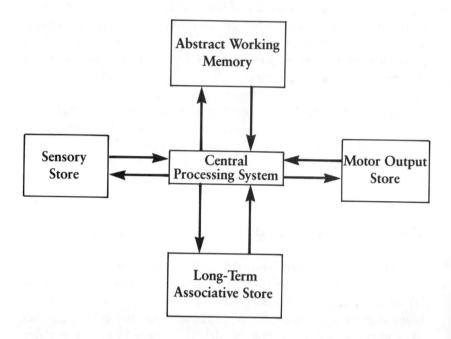

Taken from Broadbent 1984.

Indeed, Broadbent insisted that not all of our permanent memories reside in the long-term associative store. The central processing system contains permanent memories. The central processor is capable of interacting with any of the other processing units. For example, according to Broadbent, the central processing unit would handle pattern recognition. The fact that the inputs stimuli "2" and "two" are equivalent would be recognized without accessing the permanent long-term associative store. It seems likely that classical conditioning, a phenomenon discussed in detail in the previous chapter, could easily involve the central processing unit without employing material housed in long-term storage. As we have seen, classical conditioned responses are elicited very rapidly. They involve the recognition of a kind of patterning in stimuli. Thus I would think Broadbent might argue that his central processor could handle many instances of classically conditioned responses.

The *sensory store* in the Maltese cross differs from the sensory registers discussed previously. Broadbent (1984) argued that sensory storage can retain the physical information about stimuli for relatively extended periods of time. He presented evidence that iconic and echoic memories can be retained for periods longer than those described in the multistorage model. In fact, he argued that under normal circumstances material resides in the sensory store until new material "overwrites" it (60). Broadbent viewed the sensory memory as more than just a passive receptacle. He cited evidence showing that sensory memories of lip-read stimuli interact or interfere with sensory memories of auditory stimuli. In his modification of previous notions, sensory memory becomes more constructive. The material is not simply a physical translation of physical input to sensory code. Rather, the translation of input may be influenced by activity in other sensory channels. Additionally, the sensory storage system is not passive; rather, it is able to retain stimuli more actively depending on the features of the stimuli.

The *motor output store* represents an efferent, action-oriented wing of memory in the Maltese cross model. It contains plans for executing complicated sequences of motor activity. For example, a motor output program exists, and a complicated one at that, that gives children the skills to jump "double Dutch." This play activity, very popular among African-American young people, involves jumping two ropes, turned simultaneously in different directions. Often, the young people turn the rope very rapidly. A proficient jumper makes several crossings of the rope per second. No interference with performance results when participants recite short songs in rhythm with the turning of the rope. Broadbent would probably argue that this lack of suppression of performance occurs because separate memory systems, the motor output store and long-term associative storage, are involved in these activities.

Of course, if one challenges a person to learn a list of words and then insists that he or she sing the lyrics of a song while trying to memorize the material, the subject will not learn the list efficiently. The individual will perform poorly because the long-term associative store and the fourth unit, called *abstract working memory*, would be involved in the task.

The abstract working memory that Broadbent described holds information for limited periods of time. Information that is neither sensory nor motor is retained here. It appears that Broadbent developed the description of this wing of the Maltese cross almost through a kind of empirical attrition. That is, the experimental evidence suggested that, in the laboratory, performance on memory tasks was explicable through the mediation of motor and sensory memory tasks. However, residual evidence suggested that participants were employing temporary memories that were not related to motor activity or to sensory processes. In later work Hayes and Broadbent (1988) proposed that one of the primary functions of the abstract working memory is to form associations that can be labeled verbally. Hence, this working memory has "slots" for at least two concepts or entities and a third slot that describes their associations. Suppose I ask you to generate and say aloud, on my command, numbers in a random sequence. In order to do this, you have to keep in mind what numbers you said previously so that you will be sure there is nothing systematic about the numbers you are generating. That is, you have to make sure the numbers are in a random sequence. This means you will use abstract rules to monitor your own activity. Hayes and Broadbent (1988) suggested that we use abstract working memory for this task. To show it is limited in capacity, their experiment demonstrated that doing this task interfered with or reduced the efficiency of learning other abstract tasks. However, it did not interfere with learning material that was more concrete. This indicates that abstract working memory functions as a distinct entity.

The *central processing system* houses operations that transfer material to and from the four memory systems. It has the capacity to move material between the storage areas. For example, material from long-term associative memory can be moved to abstract memory to help build an association between two nonsensory and motor items. For decades, rhythm and blues vocal groups, in extended extemporaneous refrains, have fused stored language concepts with complex expressive gestures while performing. Since spontaneity is preserved in the vocal domain, it is clear that these artists are making use of long-term memory, abstract working memory, and motor output storage. On the other hand, patterns of incoming stimuli may be recognized by the processing system and a motor response executed through the motor output memory without the long-term associative memory being accessed. For example, drivers need not access long-term memory to apply the brakes when they see a red light.

Broadbent's model is inherently more flexible than the multistorage model it hoped to supplant. He argues that we can use a number of avenues and processes to integrate, store, and access information. This model seems to fit human information processing better than models that conceptualize processing as moving through a series of fixed stages. Still (and this we noted at the outset), the evidence that these memories exist is taken from performance on memory tasks. In several instances, *interference,* that is, the failed or less efficient performance on a memory task, is the criterion for the existence of a distinct storage area (Roediger 1984). Broadbent's model may eventually satisfy, in two respects, the neuropsychological criteria requiring that memory systems be based on what is known of brain functions. First, he cites studies of the hippocampal involvement in memory and suggests that motor output memory functions separately from those the hippocampus controls. Secondly, recent evidence suggests that something like Broadbent's abstract working memory may be located in the brain's prefrontal cortex (Beardsley 1997). Still, the strength of the model seems to lie in its flexibility, not in the relating of memory function to structural knowledge of the brain itself.

The notions of *automatic* and *controlled* processing can be integrated quite readily into Broadbent's (1984) cross. Shiffrin and Schneider (1977) proposed that controlled processing involved the use of a "limited capacity processor," which would include the abstract working memory that Broadbent described. We use controlled processes when we systematically employ different strategies to solve a problem. Not all controlled processing is accessible to awareness, that is, reportable by the individual using it. There are veiled controlled processes that occur outside the awareness of the individual. These are not only difficult for the person to report, they are not easily modified by following verbal instructions. For example, when we try to determine if a word in a sentence was used correctly, we use veiled controlled processes. They entail "looking up" the word in our long-term memories and comparing the current usage with these definitions. Here, the limited working memory (in Broadbent's model, abstract working memory) and the theoretically unlimited long-term storage are being used. However, the actual process of looking up the word is difficult to articulate.

Automatic processing differs from controlled processing in that working or limited capacity memory is not tapped or employed as information is exchanged, integrated, or employed. Automatic processing is an effortless process that is beyond the control of the participant (Howard 1983). The example Howard uses in her discussion of automatic processing is compelling. She instructs the reader to call out the number of digits in a box, ignoring the numerical value of the digits themselves. For example, in her first square she places two digits, each with the value of five. It is difficult to execute the task rapidly or smoothly because we tend to process automatically and call out the value of the digits themselves. This is a modification of a Stroop color-word test. The Stroop test requires readers to ignore the color of the letters that are used to write a particular color word and read the word itself. For example, the word "blue" may be written in red ink.

Again, the flexibility of the Maltese cross is in its accommodation of the fact that, on the one hand, we are able to process information immediately and rapidly; on the other, we are capable of holding material in abeyance for periods of time. Certain processes are automatic and may involve only the central processing unit before we emit an efferent. However, others are controlled and deliberate, and the processor moves material between one wing of the cross and another. For example, we might move information back and forth between long-term associative storage and abstract working memory. This, perhaps, is a more accurate reflection of the intricacies of human information processing.

In fact, we have argued already that the level of active effort involved in processing stimuli that will lead to Manichean thinking varies considerably from instance to instance. Consider the difference in terms of the cognitive effort between memorizing a poem that can clearly reinforce Manichean cognition, say Rudyard Kipling's "Gunga Din," and the construction of classically conditioned associations between groups of adolescent black boys on a city street and negative affective responses. In both instances Manichean mental structures are supported. However, the mental mechanisms used in their construction are vastly different. The Maltese cross is a step in the direction of accounting for the various forms of information processing we think take place as a Manichean way of thinking is developed.

Kihlstrom's unistore model. Kihlstrom (1987) presented an interesting and distinct alternative to the original multistage model. It is quite different from the Maltese cross as well. In fact, Kihlstrom's conceptualization is consistent with more modern notions of information processing (see Howard 1983). As is the case with the Maltese cross, notions of controlled and automatic processing can be integrated into this model. A good place to begin the explication of this system is by extending the discussion of the concepts of episodic and semantic memory. We intimated that episodic memories are autobiographical in that they represent events and contexts within the flow of our experiences. On the other hand, semantic memory is a general, abstracted knowledge of language and events. Kihlstrom accepted this distinction but partitioned information-processing activities further into *declarative* and *procedural knowledge.* Others have also made this distinction (Howard 1983). Declarative knowledge, in Kihlstrom's model, is the stored information acquired about the physical and social world that we inhabit. Procedural knowledge is a set of cognitive capacities that permits us to manipulate declarative knowledge and various forms of input and information. In Kihlstrom's view, for the most part, episodic memory is declarative, while semantic memory may be procedural or declarative (Kihlstrom 1984, 167).

In the final section of this chapter I take up the matter of the extent to which procedural and declarative knowledge, as defined in these terms, is available to consciousness. Presently, for the purpose of clarity, we will examine Kihlstrom's treatment of the relationship between consciousness and these forms of knowledge. He maintained that it is possible in certain circumstances to render declarative knowledge conscious. Activating declarative knowledge involves attentional processes and other procedural mechanisms that are involved in recall. Placing declarative knowledge in a highly active state is tantamount to bringing information to a conscious level. On the other hand, as a rule, procedural knowledge itself, though unmistakable in its impact, is not available to consciousness. One can determine quickly the equivalency of the sentences "The farmer tilled the soil" and "The soil was tilled by the farmer." However, the semantic memory or other facets of the procedural knowledge that allowed one to transform the physical events on the printed page into sentences and employ transformational grammar to determine that the "deep structures" of the two sentences were identical are not available to consciousness.

Kihlstrom's unistore model identifies four elements that are involved in mental processing (see figure 4). These include two that are largely unconscious (procedural knowledge and a sensory perceptual system), one that is available to consciousness (declarative knowledge), and a fully conscious attentional mechanism. Incoming information is retained first in the sensory perceptual system. Elements of procedural knowledge operate on it at this point. However, in Kihlstrom's formulation the sensory perceptual system remains obtuse, and the individual has no conscious access to events that take place within it. The operations of procedural knowledge with respect to the sensory system include analyzing the features of the incoming stimulation. As a function of this analysis, the perceived events activate an associated network of information in declarative memory.

FIGURE 4. Kihlstrom's Unistore Model of Information Processing

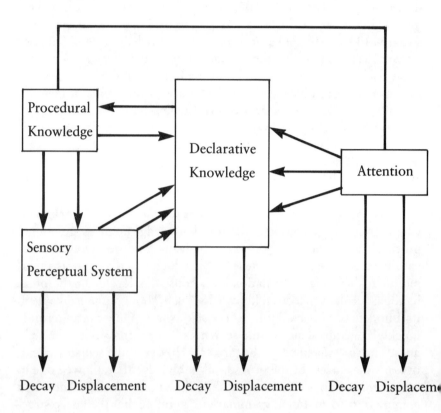

Simplified model taken from Kihlstrom 1984.

There is a second source of activation of declarative memory. It is through attentional mechanisms "corresponding to the processes of expectation" (Kihlstrom 1984, 169).

The activation of the declarative memory is pivotal in the process of interpreting and integrating the incoming information. It is this activation of our existing knowledge that permits us to make sense of the incoming material; it will represent our conscious experience. Again, according to Kihlstrom's model, our declarative knowledge can be activated in at least two ways. The first is through an analysis of the features of the input from the external environment that is executed by procedural knowledge. The second mode of activation is carried out exclusively by the internal processes of directing attention to stored elements. In essence, our conscious processing is a product of the activation of declarative knowledge from these distinct avenues.

Two implications of this model for our study of racism should be underscored. First, elements of declarative knowledge can be made active in our minds in the absence of input from the external environment. That is, the model describes the manner in which we can initiate our own experiencing of an image, concept, event, or entity that is housed in declarative knowledge. This we execute through the operation of attentional mechanisms. Second, it is likely that the fashion in which material is arranged and structured in declarative knowledge remains beyond the awareness of the individual. We remain unaware of this arrangement because, in most instances, the processes that govern how our perceptual and phenomenal world is formed occur unconsciously through the functions of procedural knowledge. The model does not hedge regarding the importance of unconscious processes. In many instances we simply do not really consider consciously the manner in which we think about the world.

The model proposed by Kihlstrom is simple and in some ways quite elegant. It provides a framework for understanding processing that, although not as detailed as Broadbent's, describes certain general features efficiently. Obviously, procedural knowledge involves a myriad of functions. Indeed, Broadbent alludes to several of these, but even his discussions are sketchy in his presentation of the Maltese cross. Broadbent has detailed elsewhere the complexities of attentional mechanisms (Broadbent 1958). In some ways, then, Kihlstrom's general presentation somewhat belies the complexity of the processes that he is describing. Additionally, as we noted at the outset, brain mechanisms involved in the systems Kihlstrom describes are not identified. Thus the neuropsychological criterion remains unmet. These criticisms notwithstanding, this model provides a useful framework within which we can structure an explanation of pivotal cognitive processes that take place within a racist society.

Appraising the models of processing. The alternative models to the traditional multistorage approaches provide more satisfactory frameworks for understanding the process through which a Manichean mind-set is inculcated. Even though neither identifies the physiological or neural substrates of the mechanisms it describes, there are several clear advantages to these reformations. However, in all fairness, there

185

are circumstances involving mental processing within the racist environment that favor the explanation that would be derived from the traditional multistorage model or at least illustrate where it is applicable. Obviously, verbal information that is twisted and crafted to be consistent with or reinforce white supremacy is in some cases learned through rote memorization by the oppressed. Again, the clearest instances of this form of information processing take place within the framework of the formal educational system. Here, sometimes even well-meaning teachers force students into the elaborate rehearsal of "facts" that are rife with distortion. King (1992) shows how the treatment of the collusion of African kings and merchants with Europeans during the West African slave trade is distorted in modern texts, although certain facts are presented accurately. She argues that if the cultural values of the groups that are involved are not presented, then the treatment of this complex chapter of social interaction will facilitate the development of "ethnocentric stereotypes" (330). It is usually the cultural values of African people that are not presented in these texts. Hence, students have no way of determining the extent to which those who were in collusion with this destructive practice were behaving in a fashion inconsistent with the African cultural ethos. Rather, these kings and merchants fit a mental representation of shrewd but greedy and morally debased individuals taking advantage of even less fortunate individuals in a primitive and depraved land. Tragically, the African moral codes they were violating simply are not presented. What King (1992) called ethnocentric stereotypes are stored in such a way that successive racist input will be accommodated readily.

The formal educational system, then, requires students to rehearse what can only be termed bad history. The cognitive structures of African people are affected accordingly. The older multistorage models adequately explain how this process might occur. As noted earlier, the circumstances under which formal, elaborative rehearsal of this kind may take place are limited both by the nature of the material and by the extent to which Manichean structures exist within the individual. Refer again to figure 1. In the final analysis, it appears that the form of processing described in the multistorage model applies to only one corner of the information processing that is the focus of this study of racism.

We must bear in mind three other facets of the processing of input that will accommodate and reinforce a racist mentality. These have been mentioned previously. First, arrays of stimuli including experiences and events that cannot be wholly represented by verbal processes constitute a significant portion of Manichean input (see chapter 3). Thus, the processing of this input does not involve elaborative rehearsal, articulation, or even rote repetition. However, these stimuli are capable of activating and interacting with the network of existing memories and eventually become part of both nonverbal and verbal structures within long-term memory. Second, though individuals have full recall of the physical features of stimuli that lead to racist thinking, they often cannot describe the manner in which this input has come to be organized into a racist way of viewing the world. Recall our discussion of the use of symbols in motion pictures. Though the colors worn by the villain in a film or even the skin color of the villain may be recalled by the viewer, even the racially conscious person may fail to recognize the Manichean aspects of the events. Third, it is evident that the oppressed experience racist memories in the absence of external input. This includes not only the activation of old memories but also the self-generation of new racist images and information. The model toward which we will gravitate must provide for the fact that racist input can involve the oppressed generating their own toxic input. Input reinforcing Manichean thinking is often constructed from behind "the veil," in Du Bois's words. Presently, we will appraise these models in light of these three considerations.

We return again to the matter of rehearsal only briefly, not to criticize this facet of the multistorage model yet again, but to show how the other models handle nonrehearsed input. The alternative information processing models of Broadbent and Kihlstrom, as well as similar models proposed by Norman (1968) and Howard (1983), accommodate this fact quite readily. The input in question can be visual, auditory, olfactory, or tactile, and much of it is not subject to rote repetition. Consider persons of African descent processing but not comprehending the root causes of disparities between their (collective) environments and those of members of more empowered groups, primarily those of European descent. A significant number of African people live in wretched conditions. Still, in these modern times, they are at least dimly aware that many people of European descent enjoy a much more tolerable existence. Indeed, even the most materially fortunate of black people see from time to time the environs of the masses of their kith. These few know that their exalted physical living conditions are an anomaly. Neither the wretched nor the spared rehearse the disparities they perceive. Rather, in the absence of an informational context that would provide an understanding of these disparities, the input activates preexisting memories that are organized along Manichean lines. Broadbent's Maltese cross may propose that this form of input moves quite rapidly from the sensory memory wing to the central processors to long-term associative storage. Kihlstrom's model might posit procedural knowledge activating existing associated units in the long-term storage as soon as the features of the stimuli are analyzed. Both show how these disparities might be processed and stored in the absence of rehearsal.

Second, the level of complexity involved in processing stimuli that have the potential for reinforcing Manichean thinking varies from situation to situation. In addition, in many instances, the oppressed may not be aware of subtle, self-deprecating facets of this information or of the manner in which it is being processed. At one extreme, the cognitive processes by which information that accommodates Manichean ideology is integrated into mental structures are quite direct and straightforward. At the other extreme, these processes are highly complex. The classical conditioning examples discussed in chapter 4 provide instances where processing involves simply determining that two stimuli are associated in a contiguous fashion. Eventually, the same efferent response is elicited by either stimulus. In contrast, often cultural symbols are veiled and the potentially toxic stimuli are subtle. For example, the world witnessed recently the utter horror of ethnic strife in Bosnia and in Rwanda. Unthinkable and completely senseless death and destruction were perpetrated in both instances. However, the term commonly used in the media to describe the situation in Bosnia was "ethnic cleansing." "Tribalism" and "savagery" are used frequently to describe the tragedy in Rwanda. *Time* magazine in an article on Rwanda used the words of a priest saying that "the devil was alive in Rwanda." The processing of these verbal descriptors involves storing stimuli in complex semantic networks, and their impact will not be straightforward. At both extremes of complexity, processing can be automatic in the sense that a working or short-term memory as well as long-term memories that are highly activated by attentional processes are not utilized as the processing is carried out. Rather, the oppressed rapidly and casually process information that will have dire consequences for the development of a healthy cognitive framework.

Another illustration of the occasionally effortless processing of Manichean stimuli is necessary. Consider for a moment the number of individuals of African descent who claim to be "hooked" on daytime television melodramas (soap operas) or the more recent talk shows. Even with a wide African-American viewership, some soaps still feature black characters on the periphery. Concern with the outcome of day-to-day conflicts in the lives of the mostly Caucasian characters becomes an obsession. On the other hand, a "sleaze factor" seems to govern the selection of topics for the talk shows. Each day they feature usually poor, very often black individuals behaving in a ridiculous fashion. The behaviors that these individuals exhibit are not remarkable. The oppressed and unfortunate in every land, perhaps partially out of frustration, tend to prey on each other. What is remarkable is that a significant number of daytime television viewers passively watch this material without asking for an explanation of its root causes.

It is best to leave aside a discussion of the literary value or cultural ethos of these serial dramas and talk shows. Instead, I would argue that submitting to the prescriptions for beauty, competence, and worth that these dramas set forth on a daily basis is not an insignificant practice. Similarly, observing the immoral and incompetent behavior of people of African descent that the talk shows parade can have a profound impact on the cognitive structures of African people. That is, black people expose themselves to a daily drubbing of story lines centered around a particular Caucasian man who is supposed to be imposing and desirable or a Caucasian woman who is portrayed as powerful, shrewd, and sexy. Additionally, we tune in channels where alienated and confused people of African descent act out, unashamedly, the symptoms of their mental illnesses. Still, from the cognitive perspective, individuals carry out the daytime viewing in the most passive, leisurely, and effortless fashion. We do not move these complex images into a working or short-term memory, the brain's "mental workbench." As people process the images, they do not activate those troubling memories of racially oppressive times, individuals, or situations. Often such memories lie within the recesses of the minds of most people of African descent. Rather, the content of the daytime shows enters long-term storage without the cognitive fanfare of elaborative rehearsal or deep processing. However—and this is crucial—the processed images take a place alongside Manichean cognitive structures. Consistent with the primary thrust of white supremacy, these structures relegate the world and the concerns of people of European descent to a status that is exalted and paramount. The lives of black people are rendered peripheral on the one hand and demonized on the other. The alternative models provide a framework for how the casual processing of complex stimuli may take place.

189

Finally, in the absence of input from the environment, declarative knowledge, that is, discrete configurations of memories, can be activated and even reevaluated. Both alternatives show how this might occur. Kihlstrom argued that by turning attention to declarative knowledge, stores of information can be experienced in our consciousness in a manner similar to the way our current sensory script is being experienced. Broadbent's executive processor can activate or call up old memories from motor memory or long-term associative stores. This spontaneous activation of stored material can have a reinforcing or detrimental impact on the viability of a Manichean mental framework. In a positive instance, the Manichean facets of these memories might be recognized and discarded. This might occur during metacognitive processes of the kind described so aptly by Earnest Gaines (1984) in his important novel *A Gathering of Old Men*. Charlie, a physically imposing but cringing fifty-year-old black man who has killed a sadistic white man, runs and hides in a swamp, leaving his own father to face the consequences. In that swamp at the edge of the cane fields of Louisiana, alone and concealed, he considers his cowardice and the nature of the Manichean world in which he lives. Later that night he returns to the quarters. In the presence of older black men who have gathered to protect his father, he explains, " 'Then I just laid there, laid there. Sometime round sundown—no, just 'fore sundown, I hear a voice calling my name. I laid there listening, listening, listening, but didn't hear it no more. But I knowed that voice was calling me back here. . . .' Charlie grinned—a great, wide-mouth, big-teeth grin. It was a deep, all-heart, true grin, a grin from a man who had been a boy fifty years" (192–93).

On the other hand, internal activation of memories can further reinforce Manichean thought. Some of the black comedians who gained popularity in the late 1980s and early 1990s tend to create characters that are similar to the damaging stereotypes of the past. In the early 1990s, on separate shows, two young black male comics, Martin Lawrence and Jamie Foxx, gained some notoriety and large national television audiences partially as a result of their portrayals of obnoxious caricatures of poor, uneducated black women. The creative process is a complex one, and certainly external exigencies including money and access to film and television are responsible in part for the products these individuals create. However, they have synthesized these characters out of their own experiences, that is, from their episodic memories. In this respect, they have produced images that are potentially supportive of Manichean thinking. The Kihlstrom and Broadbent models are able to account for those instances where material previously organized along Manichean lines can be activated and transformed in the absence of discrete current input.

From this perspective, the more modern models of information processing are more active and constructive in that they view individuals as quite capable of creating their own "input" and of restructuring previous input. At the same time, these models allow for the existence of both automatic and effortful processing of external input. Information processing flows in several directions in the two alternative models. Human beings bring new information into association with old, and old experiences can be reexamined or brought to the table in the presence or absence of new input. Thus, racist thoughts can fester and erupt in what appear to be spontaneous outbursts of self and group deprecation. Also, insights into flawed and rotten structures of racist thinking can occur and self-correcting restructuring can result. One major advantage of the Maltese cross and Kihlstrom models, then, is the flexibility of information flow. They show that through a number of avenues, processed material can be reactivated and reprocessed. Consequently, this material can exert a causal influence on our behavior.

Structure of permanent memory

The nature of schema

Obviously, our experiences—the continuous, detailed flow of the episodes and events of our lives—are not stored as isolated units in our memories. The input must be stored and made meaningful in relation to other input we have been provided. The human mind organizes and abstracts features of the world we encounter into cognitive structures. For the last sixty years, psychologists have called these mental structures schemata (Bartlett 1932). Schemata are active and constructive. They guide the processing of information and lead us to synthesize our experiences in a fashion that is efficient for social functioning and consistent with our existing schemata (Fiske and Taylor 1984).

Humans outside of experimental psychology laboratories encounter events other than lists of nonsense syllables, words, or sentences that they must commit to memory. Indeed, our human experience is largely a collision with complicated and only partially predictable circumstances. The schema, which is built on our previous experience, is activated by these encounters as we strive to make sense of a complex world. Certainly, procedural knowledge, in Kihlstrom's (1987) usage, is involved in organizing the schema. But specific experiences—that is, episodic memories—constitute the essential building blocks of schema. We organize what we experience into schemata that in turn influence our further perception, synthesis, and organization of our experiences.

With this in mind, the central and simple argument of this book can be stated more formally. Racism has a significant impact on certain key facets of the cognitive schemata of those who live under its sway. Manichean schemata, in the broadest sense, are those that contain elements that attribute, in principle, positive features of experience to whiteness and white people and negative features of experience to blackness and black people. Presently, we will examine two theories advanced to explain how long-term or permanent memories—in essence, the foundations of the schemata—are organized.

Organization of long-term storage

Network versus fragment theories. Howard (1983) described four characteristics of a class of approaches to understanding how memories are organized. These approaches are known as *network models* of semantic memory (Anderson 1976). They have been applied primarily to the manner in which semantic memory is organized. The models purport to show how semantic memory ultimately provides a working mental dictionary. We use semantic memory when we comprehend the world in linguistic terms. We have noted that only a portion of what we experience is verbal. A good measure of the input we encounter is not reducible to verbal description. Therefore, it is important to acknowledge at the outset that network models will not apply to the organization of a significant segment of our memories. To some extent, we address this limitation in our final section, where we discuss the manner in which memories not accessible to verbal channels may operate.

The first characteristic that Howard noted is that the network theories claim that long-term memory is structured around nodes. These nodes are concepts that specify properties and include relationships with other nodes. A node tells us something about the item in storage and tells us the direction of the association between that node and other nodes. For example, we can organize information about the entity "porpoise" around two nodes accordingly:

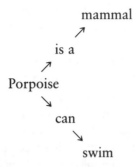

mammal

is a

Porpoise

can

swim

Notice that the node tells us of the properties of the porpoise and also gives information about the direction of the association. Therefore, we know that a mammal is not necessarily a porpoise and swimming does not make a porpoise.

Howard's (1983) second general statement about network theories is that recall (and thus comprehension) involves searching through the networks for meaning. This excursion permits us to determine the meaning of individual elements and to derive meaning from individual stimuli. Third, Howard notes that nodes, in fact, do not represent words. Rather, they are truly conceptual. Concepts are linked to a mental dictionary that includes the name. For example, I always have a great deal of difficulty recalling the name of the individual who betrayed the Denmark Vesey rebellion against slavery in Charleston, South Carolina. One individual was an enslaved African (Monday Gell) who received leniency from the court for his testimony. According to network theories, the memory might be organized in the following way:

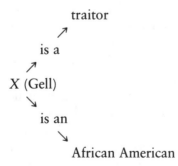

traitor

is a

X (Gell)

is an

African American

Finally, network theories distinguish between type and token nodes. This distinction is in line with that between semantic and

193

episodic memory. Type nodes are general and pertain to all instances or members of the set being defined. Token nodes are specific to one manifestation of the concept. My example of the structure related to the porpoise is a type node, while my search for the missing name is a search for a token node.

Contrast the network approaches to a second way of thinking about the organization of material in long-term storage. Broadbent (1984) endorsed this theory in his presentation of the Maltese cross. Memories are not seen as organized into networks of interrelated nodes in this approach. Rather, Broadbent, in agreement with Jones (1976, 1978), proposed that memory is represented in a distributive fashion at several locations. These *fragments* may have any number of associations with other items in storage. This model of storage presents the retrieval differently than do network approaches. For a memory to be recovered, an excursion through a directed or hierarchical network is not necessary according to this model. Instead, an item or concept can be accessed at several junctures or through any of the several fragments by which it is represented in memory. That is, a particular memory has several fragmentary representations. Cueing any of these will bring forth the entire memory.

An interesting set of studies reported by Jones (1978) actually tested the fragment hypothesis of long-term memory. The material that was to be learned in these studies was composed of discrete elements. For example, a slide would be shown describing in a phrase an object of a particular color at a particular location, e.g., yellow/cup/top left. During testing, one or several attributes of the object would be provided as cues for recall of the full slide. Similar experiments were reported where visual representations of the objects were presented. The results showed that cues involving fragments elicited full recall as predicted by the fragment hypothesis. Jones (1978) reanalyzed data from a study conducted by Anderson and Bower (1973). This reanalysis showed that the fragment hypothesis predicted performance better than a network model. Network models propose that memories are based on associations within a propositional tree.

M. Martin (1984) pointed out that the fragment hypothesis of long-term memory makes interesting predictions with respect to mood and memory. She noted that if individuals learn positive or negative trait words when their own moods are neutral, they recall this information better in pleasant and depressed moods, respectively. In studies of memory, this finding is known as a "mood congruency" effect. As Martin stated, the fragment hypothesis predicts that the memory item and its relationship to mood may be included in each fragment. Hence recall is easier in the mood state associated with that element of the fragment.

Perhaps the research work that uses brain imaging will shed greater light on the nature of memory storage. A. Martin et al. (1996) used positron emission tomography to track changes in cerebral blood flow while individuals identified tools and drawings of animals. When we identify animals, we pay a great deal of attention to physical features. However, our attention shifts more to how an object is used when we recognize tools. A. Martin and his colleagues found that the recognition of these objects resulted in changes in cerebral blood flow in several distinct brain regions. That is, not only did recognizing tools and animals elicit activation in a number of parts of the brain but also recognizing these two classes of stimuli activated different regions. They concluded that the information for recognition was located in distributed neural networks in various locations. This finding certainly leaves open possibilities of memories stored in fragmented forms or in multiple locations in the brain.

A great deal of work, both conceptual and empirical, remains before we will be able to determine whether the "network" or "fragment" approach to the organization of long-term storage is more adequate for the understanding of the structure of Manichean cognitive schema. However, drawing on experiential consciousness, one can identify certain crucial elements of the way the mental structures of the oppressed are organized within a system of white supremacy. A brief discussion of selected elements may serve to encourage and guide some of the studies of cognitive schemata in a Manichean world. I anticipate that bright students will conduct serious studies of the cognitive organization of the oppressed in the coming years.

Permanent mental representations in a Manichean world. I have argued in each chapter of this book that African people encounter potentially mentally toxic information or input in virtual barrages. This input emanates from every level of the social environment. It is a regular feature of the world African people perceive and process. Encounters with racist stimuli occur with such regularity and in such a manner that the mental structures of the oppressed begin to accommodate major tenets of white supremacy. In terms of the models we have reviewed, input tends to activate elements in long-term storage whose structures include Manichean associations. When integrated with preexisting structures, these new elements are stored in similar associations. Typical associations are illustrated in table 5 for the three main regions of Manichean thought. The power and, perhaps, the irony in the organization of Manichean schemata is the manner in which they may totally saturate certain regions and subregions in the minds of the oppressed. They may be utterly ubiquitous in this respect. On the other hand, the schemata may have abrupt and definite boundaries and be quite circumscribed. Let two examples illustrate this paradox. The first is from literature. In *A Soldier's Play*, Charles Fuller (1981) created a complex, tragic, but compelling character in Sergeant Vernon Waters. Waters recognizes the classic dimensions of blues music and values it highly. In the play, the young bluesman, a private named C. J. Memphis, says to Waters, "You really like the blues, huh?" Waters replies, "No other kind of music . . . ." (27). In addition, Waters has a profound respect for Melvin Peterson, the black GI who eventually murders him. He admires Peterson because he sees him as a black man with courage and a willingness to take a stand. At the same time, Waters views the very black folk tradition that forms the root of the blues he loves and the courage he respects as dangerous and out of step with the times. This tradition and those who represent it he despises with a "crazy hate" (89). Eventually, this complex mix of schemata drives Waters mad.

The second example emerges when we study the manner in which early (and, I would argue, present day) black scientists wrestle with matters of psychological identity. Here too, very complex schemata are readily apparent. Manning (1993) provides an interesting synopsis of the complex schemata that had to have been operative in the minds of leading scientists of African descent in the United States at the turn of the century. A fascinating case is that of Ernest Just, an embryologist born in 1883, about whom Manning wrote an entire volume (Manning 1983). Dr. Just felt the objectivity of science was of greater value for solving the problems facing black people than

TABLE 5. Three Main Regions of Manichean Thought

Efficacy/competence		Body image	
competent	incompetent	desirable	undesirable
white business	black business	light/straight hair	dark/tightly curled hair

Cultural/Historical	
classical	ephemeral
European/concert	jazz/improvisational

"intuitive and emotional" approaches he viewed as typical of people of African descent. Just's infatuation with science and its method was so deep that he would come to ignore growing fascism in Europe because Europe was the center of scientific thought (see also Gould 1985). Still, as Manning pointed out, Just was confronted with the irrational, racist manifestations of science in the journals to which he subscribed and in which he published. Vulgar articles appeared from time to time in these professional scientific sources. Just remained silent even when an article written by J. E. Wodsedalek (cited by Manning 1993) questioned the very humanity of African people on a biological level. Not only did Just remain silent publicly, but the extent to which he was privately enamored of the rigors of science and the European culture he saw as its root also was not reduced. In Just we have the tragedy of a brilliant and complicated man willing to submerge if not renounce a significant portion of his own cultural heritage in order to maintain acceptance in the scientific world. This objective world seriously entertained the absurdity that he himself was not human. How complicated the schemata that functioned in the mind of this brilliant man. Thus, the complexity of the human personality and thus the exigencies for models that describe the organization of human memory!

Jones (1978) advanced the fragment model of memory that is intriguing given the very complicated and paradoxical fashion in which Manichean schemata are organized. This is the model Broadbent (1984) endorsed. Even though we know that hierarchical networks can be quite complicated, fragment theory has the capacity to account for more associations for a given item in memory. First, in the fragment theory of storage, the direction of activation is more flexible. Specifically, the entry points to the schema are not arranged hierarchically. Memories can be elicited in several directions in the distributed theory. Hence Broadbent argues that memory A can be elicited by B and memory B by A. This seems to account for the saturation effects noted in regions of Manichean thinking. These effects occur where all stimuli in a given domain tend to be filtered through and processed by the Manichean schema. All black institutions, businesses, and educational entertainment can be viewed as inferior when saturation effects are extant.

At the same time, fragment storage theory seems to account quite readily for the complex configurations of Manichean schemata. As we have noted, the structure of the Manichean mind may not be as simple as a large network where all things black are construed as evil. Partial shields, generated from within black culture, exist and have always existed. Both theories can accommodate this reality, but, in my estimation, the hierarchical approach must stretch more to do so. Memories stored in fragmented associations are easier to circumscribe than complex networks. Hence, an argument in favor of the fragment theory.

Finally, in our discussion of novelty in the previous chapter, we argued that often certain facets of input change, but the essential elements of the Manichean cognitive processes remain the same. We intended to show that the input leading to racist schemata is often novel and dynamic, but it still activates Manichean associations. If such memories or associations are distributed in fragments and represented at multiple loci, it seems more likely that their elicitation by novel stimuli will be facilitated.

Clearly, coming to understand the organization of long-term storage is at the heart of our efforts to explore Manichean thinking. In any model of information processing, previously stored information has to be seen as having a profound impact on the manner in which we process current input. Obviously, the cognitive schemata hold the key to fathoming the manner in which people interact with their environments and circumstances. That is to say, the schemata are central to understanding personality itself.

Parallel distributive processing: A radical alternative model

The stark alternative to the Atkinson- and Schiffrin-inspired multistorage models of information processing is a relatively new view of cognition known as parallel distributed processing (PDP) (McClelland, Rumelhart, and the PDP Research Group 1986). Indeed, this approach departs radically from the alternative models of Kihlstrom and Broadbent. It is structured around knowledge of the functioning of neurons and, to that extent, speaks to the neuropsychological criterion. The approach is a stimulating and challenging one for those interested in the operation of the human brain. However, the empirical work available on the theory to date focuses on fairly basic perceptual and problem-solving processes. This is because the approach begins with an examination of the functioning rudimentary elements of the nervous system. It is difficult to foresee what utility PDP will have in coming years in studies of the development of complex social schemata including racist mental structures. I will project some possible applications after describing general features of the theory.

We intimated at the beginning of this chapter that the quantity of neurons in the human central nervous system is virtually inestimable. It is necessary at this point to take a closer look at neural organization. The complexity of arrangement is nothing short of astonishing. Neurons in the brain are equipped with *dendrites,* branching fibers that receive information from other neurons and can number in the thousands. Additionally, neurons are equipped with *axons* that also have complex branches and transmit information to other neurons. Information is transmitted in the form of small electrical charges. In the brain, the synapse is the juncture between neurons where a series of neurochemical changes result in the passing of information from the axon of one neuron to the dendrite or cell body of another neuron. A neuron can, through synaptic transmission, excite a neighboring neuron, increasing the likelihood it will fire an impulse, or inhibit this neuron, decreasing the likelihood it will transmit the electrical charge (Carlson 1994). Undaunted, even encouraged, by the vastness and complexity of neurocircuitry, PDP researchers have structured their models of thinking around the neuroanatomical characteristics of the human brain.

In PDP theory, the interrelationships of groups of neurons can be thought of as communication networks. According to theory, information is represented as these networks are activated. The messages travel through these networks rapidly, that is, within milliseconds. However, this is slow when compared to the speed at which modern computers process information (Norman 1986). The brain is impressive not for its speed of processing but because the networks function in a parallel fashion. That is, within a network, input that is processed may be the object of operations taking place simultaneously in various regions of the brain. Thus, a number of configurations of neural connections work in parallel. In an instant, hundreds of thousands of synapses are activated, processing in a few cycles what a computer may take several million cycles to execute. Clearly, PDP dismisses any notion that information processing will take place in a pipeline fashion or in a series of stages. Significant portions of specific networks, which can involve a million neurons (Haberlandt 1994), process information simultaneously.

As more components of a network become involved in processing, the network is said to be more activated. Therefore, activation in a network does not vary in a discrete, binary, off/on fashion. Rather, the level of activation of a network is thought of as constituting a continuous function (Kihlstrom 1987). As activation increases, it is more likely the information will be represented in consciousness.

Memory items are seen as represented across a number of stored elements, and these stored elements hold more than one memory. This permits a "robust" recognition of input (Haberlandt 1994). Incoming stimulus events activate a number of networks. Those that are close but less than exact fits to the input can be employed to disambiguate and process the input as belonging to a particular stimulus class. A visual image of a bird can be blurry, somewhat misshaped, and even presented in an absolutely novel fashion. Still, neural networks holding this representation will recognize it persistently. PDP sees this flexibility as one source of the brain's formidable power. Relatedly, schemata in PDP theory are conceptualized to be flexible, as opposed to fixed, cognitive structures (see Norman 1986; Rumelhart et al. 1986). The strong form of this view is that schemata come into existence "at the moment they are needed" (Rumelhart et al. 1986, 20).

The process of perception and the use of schemata can be summarized accordingly. Input will activate sets of networks until a good "fit" for the input is found in the neural interconnections. Once this fit is achieved, an interpretation of input is possible. In any case, PDP maintains that tight interrelations among neurons where clusters tend to be activated as units exist in the brain and function in a schema-like fashion. However, looser interconnections also exist in which units are activated simultaneously on a less regular basis. Here the networks function in a far less structured fashion as input is interpreted. Finally, as a function of input, connections can be strengthened in the looser networks or weakened in the more schema-like networks. This strength adjustment defines learning in the PDP system.

Presently, researchers are developing sophisticated artificial neural networks in laboratories. In these, a modifiable mathematical weight is given to each of the interconnections between the units in the system. These networks can be "trained" to recognize various forms of input, which can be complex and ambiguous. Hinton (1992) discusses neural networks capable of recognizing handwritten digits and parts of the human face.

I provide this very brief outline of the theory of parallel distributive processing as an instance of a "new look" in theories of human cognitive functioning. Its starting point is different than that of the other theories we have discussed. It begins with knowledge of how individual neurons work and moves forward to posit models of human brain functioning. The other models we discussed began at the opposite end of this process. They used evidence from experimental and sometimes clinical studies of performance on cognitive tasks and developed models of how the brain is operating. These models do not concern themselves as much with the functioning of individual neurons.

Because they begin on a micro level and then move to models of human thought, PDP research activities are not yet concerned with functioning in the social milieu. Indeed, the manner in which affect or emotions influence functioning is not addressed in several reviews on the subject (see McClelland, Rumelhart, and the PDP Research Group 1986). At this point, then, PDP theories are a bit sterile to be applied to the rich and complex human interactions involved in the development of a Manichean mentality. However, two facets of this approach hold promise for the study of racism.

First, the neural networks are seen as flexible processors or representations of information. In chapter 4 we discussed how elements of Manichean stimuli change and preserve novelty though they continue to reinforce cognitive frameworks saturated with white supremacy. PDP holds that networks represent information in a distributed fashion, and a number of forms of a Manichean stimulus could activate and indeed strengthen existing networks that are fraught with racist representations. The schemata themselves are flexible and therefore capable of processing stimuli that may be at variance with earlier representations.

Second, PDP is an interesting theory for those concerned with the effects of racism on cognition, because it posits that activation results in structural modification in synaptic junctures. Physiological evidence is the basis of this notion. Neural pathways actually do show a kind of plasticity in the sense that they are altered as a function of activation (see Fischbach 1992; Shatz 1992). Importantly, PDP theory approaches information processing from a perspective that tends to specify the biological substrate of Manichean thought. Those associations that represent the linking of negative concepts to people or entities associated with Africa have counterparts in the brain. The challenge will be to identify or model associative networks of this kind.

In short, PDP is a new approach, and its utility in the areas of social cognition is unclear. In their present states, the models being generated by PDP researchers may not represent the manner in which the brain works in complex social situations. Still, serious students of

201

racist cognition should not ignore this approach to information processing. Manichean schemata can be thought of as flexible and dynamic neural networks that are strengthened and weakened as a function of exchanges in a racist environment.

The special problem of consciousness

To what extent is conscious awareness necessary when human beings process information? In the previous discussion of information-processing models and the structure of long-term storage, we have broached this controversial topic. In fact, in chapter 4, questions about the status of consciousness hovered over the treatment of both classical conditioning and orienting responses. In each instance, I avoided a direct discussion of this topic, which is an unsettled issue that deserves treatment under its own rubric. For our purposes, the central question can be stated in stark terms. Do the oppressed, living in a modern system of white supremacy, consciously process all of the input and information that contributes to the construction and utilization of Manichean schemata? If the answer is negative, the task becomes to identify the stages of information processing where unconscious processing might take place. We are forced to examine general experimental research findings rather than data directly related to the processing of the kind of information that might lead to Manichean thinking. The latter evidence is not available. Perhaps in the near future investigators will provide empirical evidence related to the unconscious processing of racist information. These studies will have to focus on input from a variety of external environmental sources. Additionally, they will examine several different cognitive regions where white supremacist ideology tends to flourish.

I have provided information that is relevant to the question of the role of consciousness. Perhaps, to an extent, this information answers the question. I agree with those who wish to supplant the older, multistage "pipeline" model of memory. This model proposes that information is moved from one stage of memory to the next by attention and rehearsal. Both processes involve conscious awareness. The alternative models, namely Broadbent's Maltese cross, Kihlstrom's unistore approach, and PDP, do not require consciousness for information to be processed. Recall that Broadbent's central processor, as well as procedural knowledge as described by Kihlstrom, can operate in the absence of awareness. Consciousness, within the theory of PDP, occurs when neural networks are highly activated. However, stimuli may undergo considerable processing before reaching this highly activated state.

Indeed, we are aware of our own existence and of the world around us. Some argue that awareness—that is, sentience—is a hallmark of being human (Dulany 1968). Perhaps the capacity to talk to others about our awareness sets us apart from other creatures. We spend a significant portion of our waking processing time focusing our attention on problems, selectively filtering sensory input, and actively integrating and retrieving information. Must we process information only in this "effortful" fashion? Apparently, the answer is no.

I will begin with a brief biographical statement related to the study of unconscious processing. Then, I will examine the status of awareness as cognitive activity takes place at several stages of processing. These stages include (1) the initial sensory input, (2) construction of simple associations between stimuli, (3) processing of semantic information, and (4) in classical conditioning, more complex learning and the construction of rules that govern our responses to the environment. At each stage, the evidence suggests that unconscious processing takes place.

Several years ago in New Orleans, a scientific poster presented to the twenty-ninth annual meeting of the Society for Psychophysiological Research caught my attention. These meetings feature hundreds of presentations of research findings from studies conducted in laboratories in the United States, Canada, and Europe. But there was something intriguing about this particular report. It jolted me, intellectually speaking, and set me on a course of reading that would change my own position on unconscious processing in general and awareness in emotional response in particular.

The authors of the report (Warrenburg, Wexler, and Schwartz 1989) described an experimental procedure in which participants were presented different short words simultaneously to the left and right ears over stereo headphones in a dichotic listening task. Volume and word length were the same for the word pairs. Not only were the words that were presented simultaneously of exactly the same length but they were also acoustically identical in all respects except for the first phoneme or sound unit, for example, "dug-tug." Under these carefully controlled conditions, participants were expected to report hearing only one of the words. As anticipated, in most instances they reported hearing a single word.

In one condition, the researchers presented two words that were emotionally neutral like the "dug-tug" pair. In another condition, they provided a neutral and an emotionally positive word (e.g., rug-hug). In the remaining condition, a neutral and an emotionally negative word were presented (e.g., bide-died).

The experimenters obtained measures of facial muscle activity using an electromyograph. They assessed activity from the muscles in the regions associated with frowning or unpleasant expressions (corrugator muscles). In addition, the investigators measured brain activity using an electroencephalograph (EEG). They assessed activity in the right frontal area, a region of the brain associated with unpleasant emotions, and the left frontal area, a region associated with positive emotions.

When the participants reported hearing the emotional words, that is, when these words were perceived consciously and there was no recall of the nonemotional word, the impact on physiological responses was somewhat complicated. Both positive and negative words activated the left hemisphere, but the activity in the corrugator regions tended to reach higher levels when negative words were reported than when neutral or positive words were reported. However—and this was the most relevant and startling finding for me at that time—when participants were provided the emotionally neutral pair and reported hearing the *neutral* word only, EEG activity consistent with the emotional tone of the unreported word was observed. That is, if the emotional word was negative, right hemispheric activation resulted. If the emotional word was positive, left hemispheric activation tended to occur. Further, when the negative-neutral pair was presented and the subjects reported hearing the neutral word, activation of muscles in the corrugator region persisted. These remarkable findings suggest that even when the participants did not process the negative emotional word consciously, they processed it at the sensory level as well as the semantic level. This processing involved an activation of the brain region normally associated with the word's emotional valence. In the case of the negative words, the processing generated efferent activity in the form of activating the appropriate facial muscles!

This finding, along with several others I will discuss presently, invited me to reconsider my skepticism about unconscious information processing. It appeared plausible that thinking, even fairly complex emotional and cognitive processing, may occur outside of awareness. Could it be that the negative images found in film need not be processed consciously to have an impact on the oppressed? Perhaps witnessing the presence of people of African descent in crime-ridden areas or in undesirable living conditions influences our thinking in ways we do not recognize. We have to consider the possibility that unconscious processes may be in operation. But I am getting ahead of myself. What kind of evidence is available?

Sensory input and semantic processing

Subliminal activation refers to a process in which stimuli of which we are not aware elicit responses in sensory and higher level processing mechanisms. Dixon (1981) discussed the manner in which the orthodox scientific community first hastily refuted and then ignored the evidence in favor of subliminal activation. He argued (182) that, in many instances, evidence that individuals may process stimuli of which they are not conscious was rejected for a reason other than methodological flaws in the research designs that were employed to produce the evidence. The detractors belittled the findings because the very notion of subliminal activation is disquieting to the scientific community. In his book, Dixon (1981) marshaled a formidable array of findings demonstrating that where the signal-to-noise ratio of stimulation is low, processing the stimulus may take place out of awareness. A low signal-to-noise ratio can result from the presentation of information at or near sensory threshold (lowering the gain on the signal); the failure of the person to ignore or screen out background stimulation (subject-initiated subliminal effects); and the inundation of the setting with a myriad of candidates for processing (increasing the noise). Hence, those concerned with unconscious processes at the stage of sensory processing will find Dixon's empirically supported position very interesting. He shows that signals embedded in "noisy" backgrounds can be processed out of awareness.

Velmans (1991) provided a detailed discussion of the role consciousness plays at various stages of information processing. In fact, Velmans's position is more radical than the one I will advocate here. He viewed consciousness as a kind of byproduct of information processing, not as a causal factor facilitating cognitive work. I feel it is appropriate to afford the role of consciousness in information processing more status than this, though its role is probably less than what those on the other extreme might claim (see Searle 1990).

Velmans discussed the findings from a body of literature that employed shadowing techniques to study the allocation of attention to incoming information. As we noted earlier, in these studies participants are given different messages in each ear and are instructed to repeat the material provided to one of the ears only. The nonattended ear is the one presented the message that the researcher instructs the participants to ignore. The findings Velmans (1991) examined showed that not only was the information in the nonattended channel processed but, in instances in which the message was presented to the nonattended ear below the sensory threshold, it was also processed semantically, that is, in terms of meaning. The subjects processed the physical characteristics of the material in the nonattended channel that was presented above threshold. Here is how this was demonstrated in a study Groeger (1986) reported. Participants were challenged to complete a sentence with one of two words, for example, "They accepted (blame:compensation) for the accident." As they listened to the sentence, the participants were presented a "prompt" word in the nonattended ear either 5 decibels above or 5 decibels below the auditory threshold. In the present example, the experimenter presented the word "condemnation." Notice that "condemnation" is similar physically to the choice word "compensation" but is semantically similar to the word "blame." When the prompt (e.g., condemnation) was presented above threshold, participants tended to select the physically similar word (e.g., compensation) to complete the sentence. When it was presented below threshold, they tended to select the word that was semantically similar (e.g., blame). If the words presented in the nonattended ear were having no impact, the two option words would be selected at chance levels, or about 50 percent of the time. The findings of this study indicate that not only were the words in the nonattended channel processed, but they also tended to be processed at different levels (acoustically and semantically) depending on whether the experimenter presented them above or below auditory threshold.

Researchers use another technique, called priming, to show that preconscious effects on perception are reliable phenomena. Priming tasks require participants to determine if a string of letters is a word. Contrast the letters "EOT" with "EAT." A "prime" word is presented several hundred milliseconds (msec) before the target sequence of letters is shown. Sometimes the prime word is related conceptually to the target letter sequence; in other instances the prime is unrelated to the target. For example, the prime might be "legs" and the target "body" (related instance) versus the prime "wall" for the target "body" (unrelated instance). When the interval between the two stimuli is short (250 msec), conscious expectations for the target word cannot operate. There is simply not enough time. However, even at short intervals, people tend to recognize the target as a word more rapidly when the prime word was related to the target than when it was unrelated to it. It is likely that an unconscious or preconscious network of associations has been activated by the prime. This facilitates the recognition of the target. However, it does so out of awareness.

The priming studies can be used to demonstrate a number of cognitive phenomena that are germane to the present discussion. For example, Velmans cited the work of Neeley (1977), in which participants were told to expect words that were unrelated semantically to the prime word. This instruction influenced recognition only when the intervals between the prime and the target were longer (750 msec). In this case, there is time for the prime to be consciously processed and expectations for the coming word to function. When the target that is unrelated to the prime is expected, the participants recognize it as a word more rapidly.

The findings emerging from the priming experiments are of importance to a psychological study of racism. They suggest that the perception of prior events may speed the processing of subsequent related stimuli. The drawing of relevance from these findings involves a logical leap, because the direct buttressing evidence is not available. However, I hypothesize that in an environment saturated with stimuli and input that can be accommodated by or can support racism schemata, the processing of one racist event "primes" the processing of a second. A kind of unconscious "greasing" of the input runway for Manichean stimuli is set up. Future research will have to determine the validity of my hypothesis.

Another of the many examples of processing without awareness that Velmans (1991) cites takes place at the level of semantic processing. One focus of language studies of mental chronometry is the rate at which the meaning of words is determined by the brain. Velmans reviewed evidence that suggests that words, on the average, take 400 msecs to say in isolation. However, their meaning is recognized before the last sounds are articulated. Hearers process meaning in about 300 msecs. If the words are presented in a context, people tend to recognize them after articulated fragments of 200 msecs. Other evidence (Neeley 1977; Posner and Snyder 1975) suggests that consciousness occurs 200 msecs after the arrival of the information in the association areas of the cerebral cortex. Hence, the processing of information—looking it up in the mental dictionary—must occur preconsciously, because consciousness of words' meanings has to occur subsequent to the processing activity that identifies the words (Velmans 1991, 657).

These findings are consistent with Chomsky's (1980) notion that complex verbally related processing occurs preconsciously. Chomsky argued that we use the complex rules that determine the grammatical status and the meaning of sentences out of awareness (Chomsky 1957, 1980). He argued that normally we do not have "access" to all the rules we use in decoding linguistic communications. Therefore, at least according to Chomsky, portions of this very complex aspect of information processing take place in a realm that is beyond our awareness.

Learning simple and more complicated associations

In the previous chapter we discussed the impact of classical conditioning on emotional responding. From a cognitive perspective, classical conditioning involves the "recognition" of an association between the presentation of an unconditioned and a conditioned stimulus. In many instances of human classical conditioning, individuals are able to report that the conditioned stimulus is associated with the onset of the unconditioned stimulus (see Roberts et al. 1993). However, conditioning can occur where there is no such awareness. For example, Daum, Channon, and Canavan (1989; Daum et al. 1991) studied conditioning in patients with severe memory disorders that resulted from brain injury or surgery. The authors reported that conditioned stimuli in the form of lights and tones could be used to elicit eyeblinks. The unconditioned stimulus in these studies was a puff of air to the eyeball. The patients' memory impairments were so profound that they could not report that the puffs of air were followed by tones or lights. Still, patients showed the conditioned eyeblinks.

Recently, a series of very interesting conditioning studies has employed what are referred to as masking procedures. The findings from these studies show that individuals do not have to fully recognize conditioned stimuli for conditioned responses to occur. That is, these studies suggest that not only is it unnecessary for the association between the conditioned and unconditioned stimulus to be recognized, but also the stimulus itself may have an impact without being recognized. Öhman and his colleagues (1993) reported several examples based on work they conducted in their laboratory in Sweden. The studies are somewhat complex and are based on the theoretical work of Marcel (1983). Marcel proposed that the processing of input by the human brain involves matching information received by the senses with the brain's representations of similar input. He theorized that we rapidly and automatically construct hypotheses about the nature of incoming information. Equally rapidly, we test to see if the input fits the brain's hypothesis about what the input actually is. Consciousness occurs when our hypothesis about input fits the sensory information. He wrote that "a conscious precept is obtained by a constructive act of fitting perceptual hypothesis to its sensory source" (245). However, we may generate many incorrect hypotheses about input that will never become conscious. They fail to reach consciousness precisely because they do not fit the incoming information.

Soares and Öhman (1993) recruited thirty-two individuals who feared either snakes or spiders and thirty-two who feared neither to participate in an experiment. They used an electrical shock as an unconditioned stimulus to elicit changes in electrodermal activity. (Researchers obtain measures of electrodermal activity or skin responses from the palms of the hand or soles of the feet. The responses are related to the activity of sweat glands and are often seen as useful measures of psychological arousal or emotionality [see Harrell, Morris, and Rasayon 1996; Edelberg, 1993]). The conditioned stimuli were pictures of snakes, spiders, or flowers and mushrooms. That is, Soares and Öhman gave some of the participants shocks subsequent to the presentation of snakes. They also gave shocks after pictures of spiders or of flowers and mushrooms. As expected, classical conditioning occurred. That is, the snakes, spiders, and flowers and mushroom scene elicited conditioned electrodermal responses as did the more pleasant flower scene. More important, in a final phase, masked pictures of these stimuli were presented. Masking was effected by cutting the stimulus pictures into puzzle-like pieces and reassembling them into unrecognizable collages. Both phobics and normal participants showed conditioned electrodermal responses to the "fear-relevant" masked stimuli but not to masked flowers and mushrooms.

Esteves et al. (1994) used a different masking strategy to demonstrate the manner in which classical conditioning operates. Again, in this study, they used shocks as unconditioned stimuli and electrodermal responses were measured. This time, the conditioned stimuli were either happy or angry faces. However, these were presented for very brief periods, that is, 30 msecs, and followed immediately by a neutral face for 30 msecs. Under these conditions, the brain is unable to consciously perceive the expression on the face. In general, people cannot say if the face was happy or angry when it is presented for this duration. However, when the angry face was paired with a shock during the conditioning phase, even though it was not recognized later when presented alone, it still elicited a conditioned electrodermal response. These studies show dramatically that it is not necessary for individuals to be aware of or to think about the relationship between conditioned and unconditioned stimuli in order for conditioned responses to be elicited.

Researchers are very close to uncovering the brain mechanisms involved in classical conditioning. Scientists are using animals in these studies, primarily rats. The purpose of the studies is to identify the brain structures that are involved in classical conditioning. The thrust of these studies has curious and revealing implications for the present discussion of consciousness. LeDoux (1994) summarized a series of experiments in which an experimenter conditioned rats to exhibit a fear response to an auditory stimulus. He measured fear in terms of blood pressure increases and temporary immobility, or freezing. On several earlier occasions, he had presented the sound as the animal received a mild shock to its foot. Subsequently, the rats underwent surgery on various parts of their brains. LeDoux showed that the conditioned effect did not occur after he destroyed portions of structures in the midbrain and the thalamus that are known to receive auditory input. However, when portions of the higher brain structures (specifically, structures in the auditory cortex) were damaged, the animals continued to show the classically conditioned fear response. This finding suggests that the higher brain centers are not necessary for the conditioned fear response to occur. LeDoux (1996) concluded that classically conditioned responses are not influenced by higher brain centers. However, he argued that lower brain structures, including those in a structure called the amygdala, can mediate physiological changes associated with conditioned emotional changes quite independently of the higher brain centers. With respect to humans, it is safe to propose that awareness is likely involved in many conditioned emotional reactions. Nevertheless, these responses can and probably do occur very rapidly and through the mediations of lower brain centers. The lower brain centers are able to function independently of effort or conscious awareness on the part of the individual.

In summary, one might argue that awareness of the relationship between an eliciting conditional stimulus and the unconditional stimulus is an important component of classical conditioning in human beings. However, the evidence suggests that this awareness is not *essential* to the occurrence of conditioned responses. It is possible that the oppressed may not be aware of the conditioned bases of emotional responses they evidence in certain crucial situations. As we outlined in chapter 4, black adolescent males may become conditioned stimuli for very short-latency, negative emotional reactions. We argued that this occurs after these young men have been paired with crime scenes in television news portrayals. There is no reason to believe that those who exhibit the emotional response consciously recognize the *contiguity* between the presence of the boys and the crime scenes on television. It is even less likely that one will be able to articulate the steps involved in the conditioning process. In the 1990s, the faces of well-known black adult males have been paired with stories of spousal murder and abuse, rape, sexual harassment, political corruption, and cocaine use. Quite possibly, black males might carry the baggage of having become conditioned stimuli for the negative emotional reactions these criminal acts elicit. There is adequate reason to suspect that these associations occur unconsciously. Simple classical conditioning, then, in the absence of awareness, may reinforce Manichean mental structures in people of African descent.

With respect to more complex forms of learning, there is considerable evidence showing that as we store memories, unconscious processes operate. These findings were generated in experimental psychological studies and have captured the attention of a large number of researchers. Seger (1994) discussed the role of implicit learning, one of the unconscious processes that operate as human beings store memories. Implicit learning, according to Seger, is (1) not accessible to consciousness, (2) abstract in nature (that is, more than a simple association between two events), and (3) the "incidental" result of or consequence of cognitive processing. Implicit learning can take place even in patients with severe "amnesia," for example, in those suffering from the inability to develop new conscious memories like the patient H.M. Among the striking examples of implicit learning cited by Seger (1994) are the stories of H.M. and other amnesiacs. These unfortunate individuals show improvement at solving various very short mazes or in learning very short strings of numbers. However, they have no memory of practicing the tasks. This suggests that memory is formed independent of the conscious storage of memory in which the hippocampus is involved. Indeed, most of the experimental evidence Seger (1994) cites involves normal individuals, not patients with neurological disorders like H.M. and other amnesiacs.

Jacoby (see Jacoby, Toth, and Yonelinas 1993; Debner and Jacoby 1994) argues that we often overestimate the extent to which conscious processes are involved as memories are stored and as perception occurs. Jacoby uses a process-dissociation procedure to separate conscious from unconscious processes. This procedure exposes participants to a stimulus—a word, for example. The participants may or may not learn or perceive the word. In the second part of the study they have to complete a sentence. In some conditions Jacoby and his associates tell the subjects to include the word if they saw it or remember it. However, in an "exclusion condition," the experimenters tell the subjects that if information that they picked up in the first session comes to mind, they are not to use it in completing the sentence. Hence the participant would use the word only if it came to mind automatically and the individual had no memory of being exposed to it. Jacoby's research shows that often people employ the material they have picked up "implicitly" to complete the sentences. They do not recall processing it.

Finally, Pawel Lewicki first reported from Poland (1986) and later from a laboratory in the United States that individuals function and behave according to rules they are not able to articulate. Lewicki uses several rather straightforward experimental manipulations to demonstrate how this occurs (Hill and Lewicki 1991; Lewicki, Hill, and Czyzwska 1992). In the studies Lewicki reports, participants are given experience with a set of circumstances that entails an association between two events or concepts. This experience sets up an "encoding bias," because the researchers show the participants only instances in which the association is true. Subsequently, the participants are exposed to a novel situation, and Lewicki assesses their tendency to function according to the rule or bias they have encountered on earlier experiences. Often the participants operate according to the bias. However, usually they cannot articulate the nature of the association between the events.

For example, Lewicki and his associates set up a series of events in which a research assistant with short hair interacted repeatedly with the participants in a kind fashion. Then, in novel circumstances, the participants interacted with both short- and long-haired individuals. Appropriate controls for familiarity were employed. The usual response was that the behavior of the short-haired person was evaluated as kind. The participants could not provide the basis of their judgment. In another instance, the experimenters showed participants complex computerized axial tomography (CAT) scans of the human brain. The experimenters told the participants that some of the scans were from extremely bright people. The participants' job was to select the "bright scans." On practice trials, when the experimenters told subjects that the scan was of a "bright" brain, in all cases one region of the scan was identical. When asked to make independent judgments later in the experiment, participants showed the bias toward scans with the particular configuration in this region. However, they were unable to identify this region as being the basis of their judgment.

In the body of evidence that Lewicki and associates generated, we have evidence that efferent activity, that is, the behavioral output itself, can be influenced by unconscious processes. It is not only the integration of input, but the execution of responses that may be affected by processes beyond our awareness.

Recently, Greenwald and Banaji (1995) reviewed research that examined unconscious aspects of social attitudes and beliefs. They used the term "implicit" to designate information-processing activities that individuals cannot report or gain access to through introspection. That is, implicit social cognitive processes are those that experimental psychologists can identify in the laboratory. However, the participants in the studies are not aware that these processes are taking place. Greenwald and Banaji cited work showing how stereotypic attitudes operate implicitly. Gaertner and McLaughlin (1983) showed that whites were able to identify strings of letters as words more rapidly when the word pairs involved *white* being associated with a positive word than when *black* was associated with a positive word. In a priming study that Greenwald and Banaji cite, when the prime was *black*, subjects recognized positive trait descriptors as words more slowly than when a positive descriptor followed the prime *white* (Dovido, Evans, and Tyler 1986). Greenwald and Banaji (1995) concluded that "much social cognition occurs in an implicit mode" (20). The findings they reviewed suggest that unconscious processes occur in important social realms, including attitudes toward self, other individuals, and groups.

The status of unconscious processing

Obviously, the evidence suggests that we should phrase the question regarding unconscious information not in terms of if it occurs but rather in terms of when and where it operates. The research findings lead us to conclude that we should not claim full awareness of all aspects of our mental activity at any stage of information processing.

213

There is evidence for unconscious priming activities. Here the reception of one stimulus or form of input may speed the processing of a second stimulus, though we are not aware that this is happening. Further, a number of different experimental paradigms have provided evidence that the meaning of words can be processed outside conscious awareness. Also, studies of classical conditioning show that one need not be aware of the relationship between the occurrence of the conditioned stimulus and the unconditioned stimulus for conditioned responses to be elicited. The studies of more complex learning show that as we engage in the ordinary process of learning and remembering, we "pick up" additional material implicitly. Finally, findings from a variety of studies show that the learning of complex rules and relationships among concepts takes place outside awareness. This seems to occur as individuals encode specific events into memory. The unconscious rules have been shown to influence behavioral output. To believe that awareness is a kind of sine qua non of human information processing would be to disregard experimental evidence that is forthcoming from many different paradigms. By extension, it would be naive to posit that in an environment replete with input that facilitates the development of Manichean schemata, we process all information consciously.

Understanding brain functioning in a Manichean world

Gould (1985) discussed a philosophical problem encountered by Ernest Just and other biologists of his day. The essence of this problem was how to view life itself. The extreme positions were these: Life is but a summation of mechanistic laws; life has a component to it that transcends the physical entities studied by the scientist. There is an analogous problem for those of us concerned with the cognitive impact of racism. How should we view the brain? Some models talk of central executives, discrete memory systems, and identifiable processes. All these entities are discussed as if they are embedded in a real existence. On the other hand, we might look at the brain as a massive collection of very dynamic electrical circuits. It is inappropriate to give names to and anthropomorphize these circuits. Gould praised Just's wise choice in solving the dilemma of his time. He found a middle ground between the two positions in his quest for truth. Our search is for a model that facilitates our understanding of the manner in which a modern, some say postmodern, racist society acts on the cognitive processes of its victims. Interestingly enough, our excursion into the area of cognitive psychology has resulted in our taking a tolerant position with respect to the models that are being promoted. Hopefully, we are behaving within Just's tradition.

It is useful to summarize some features of brain activity in terms of components that may not actually exist on the level of neural circuitry. I am not sure we will ever identify procedural knowledge or central processing systems in the biological sense. Still, these concepts are helpful when we study how people might be victimized by racist input. Similarly, there is something attractive about being able to identify how Manichean concepts may be organized in neural networks as PDP approaches may one day be able to do. It is productive to propose and discuss the functioning of macrosystems and to encourage the examination of microsystems in studying brain functioning.

We know that Manichean memories are durable. It is crucial that we come to know how they are stored. I think a good lead is to suppose they are stored in a fragmented and distributive fashion. We should assume that Manichean concepts are accessible from many avenues or by many forms of stimuli. We are in need of studies that focus on how Manichean concepts are organized in the minds of those on oppression's receiving end.

Finally, the case in favor of the unconscious processing of Manichean stimuli is most clear. It is more than likely that people of African descent frequently are no more aware of internalizing Manichean stimuli than one is conscious of an influenza virus when it initially enters the body. Quite probably, extensive processing of these stimuli takes place automatically, and the schemata they engender may in fact influence our behavior in an unconscious fashion. This does not imply that processes at any stage must remain unconscious. However, methods useful in increasing awareness of the forms of stimuli that are potentially toxic will prove therapeutic. This we will see in the final chapter.

The wonder that the biological psychologists experience is understandable. Breakthroughs in brain sciences, like those that show us the neuropathways of classical conditioning (LeDoux 1994, 1996) or the various kinds of memories that may exist in the brain (Seger 1994), serve as vivid reminders of the remarkable complexity of the human brain. So much remains to be discovered about the manner in which the brain functions. Even our little peek, carried out for our own parochial purpose of coming to a better understanding of Manichean thinking, gives some idea of how involved and intricate these studies will be and the brain itself is. As far as we know, the brain is the most sophisticated of nature's creations. Its growth and development are affected directly by racist stimuli, be they vulgar and overt or subtle and polite. These stimuli set in motion complex processes that we must continue to struggle to understand if we wish to make sense of the behavior of African people and rectify the harmful effects of racist stimuli. The last two chapters are directed toward these ends.

References

Anderson, J. R. 1976. *Language, Memory and Thought*. Hillsdale, N.J.: Erlbaum.

Anderson, J. R., and Bower, G. H. 1973. *Human Associative Memory*. Washington, D. C.: Winston.

Atkinson, R. C., and Shiffrin, R. M. 1968. Human Memory: A Proposed System and Its Control Processes. In *The Psychology of Learning and Motivation: Advances in Research and Theory, Vol. 2*, ed. K. W. Spence and J. T. Spence, 89–195. New York: Academic Press.

Bartlett, F. C. 1932. *Remembering: A Study in Experimental and Social Psychology*. London: Cambridge University Press.

Beardsley, T. 1997. The Machinery of Thought. *Scientific American* (August): 78–83.

Best, J. B. 1989. *Cognitive Psychology*. 2d ed. St. Paul: West Publishing.

Broadbent, D. E. 1958. *Perception and Communication*. London: Pergamon Press.

———. 1984. The Maltese Cross: A New Simplistic Model for Memory. *Behavioral and Brain Sciences* 7: 55–94.

Carlson, N. 1994. *Physiology of Behavior*. 5th ed. Boston: Allyn and Bacon.

Cherry, E. C. 1953. Some Experiments on the Recognition of Speech, with One and Two Ears. *Journal of the Acoustical Society of America* 25: 975–79.

Chomsky, N. 1957. *Syntactic Structures*. The Hague: Mouton.

———. 1980. Language and Unconscious Knowledge. In *Rules and Representations*, ed. N. Chomsky, 217–54. New York: Columbia University Press.

Craik, F. I. M., and Lockhart, R. S. 1972. Levels of Processing: A Framework for Memory Research. *Journal of Verbal Learning and Verbal Behavior* 11: 671–84.

Craik, F. I. M., and Tulving, E. 1975. Depth of Processing and the Retention of Words in Episodic Memory. *Journal of Experimental Psychology: General* 104: 268–94.

Craik, F. I. M., and Watkins, M. J. 1973. The Role of Rehearsal in Short-Term Memory. *Journal of Verbal Learning and Verbal Behavior* 12: 559–607.

Daum, I., Channon, S., and Canavan, A. G. M. 1989. Classical Conditioning in Patients with Severe Memory Problems. *Journal of Neurology, Neurosurgery, and Psychiatry* 52: 47–51.

Daum, I., Channon, S., Polkey, C. E., and Gray, J. A. 1991. Classical Conditioning after Temporal Lobe Lesions in Man: Impairment in Conditional Discriminations. *Behavioral Neurosciences* 105: 396–408.

Dawson, M. E., and Schell, A. M. 1987. Human Autonomic and Skeletal Classical Conditioning: The Role of Conscious Cognitive Factors. In *Cognitive Processes and Pavlovian Conditioning in Humans*, ed. G. Davey, 27–56. New York: Wiley.

Debner, J. A., and Jacoby, L. L. 1994. Unconscious Perception: Attention, Awareness, and Control. *Journal of Experimental Psychology: Learning, Memory and Cognition* 20: 304–17.

Dixon, N. F. 1981. *Preconscious Processing.* Chichester, N.Y.: Wiley.

Dovido, J. F., Evans, N. E., and Tyler, R. B. 1986. Racial Stereotypes: The Contents of Their Cognitive Representations. *Journal of Experimental Social Psychology* 22: 22–37.

Dulany, D. E. 1968. Awareness, Rules, and Propositional Control: A Confrontation with S-R Behavior Theory. In *Verbal Behavior and General Behavior Theory*, ed. T. R. Dixon and D. L. Horton, 340–87. New York: Prentice Hall.

Edelberg, R. 1993. Electrodermal Mechanisms: A Critique of the Two-effector Hypothesis and a Proposed Replacement. In *Progress in Electrodermal Research*, ed. J. Roy, W. Boucsein, D. Fowles, and J. Gruzelier, 7–31. New York: Plenum Press.

Esteves, F., Parra, C., Dimberg, U., and Öhman, A. 1994. Nonconscious Associative Learning: Pavlovian Conditioning of Skin Conductance Responses to Masked Fear-relevant Facial Stimuli. *Psychophysiology* 31: 375–85.

Fischbach, G. D. 1992. Mind and Brain. *Scientific American* 267: 48–57.

Fiske, S. T., and Taylor, S. E. 1984. *Social Cognition.* Reading, Mass.: Addison-Wesley.

Fuller, C. 1981. *A Soldier's Play.* New York: Hill and Wang.

Gaertner, S. L., and McLaughlin, J. P. 1983. Racial Stereotypes: Associations and Ascriptions of Positive and Negative Characteristics. *Social Psychology Quarterly* 46: 23–30.

Gaines, E. J. 1984. *A Gathering of Old Men.* New York: Vintage Books.

Gould, S. 1985. *The Flamingo's Smile: Reflections in Natural History.* New York: W. W. Norton.

Greenwald, A. G., and Banaji, M. R. 1995. Implicit Social Cognition: Attitudes, Self-esteem and Stereotypes. *Psychological Review* 102: 4–27.

Groeger, J. A. 1986. Predominant and Non-predominant Analysis: Effects of Level of Presentation. *British Journal of Psychology* 77: 109–16.

Haberlandt, K. 1994. *Cognitive Psychology.* Boston: Allyn and Bacon.

Harrell, J. P., Morris, C. E., and Rasayon, N. K. B. 1996. Physiological Measures in Studies of Psychological Stress in Black Populations. In *Handbook of Tests and Measurements for Black Populations*, ed. R. Jones, 59–74. Berkeley: Cobb and Henry.

Hayes, and Broadbent, D. E. 1988. Two Modes of Learning for Interactive Tasks. *Cognition* 28: 249–76.

Hill, T., and Lewicki, P. 1991. The Unconscious. In *Personality: Contemporary Theory and Research,* ed. V. Derlega, B. Winstead, and W. Jones, 207–29. Chicago: Nelson-Hall.

Hinton, G. E. 1992. How Neural Networks Learn from Experience. *Scientific American* 267: 145–51.

Howard, D. V. 1983. *Cognitive Psychology: Memory, Language and Thought.* New York: Macmillan.

Hubel, D. H. 1979. The Brain. In *The Brain: A Scientific American Book.* 1979. Reprint, San Francisco: W. H. Freeman.

Jacoby, L. L., Toth, J. P., and Yonelinas, A. P. 1993. Separating Conscious and Unconscious Influences of Memory: Measuring Recollection. *Journal of Experimental Psychology: General* 122: 139–54.

Jones, G. V. 1976. A Fragmentation Hypothesis of Memory: Cued Recall of Pictures and of Sequential Position. *Journal of Experimental Psychology: General* 105: 277–93.

———. 1978. Tests of a Structural Theory of the Memory Trace. *British Journal of Psychology* 69: 351–67.

Kihlstrom, J. F. 1984. Conscious, Subconscious, Unconscious: A Cognitive Perspective. In *The Unconscious Reconsidered,* ed. K. Bowers and D. Meichenbaum, 149–211. New York: John Wiley.

———. 1987. The Cognitive Unconscious. *Science* 237: 1445–52.

King, J. E. 1992. Diaspora Literacy and Consciousness in the Struggle against Miseducation in the Black Community. *The Journal of Negro Education* 61: 317–40.

LeDoux, J. E. 1994. Emotion, Memory and the Brain. *Scientific American* 270: 50–57.

———. 1996. *The Emotional Brain: The Mysterious Underpinnings of Emotional Life.* New York: Simon and Schuster.

Leukel, F. 1976. *Introduction to Physiological Psychology.* St. Louis: C. V. Mosby.

Lewicki, P. 1986. *Nonconscious Social Information Processing.* New York: Academic Press.

Lewicki, P., Hill, T., and Czyzewska, M. 1992. Nonconscious Acquisition of Information. *American Psychologist* 47: 796–801.

Lewis, D. L. 1993. *W. E. B. Du Bois: Biography of a Race 1868–1919.* New York: Henry Holt.

Lewis, J. 1970. Semantic Processing of Unattended Messages Using Dichotic Listening. *Journal of Experimental Psychology* 85: 225–28.

Mackay, D. G. 1973. Aspects of the Theory of Comprehension, Memory and Attention. *Quarterly Journal of Experimental Psychology* 25: 22–40.

Marcel, A. J. 1983. Conscious and Unconscious Perception: An Approach to the Relations between Phenomenal Experience and Perceptual Processes. *Cognitive Psychology* 15: 238–300.

Martin, A., Wiggs, C. L., Ungerlieider, L. G., and Haxby, J. V. 1996. Neural Correlates of Specific Knowledge. *Nature* 379: 649–52.

Martin, M. 1984. Memory and Mood. *Behavioral and Brain Sciences* 7: 75.

Manning, K. R. 1983. Black Apollo of Science: The Life of Ernest Everett Just. New York: Oxford University Press.

———. 1993. Race, Science, and Identity. In *Lure and Loathing: Essays on Race, Identity, and the Ambivalence of Assimilation,* ed. G. Early, 317–36. New York: Penguin.

McClelland, J. L., Rumelhart, D. E., and the PDP Research Group. 1986. *Parallel Distributed Processing: Explorations in the Microstructure of Cognition, Vol. 2: Psychological and Biological Models.* Cambridge, Mass.: MIT Press.

Neeley, J. H. 1977. Semantic Priming and Retrieval from Lexical Memory: Role of Inhibitionless Spreading Activation and Limited Capacity Attention. *Journal of Experimental Psychology: General* 106: 226–54.

Neisser, U. 1967. *Cognitive Psychology.* New York: Appleton-Century-Crofts.

Nilsson, L. 1989. Classification of Human Memory: Comments on the Third Section. In *Varieties of Memory and Consciousness: Essays in Honour of Endel Tulving,* eds. H. L. Roediger and F. M. Craik, 295–305. Hillsdale, N.J.: Erlbaum.

Norman, D. A. 1968. Toward a Theory of Memory and Attention. *Psychological Review* 75: 522–36.

———. 1986. Reflections on Cognition and Parallel Distributed Processing. In *Parallel Distributed Processing: Explorations in the Microstructure of Cognition, Vol. 2: Psychological and Biological Models,* ed. J. McClelland, D. Rumelhart, and the PDP Research Group, 531–46. Cambridge, Mass.: MIT Press.

Öhman, A., Esteves, F., Flykt, A., and Soares, J. J. F. 1993. Gateways to Consciousness: Emotion Attention and Electrodermal Activity. In *Progress in Electrodermal Research,* ed. J. Roy, W. Boucsein, D. Fowles, and J. Gruzelier, 137–58. New York: Plenum Press.

Peterson, L. R., and Peterson, M. J. 1959. Short-term Retention of Individual Verbal Items. *Journal of Experimental Psychology* 58: 193–98.

Posner, M. I., and Snyder, C. R. R. 1975. Attention and Cognitive Control. In *Information Processing and Cognition: The Loyola Symposium,* ed. R. Solso. Potomac, Md.: Erlbaum.

Roberts, L. E., Rau, H., Furedy, J. J., and Birbaumer, N. 1993. Does Activation of the Baroreceptors Reinforce Differential Pavlovian Conditioning of Heart Rate Responses? *Psychophysiology* 30: 531–36.

Robinson, C. 1983. *Black Marxism: The Making of the Radical Black Tradition.* London: Zed Press.

Roediger, H. L. 1984. The Use of Interference Paradigms as a Criterion for Separating Memory Systems. *Behavioral and Brain Sciences* 7: 78–79.

Rumelhart, D. E., Smolensky, P., McClelland, J. L., and Hinton, G. E. 1986. Schemata and Sequential Thought Process in PDP Models. In *Parallel Distributed Processing: Explorations in the Microstructure of Cognition, Vol. 2: Psychological and Biological Models,* ed. J. McClelland, D. Rumelhart, and the PDP Research Group, 7–57. Cambridge, Mass.: MIT Press.

Searle, J. R. 1990. Consciousness, Explanatory Inversion and Cognitive Science. *Behavioral and Brain Sciences* 13: 585–642.

Seger, C. A. 1994. Implicit Learning. *Psychological Bulletin* 115: 163–96.

Shatz, C. J. 1992. The Developing Brain. *Scientific American* 267: 60–67.

Shiffrin, R. M., and Schneider, W. 1977. Controlled and Automatic Human Information Processing: II. Perceptual Learning, Automatic Attending, and a General Theory. *Psychological Review* 84: 127–90.

Soares, J. J. F., and Öhman, A. 1993. Backward Masking and Skin Conductance Responses after Conditioning to Nonfeared but Fear-relevant Stimuli in Fearful Subjects. *Psychophysiology* 30: 460–66.

Tulving, E. 1972. Episodic and Semantic Memory. In *Organization of Memory,* ed. E. Tulving and W. Donaldson. New York: Academic Press.

———. 1985. On the Classification Problem in Learning and Memory. In *Perspectives on Learning and Memory,* ed. L. Nilsson and R. Archer, 67–94. Hillsdale, N.J.: Erlbaum.

Velmans, M. 1991. Is Human Information Processing Conscious? *Behavioral and Brain Sciences* 14: 651–69.

Warrenburg, S., Wexler, B., and Schwartz, G. E. 1989. EEG and EMG Responses to Unconsciously Processed Emotion-evoking Stimuli. Presented to the annual meeting of the Society for Psychophysiological Research, 1989. Abstracted as Frontal EEG and Corrugator EMG Responses to Dichotically Presented Emotional Words. *Psychophysiology* 26: S64.

CHAPTER SIX

Diagnostic Systems and Responses to Racism

My uncle was very ill. I knew that his cancer was at a stage where he might have some good days sprinkled in with the bad ones. I knew also that he would not be well again. So I was filled with a keen awareness that each moment I could spend with him was desperately precious. Because I wanted my children to remember him, we took some summer travel time to pay a visit. Most of all, perhaps selfishly, I wanted to know him better. If only he would talk to me about life as he did when I was making uncertain steps into manhood. But it was too late for that. Now, in a small Louisiana town with the other members of the family—the cousins, nephews, and grandchildren—I perched by his bedside to do his rather small bidding. In exchange, I probed him for words that might reveal to me something of myself.

At one point during my youth, my uncle had come to live with us in the small Montana city where I was raised. He was my mother's older brother, and he arrived from the deep, deep South with an accent and a style that were very different. These differences made me uncomfortable and intrigued me at the same time. He was not a large man like my very controlled, restrained father. His was a frame of wire that housed a disposition composed of a curious mixture of tenderness and fire. He could bend over and touch the floor with the palms of his hands without effort. Just as effortlessly he could move a wheelbarrow full of cement across a 2 by 10 inch plank of wood, dump it, and then smooth it artfully into anything from a sidewalk to a basement for a church. He could also "go upside the head" of any of the local men, black or white, who might say something out of line to him. And during my early teenage years, when my father died, he and several other uncles stood by with their calloused hands extended to my mother, my two brothers, my sister, and me.

But that was a different time and place, and now we were back in the South, in a plywood home that he had built and in a room where he would eventually die. I was careful with the things I said—again, the time factor. I wanted to waste not a second. Of course, I reminded him of the things he had said to me and done for me after my father's death. I assured him that these things had become part of me as I structured my own definition of manhood. I wanted him to know of the mark he made on me. But quite suddenly, I heard myself put a question to him that probably surprised both of us in equal measure. "What," I asked, "what really happened to William?"

William was a black high school student in my home town who was probably five or six years older than I. He was one of the few black high school students in a city where the number of black families was never large. Even then the black population was declining because of migration to larger cities in the Northwest. William's family was very poor. His mother had three children and no spouse. Each child had a different last name. But my older brother and I idolized William. My discerning father had the highest respect for him. William was a good student, a well-spoken gentleman, and a formidable athlete, even though he, like us, suffered from bronchial asthma.

On what I remember to be a cold spring morning—indeed, most mornings I remember in Montana were cold—we received the news that William had died. The adults told us that he had been dressing for school in his bedroom. A shotgun that was propped up close to his bed discharged accidentally and killed him instantly. I recall distinctly that he was finishing his senior year in high school when this occurred. It was not unusual for a loaded rifle or shotgun to be in a bedroom in Montana. Guns, especially rifles and shotguns, were common around a household. Usually people stored them behind glass in cabinets or on racks that were out of immediate reach. At the time I did not wonder about or question the description of events that the adults gave us. We had lost a hero and a poor black mother had lost her prized son.

But, as I grew older and gravitated away from the mountains and valley that I first knew as home, I became suspicious. I reflected on what so often happened to talented black youth there and elsewhere. Something about this story seemed odd. I suspected my uncle knew more, and I wondered if he would tell me now. He lay on his back and did not hesitate in responding to my question. "Maybe William was depressed," he said. "Could be that somebody said something that hurt him real bad, and that made him do what he did." Of course, I did not ask the obvious, indignant follow-up question, "Why didn't you all tell us the facts of the matter back then?" The answer is itself a question. It is frightening for me to ponder even now, over thirty years later. If William, the most accomplished, talented, and motivated among us, opted for suicide, what hope remained for those, perhaps less gifted, who would come after him?

This question, raised at my uncle's bedside, was burning in me when I posed it. However, once I had the answer, it seemed far less important. The implicit argument in this book is that the ultimate and most ostensible responses of the oppressed in racist environments are less important than one might think. These responses are part of a much larger social and psychological equation. The behaviors of oppressed people are but one of several areas worthy of consideration. That is, William was more than an African-American youth living in an isolated setting in the United States in the 1960s who may have committed suicide. He was, at least, a young man who faced and resisted the dehumanization of that period. For some time, he overcame obstacle after obstacle, achieved and inspired. In striving to understand him and us, I have been arguing that we must look at the input side of the equation, that is, at the stimuli. Then we should focus our attention on the way the remarkable human nervous system processes this input.

But the question of the efferent response remains salient in the minds of many who study oppression from a psychological perspective. These efferents comprise the behavioral, emotional, and physiological output that results from experiencing racism. In this chapter, we will dedicate some time to examining the principles psychologists and psychiatrists use to organize some of the less healthy patterns of behavior people of African descent may exhibit under white supremacy. Others have treated various facets of this topic adequately (Bulhan 1985; Akbar 1984, 1991; Cross 1991). Our approach is somewhat different. We are advancing a more general critique of the classification of mental disorders among people of African descent.

We will take on four basic tasks. In the first section, we will discuss the reasons mental health workers develop nosological systems. Nosological systems are conceptual frameworks directed toward organizing behavioral responses. To develop such a system for classifying abnormal behavior, one must generate a general definition of abnormal behavior. The second part of this chapter examines recent thinking within traditional Western psychiatric approaches about the definition of abnormal behavior. Even a cursory look at traditional psychiatric approaches to classification uncovers the need for a different approach when we consider "oppression disorders." In the third section, I will examine the definitions of mental disorders and the nosological systems provided by two constructionistic African-American psychologists. I conclude with a review of four principal dimensions related to mental wellness that can be affected adversely when one lives in a Manichean world. I argue that these might provide useful axes to include as investigators refine the diagnostic system for disorders related to racism.

Nosology: Pros and cons

Diagnostic systems for both physical and mental disorders have descriptive, prescriptive, and heuristic functions. That is, a good diagnostic system will provide an accurate and compelling catalog of the existing or known clusters of symptoms and diseases. The descriptions of the disorders should be comprehensive. The definitions of each illness should be rich and precise enough to ensure that clinicians can distinguish the various diseases from one another. As the descriptions are set forth, the structure of the diagnostic system emerges. Systems may contain hierarchical components. In these instances, one or more of the characteristics for a superordinate disorder forms a portion of the defined characteristics of subordinate disorders. In other instances, mutually exclusive disorders compose the system. Here there is very little overlap between diagnostic categories. A particular system can include both hierarchical and mutually exclusive elements.

The prescriptive aspect of diagnostic systems is very straightforward. Good diagnostic systems suggest avenues for effective therapeutic intervention. A cogent description of a disorder identifies elements of pathology that therapists can match to particular types of treatment. The ideal circumstance is a parallel development of noso-logical and therapeutic options. Theoretically, exact fits between dis-eases and treatment strategies are possible when this occurs.

Finally, nosological systems generate research questions. Accord-ingly, they facilitate the discovery of new knowledge. In this respect, they are very much like scientific theories. The usefulness and validity of a diagnostic approach hinge on the outcome of studies of its valid-ity. This research will range from purely experimental research to clinical investigations. The experimental studies will often take the form of rather circumscribed, controlled basic research into causal mechanisms and symptomatic manifestations of the disorders. The diagnostic system can be refined further based on findings from field studies of the diseases. Clinical studies of the utility of the classifica-tion procedure in facilitating therapeutic process are the final test of the system. Ultimately, diagnostic systems for classifying diseases are not theoretical pronouncements to be judged only by their logical structure. Concerning behavioral disorders, it is very important to remember this. It is more fitting to think of nosology as a set of theories. Relentless analyses, testing, and scrutiny must determine the logical and empirical status of these theories.

In the best of circumstances, nosological systems serve these three ends. To this extent they are extremely valuable to both clinicians and scholars. However, there is a downside to classification systems, especially when we consider mental disorders. There is an important difference between classifying a mental disorder and classifying a *person* who suffers from a mental disorder. As we noted in the open-ing narrative of this chapter, each day individuals engage in a full range of behaviors. People execute behaviors other than the small subset of actions that occur in troubled moments and cause them to be classified "mentally ill." A failure to acknowledge this distinction causes *stigmatization* of those with mental disorders. When stigma-tization occurs, the world regards every behavior of the individual, and indeed, the very essence of the person negatively simply because a mental health professional has applied a diagnostic label to the person.

We can glean a related downside of classification systems from Ani's (1994) discussion of dominant motifs in European thought. These themes ultimately support what Ani sees as the thrust of Eu-ropean culture, "the will-to-power" (105). Ani conceded that the formulation of concepts, that is, developing systematic ways of classifying and responding to the environment, is part of all human information processing. Therefore, developing concepts and the process of classifying itself represent essential components of interacting with the environment. However, if one's thinking is characterized by objectification and hierarchical segmentation, classification can become a destructive enterprise. For Ani, objectification entails the construction of an emotionless self that creates objects of knowledge that are capable of being controlled. People come to exalt the very mental process of knowing. Europeans see knowing as residing at the top of a hierarchy of existence. All realities become objects in a stratified system under knowing. Objectifying and stratifying reality become crucial links in a philosophical chain of means that will serve the ultimate end—expanding one's power to control reality.

If one approaches the classification of mental disorders within a European mode of thinking, the risks are clear. Clinicians may be prone to reduce the disorders and, by extension, the humans who suffer them, to objects. Both the diseases and the human beings become types, codes, or members of compartments in a diagnostic scheme. The goal is to exert control over the disease and the sufferer. Several crucial relationships become lost as the disease becomes an object that the clinician must pursue aggressively. One may lose sight of the interdependent relationship between the disease and other aspects of the individual's personality. Also, we tend to neglect the relationship between the individual as a whole person and others in her or his world. Finally, by objectifying disease and patient, we might forget the very complex interrelationships among the diagnostician, the disease, and the patient.

Ani's observations are sobering. Almost by necessity, classifying behaviors and placing them in disorder categories is a reductionistic enterprise. It involves ignoring central elements of the person. This tunnel vision allows us to match patterns of behaviors and symptoms that we may observe to the defining elements of the diagnostic category. Consequently, we create a fiction. This fiction suggests that people within categories will, in the normal walk of life, behave in a fashion distinguishable from those we have placed in other categories or from those we have anointed "normal." Indeed, we may actually be able to make such distinctions in a subset of instances. People suffering mental disorders do engage in some behaviors that are troubling, strange, and bizarre. However, not everything they do is abnormal. If we sample the full range of actions in which humans engage across a day or a week, people in the various diagnostic classes and people we call normal will behave in remarkably similar fashion. Thus, we witness the complexity of human behaviors and the limits of attempts to stuff patterns of behavior into categories.

Traditional psychiatric nosology: Status and issues

Overview of psychiatric diagnosis

In the United States, psychiatrists and clinical psychologists commonly use the Diagnostic and Statistical Manual (DSM) to classify mental disorders. Over the past forty years the DSM has undergone a dizzying volley of revisions. These alterations have stemmed from empirical and conceptual advances and from shifts in philosophical and political perspectives. Mental health professionals are largely resigned to the notion that it is difficult to define the concept, mental disorder. By definition, abnormal behaviors are actions that fall outside the range of actions in which people "normally" engage. Obviously, we are not able to consider all abnormal behavior disordered. Uniquely creative behavior and cogent critical thinking are clearly outside the norm (abnormal). Neither is a form of mental disorder. One might argue, to the contrary, that these forms of behavior are essential to the growth of cultures.

In addition, behavioral scientists generally accept the notion that contextual variables influence our judgments of what is disordered or deranged behavior. Americans, in the main, accepted and even applauded the slaughter of Iraqi soldiers attempting to flee Kuwait on the highway of death in the 1991 Gulf War. On the other hand, when unarmed Nation of Islam "dope-buster" security forces aggressively pursued drug pushers in public housing in Washington, D.C., many in the mainstream media viewed their behavior as abnormally aggressive.

Textbooks on abnormal psychology define psychopathology in terms of the socially inappropriate nature of the behavior and its destructive consequences for oneself or others. In this section, we will explore the definitional question further. It is one that is far from settled in traditional Western nosology. Nevertheless, major classes of disorders are described in the most recent revisions of the DSM (DSM IV). The system describes a host of conditions including anxiety, somatoform, dissociative, mood, schizophrenic, and personality disorders.

What is a mental disorder?

Psychology is not a developed discipline. Therefore, it is far from a unified one. A variety of approaches or theoretical models exist. The approach one takes will influence one's descriptions of behavior and its causes. That approach may be neurobiological, psychoanalytic, sociobiological, behavioral, humanistic, or any combination of these perspectives. Accordingly, when behavioral scientists approach the study of troubling or pathological behavioral patterns, one should expect anything but unanimity and accord on content or method. This is reflected in the volatile state of the DSM and the contentious literature surrounding the categories set forth in it. The unsettled and developing state of affairs in traditional psychiatric nosology was revealed in the exchange over the definition of mental disorder. We present the terms of the discussion below. It is evident that arriving at unanimity regarding the conceptual nature of rudimentary terms including *disorder, dysfunction, distress,* and *harm* is far from easy. This is especially the case when we apply these terms to patterns of human behavior.

The thinking of psychiatrist Robert Spitzer has strongly influenced recent revisions of the DSM. He (Spitzer and Endicott 1978) urged practitioners to consider mental disorders a subclass of medical disorders. Within this formulation, Spitzer framed medical disorders as identifiable conditions that are extensions of an "organismic dysfunction." Medical disorders, fully expressed, place the organism in a state of disadvantage, distress, or disability. Spitzer and Endicott wrote that mental disorders were medical disorders with predominant psychological manifestations. In the case of psychosomatic disorders, mental disorders are physical symptoms rooted in psychological causes.

Jerome Wakefield (1992a, b, 1993) published several thorough and helpful reflections on the metamorphosis in thinking about the nature of mental disorders. He (Wakefield 1993) analyzed Spitzer and Endicott's (1978) painstaking attempt to "operationalize" a number of terms in their definition of mental disorders. Operationalization involves outlining the manner or the operations by which we can measure a particular psychological concept. In the case of mental disorders, operationalizing terms entails listing particular instances and circumstances. These instances represent some facet or phase of a particular disorder. The presence of several of the instances or circumstances in an individual case increases the likelihood that the disorder is present. Hence, the disorder is operationalized in terms of specific measurable events. For example, Hare (1985) operationalized psychopathy or antisocial personality disorders using a fifteen-item checklist. Psychologists and psychiatrists who are familiar with the cases of candidates for the dubious honor of being diagnosed with this disorder rate them on these items. The items assess a number of characteristics of antisocial individuals. These include the extent to which the person seems to experience little guilt or remorse, treats people like objects, shows high levels of hedonism, and lacks emotional depth.

The advantages of operationalization seemed clear. Obviously, if Spitzer and Endicott could operationalize both the concept "mental disorder" and the "candidate" disorder classes, the clinicians using the diagnostic system would tend to be more consistent in making their judgments. In addition, operationalization appeared to be a way around long disputes among the various approaches to psychopathology. Using this approach, one specifies the parameters of disorders. The clinician can measure the presence or absence of mental illness against these parameters. Thus, operationalization seemed to be a prudent intellectual course to pursue.

However, Wakefield (1993) pointed out that the operationalization of the concept of mental disorder resulted in incorrect specification or overspecification. That is, often the listed instances and circumstances fail to cover the range of manifestations of disorders. Thus, the operationalization was far too rigid or narrow to accommodate the behavioral syndromes that may be disorders. For example, Spitzer and Endicott (1978) defined mental disorders in terms of problems that reside *within* the person. They operationalized this concept by saying that "in the person" means the mental disorder exists "in all environments." Wakefield contended that this attempt to operationalize may have gone too far. He argued that we can infer dysfunction only when mental mechanisms break down "in a particular range of environments." He argued that we should focus on the environments in which the mechanisms were selected to function (1993, 166).

This is a complex and thorny problem for those concerned with the psychological impact of racism. Fanon (1967) wrestled with a variation on this theme: "A normal Negro child, having grown up within a normal family, will become abnormal on the slightest contact with the white world" (143). Fanon seemed to be arguing, perhaps in a facetious tone, that mental illness can appear in one who behaves perfectly normally in the environment that shaped one's coping skills

229

and personality traits. If this is the case, the salient issue in defining mental illness becomes to delineate the range of environments in which we should expect mental mechanisms to function. Certainly, the socializing agents and institutions of a given society strive to prepare the young to negotiate the full range of environmental challenges. Adult members of a society, to the best of their ability, envision challenges that the young will meet and prepare them accordingly. Even though the labor conditions in post-slavery, colonial Martinique were most harsh, adults and elders could not conceive of the psychologically brutal, dehumanizing world that existed beyond their quarters, communities, or island shores. This was the subject of Fanon's analysis. He argued that the mental mechanisms an individual developed on her or his island failed utterly in the mother country, France. This failure leads the individual to "become abnormal," in Fanon's terms. The breakdown, however, appears to take place ultimately "within the person." Still, the disorder seems to be of a different quality than the one suffered in an environment more proximal to the setting in which the mental mechanisms developed.

Are mental mechanisms selected to function in all environments? Obviously, no. Still, we tend to attribute a good measure of resiliency to the human mind. What was not clearly a disorder in one generation, because of novel or "first contact" with the Manichean world, we may judge more stringently in subsequent instances. In Achebe's *Things Fall Apart* (1959), the central character Okonkwo is an excellent study of the psychological impact of the initial contact with white supremacy. Ultimately, he commits both homicide and suicide. However, I am reluctant to conclude that he suffered from a mental disorder. Still, I doubt we would be so generous in appraising the actions of his great great grandchildren's generation if they were to commit these acts. Once the visionary members of the collective know and inspect the forces and factors impinging on the culture, patterns of socialization change. Subsequently, when an individual's mental mechanisms fail, we may see the diagnosis of psychopathology as appropriate. We are prone to call the individual's failures to meet environmental demands mental illness. I believe that Fanon's statement that the African becomes ill upon first and sudden contact within the stultifying Manichean world was as much an indictment of the Western world as it was a clinical judgment of the mental status of the "Negro."

In the end, the committee that developed DSM III-R opted for a simpler definition of mental disorder than the one Spitzer and

Endicott (1978) advocated, and the authors of DSM IV (1994) did not change this definition substantially. Notions of statistical uncommonness, internal mental dysfunction, and distress and disability are the principal themes of the definition (xxii). Wakefield (1992a) reconstructed the DSM III-R definition as follows: "Mental disorder is a mental condition that (a) causes significant distress or disability, (b) is not merely an expectable response to a particular event and (c) is a manifestation of a mental dysfunction" (235). This seems to be a fair interpretation of the DSM III-R version.

Wakefield advanced a three-pronged critique of the DSM III-R definition. First, this critique analyzed the extent to which we can be certain that mental conditions that result in statistically unusual distress are mental disorders. He pointed out that people can be insensitive, lazy, or cowardly, or suffer from any variety of mental conditions of this kind. They may cause harm and distress to themselves or others. However, it is not likely that a clinician would consider these individuals "mentally disordered." Similarly, the definition runs the risk of excluding conditions that are disorders even though we might expect them to occur in view of the horrific nature of the environmental stress. Posttraumatic stress disorders often are reasonable reactions to one's circumstances. They are both expectable and distressing. Still, we designate these mental disorders.

Wakefield's (1992a) second critical thrust centered on the problem of distinguishing the concept "disability" from the notion of "inability." The latter is not a part of the definition of disorder. The existence of a disability implies the presence of some form of dysfunction. An inability suggests that there is a continuous range of abilities distributed in a population. The inability exists beyond an extreme point on this range. It does not necessarily mean that a pathological state is a core cause of the failure in capability. On the other hand, a disability is generally seen as resulting from a breakdown in a functioning system. The nosological problem, from the standpoint of physiology and philosophy, is distinguishing inabilities from disabilities. Some individuals find it impossible to eat and even become nauseated when the conversation at dinner involves a gory description of injuries or maladies. Does this statistically rare condition constitute an inability or disability? Should we consider it a mental disorder? The modern DSM definition does not resolve this problem. Wakefield (1992a) proposed an alternative formulation that will prove to be helpful in this respect. After we examine Wakefield's third line of criticism, we will examine his formulation in detail.

Wakefield took issue with the manner in which the definition locates the cause of the mental disorder "in the person." Modern definitions of abnormal behavior tend to take the position that a disorder resides within the person. This strategy appears to help distinguish mental disorders from normal reactions to extreme environmental conditions. Wakefield observed that cognitive construel processes are always at work as part of the person's environmental interaction. Psychologists have argued for a long time that if the person is a function of the environment, then, indeed, the environment is a function of the person. Therefore, it is difficult to separate the environment in an objective sense from the mediating cognitive events that may cause distress and disability. That is, it is hard to say with certainty if the situation itself or one's appraisal of the circumstance caused an extreme reaction. Because of this uncertainty, Wakefield argued, it is important that causal events within the person be *dysfunctional,* not merely identifiable mental conditions. Indeed, mental conditions, in the broad sense, direct functional as well as dysfunctional construel processes. The DSM III-R definition lacks precision because it fails to identify mental dysfunction as a mediator of the disordered behavior.

In summary, Wakefield's (1992a) criticisms focus on two facets of the definition of mental disorders developed in DSM III through DSM IV. He criticized the manner in which the definition sets forth the mental mechanisms purported to cause disorders. This is the essence of criticisms one and three. Additionally, he found fault with the manner in which the disordered behaviors themselves are described in the definition—criticism two. In the former instance, he argued that the existing definition pays insufficient attention to delineating the nature of the mental conditions thought to underlie disorders. In the latter, he claimed that the guidelines for making judgments about the possible pathological nature of selected behavioral patterns are inadequate. The more compelling definition, in his estimation, will allow one to distinguish inabilities from disabilities when considering behaviors that are candidates for the designation *disordered.* Wakefield attempted to correct these deficiencies with his definition of mental disorders.

Wakefield (1992b) proposed that we conceptualize mental disorders as "harmful dysfunctions" (381). "Harmful," he emphasized, is the subjective aspect of the definition. If we employ this term, we must make a value judgment of what is harmful. He acknowledged that cultural values influence the determination of harm. Behaviors that people in one culture call harmful, individuals in another culture may judge to be quite innocuous.

The second matter taken up in this definition is the matter of the mental condition that leads to the behavior in question. The conceptualization of the internal mechanisms involved in mental disorders that Wakefield encourages us to accept is an intriguing extension of an evolutionary approach to mental processes. He argued that we can specify the function and therefore dysfunction of mental processes. He claimed "a natural function is an effect that is part of the evolutionary explanation of the existence and structure of the mechanism" (Wakefield 1992b, 384). Consistent with a Darwinian view, Wakefield thinks that environmental contingencies select our mental structures. The mental structures emerge because they (the mechanisms) facilitate particular adaptive behaviors. Wakefield claims that this facet of the definition, the description of dysfunction, is less judgmental and subjective. First, one must determine the function for which a mental mechanism was selected. Subsequently, one can designate as dysfunctional the failure of the mental structure to execute this function.

An appraisal

Indeed, the volley of revisions of the DSM mark refinements in the knowledge of mental disorders. However, the diagnostic manuals cannot incorporate all the advances that surface in the literature on abnormal psychology. Wakefield pointed out inherent problems that surface because large committees construct the revised forms of the DSM. The process itself would be an interesting study in social psychology. In the end, political and theoretical forces, as well as academic clarity, are at play. Further, leading thinkers state rather bluntly that cultural factors reduce the likelihood that a universal diagnostic system for mental disorders, founded in the Western approach to medicine, is imminent or possible (Fabrega 1992). This is a rather humble admission, and a stark contrast to the hegemonic swagger that psychiatric diagnosticians displayed during Fanon's time and before. Then we would have witnessed Western clinicians applying, willy-nilly, their diagnostic labels. This they would do irrespective of the cultural background of the patients they met.

In the writings of Wakefield (1992a, 1992b, 1993) and Spitzer (Spitzer and Endicott 1978, Spitzer 1991) one can detect movement toward a clarification of what Western psychiatry and clinical psychology mean by the concept "mental disorder." The DSM III-R definition, as described here, has encouraged an operational approach to the concept. This will certainly increase the reliability of diagnoses. Wakefield's writings have been helpful in analyzing the meaning of internal dysfunction when applied to mental illness. He has deconstructed the existing definition of mental disorders and illuminated our thinking on very basic notions of "abnormal" and "dysfunctional." The body of writings on nosology summarized here reflect a serious attempt among Western clinicians and scholars to come to grips with the concept of mental disease. We should not dismiss them out of hand because of flagrant and frequent misuses and misapplications of the accepted diagnostic systems.

Still, our concern is developing a conceptual base on which we can construct a nosology for mental disorders of African people living in a modern racist environment. The definitions of mental disorders provided in the DSM, Spitzer and Endicott (1978), and Wakefield (1992b) all fail to provide this conceptual foundation. Indeed, the current tendency in all three definitions to locate a dysfunction within the person is consistent with the thrust of this book. We have argued that Manichean cognitive schemata are mental events that have an environmental origin and physiological substrate (see chapter 5).

Obviously, the problem revolves around defining dysfunction. Wakefield, after roundly and correctly criticizing Spitzer's acceptance of the traditional medical view of dysfunction (i.e., failings within the organism that impede activities), suggested clinicians adopt a Darwinian view of functioning. His is, arguably, one of the more lucid statements available in Western psychology on the meaning of dysfunction. At the same time, it is wholly unsatisfactory for our purposes. African people develop and use Manichean schemata because the biologically selected mental mechanisms of human beings are so remarkably flexible. That is, the human nervous system is extraordinarily adroit in processing and internalizing a seemingly infinite array of information from the environment that ranges from the simple to the complex. Humans are able to process an endless panoply of configurations. No two sunrises are identical. It is unlikely that any two sentences we hear have the same words, inflections, or meaning. Because of a certain "looseness" in our mental structures, we are able to decode all these events and divine their essential elements. The Manichean world exposes African people to an alien and toxic socialization agenda. It is possible for black people to accept and internalize this destructive script, ironically, because of the flexibility of the mental mechanisms of humans. From the evolutionary perspective, then, it is difficult to say that the selected mechanism is dysfunctional.

Still, Western thinking about mental illness has advanced. Wakefield's (1992a) writings are an example of the growth in knowledge. Wakefield's definition of mental illness embodies an objective (evolutionary) term—"dysfunction"—and a subjective (social judgmental) term—"harmful." The second part of his definition is worthy of further consideration. He sees the mental dysfunction as a cause of behavior that is harmful, distressing, or disadvantageous. Recall that this is the point where the social judgment becomes part of not only the diagnostic process but of defining what a mental illness is in global terms. However, it is neither difficult nor far-fetched to envision how Manichean cognitive schemata facilitate one's adaptation to the racist social environment. These mental structures may reduce distress and increase one's social advantage. The dominant culture, and those who endorse it, will not judge behaviors harmful when they are an outgrowth of Manichean thought. In fact, when one's actions represent a critique of white supremacist ideas of Western cultural superiority, Caucasian aesthetic preeminence, and intrinsic white competence, they run a risk of being personally disadvantageous to the individual. Behaviors that are an extension of Manichean values are much safer in this regard. This is true especially where racism is firmly grounded in the social environment.

There are black teachers who insist African children be taught to view history and culture from their own perspective "as subjects" (Asante 1987) rather than peripheralized objects. Often, mainstream peers and the school systems themselves tend to ridicule these individuals. On the other hand, social ostracism stalks the young African woman who refuses to chemically process her hair. Indeed, employers have been so bold as to deny work to black women because these women failed to ape the hairstyles of European women. Finally, we are surprised when the bright, "blue-chip," young black scholar opts to attend the historically black college. We know the "normal" thing to do is to place this young mind in the hands of highly competent white educators and their hospitable institutions. What if a well-to-do individual of African descent questions the parents' judgment for sending their talented offspring to a black college? The clinician may designate the questioner well-adjusted and normal. Indeed, the mind that spawned the question seems to be serving the individual well in an economic sense. There are simply too many counter instances for us to conclude that the effects of Manichean schemata are, in the surface sense of the words, distressing, disadvantageous, and harmful. On the contrary, they may be very adaptive in the Darwinian sense. They will allow individuals to survive, reproduce, and exist in a greater degree of comfort.

To summarize, there is agreement that a sociocultural judgment is involved in defining mental disorders. Those who adhere to Western nosology no longer dispute that when clinicians judge behaviors to be harmful, disadvantageous, and distressing, they are making cultural value judgments. In fact, even traditional diagnosticians may agree that behaviors consistent with Manichean values are appropriate from the perspective of the cultural mainstream. They may be able to view this situation as part of the cultural relativity of the diagnostic process. Therefore, they would allow that these behaviors are quite inappropriate from the standpoint of an African value system. This represents a significant liberalization of thinking.

However, when we grapple with the concept "dysfunction," we must make a judgment of a different kind. We are forced to take a different kind of philosophical stand. Here, too, cultural perspective will influence the intellectual posture that we assume, but the cultural influences will have more of an academic stripe. Wakefield was quite straightforward concerning the bases he uses for judging behavior dysfunctional. He viewed dysfunction as a failure of a brain mechanism to function in the fashion set forth by evolutionary processes. However, what if the "naturally selected" mechanism is functioning in the manner that nature intended? Further, what if the individual, and those around her or him, are reporting no unusual levels of distress or harm? Does this force us to conclude that no pathology exists? It is this proposition that may be untenable when we examine the impact of racism on people of African descent. This paradox compels and fuels an examination of alternative definitions of mental disorders. Black psychologists have provided several, along with fledgling nosological systems.

Nosological systems from behind the veil

The fabric of black life

One lesson from the last section is that we judge the appropriateness of behaviors according to cultural norms and values. If circumstances challenge us to decide if the behavior of an individual is disordered or pathological, we consider the factors that we believe influence behavior. That is, we base our judgment on our subjective sense of the causes of people's actions. Some psychologists believe the spirits of ancestors can have a causal influence on one's actions, others do not. Suppose a person dances and shouts as part of a ritual and claims that the spirit of a deity or ancestor is controlling the action. The psychologist who is sympathetic to spiritual causes of behavior will not reach reflexively for the closest copy of the DSM. This diagnostician may see the actions as normal.

Part of social living—that is, living in a particular culture—entails developing our set of psychological theories. These theories ultimately influence the manner in which we attribute causes to behaviors (see Weiner 1974). They form the backdrop for making judgments of the appropriateness or normality of the behavior.

Typically, we find that social scientists place the causes of behavior into three large domains. These are psychogenic, sociogenic, and biogenic spheres. As part of developing an alternative view of nosology, it is necessary to reconsider the matrices of causes within each domain. It is conceivable that an alternative system may point up causes beyond these spheres of influence. Those generating the alternative systems reveal in the process the specific forces that they feel determine behavior.

During this century, social scientists from a number of disciplines have argued that the social ecology of African Americans is particularly complex. Indeed, we are likely to find many of these complexities in the social fabric of African people living in other parts of the world. In his frequently cited passage, Du Bois (1903) described in a lyrical fashion the notion of *double consciousness:* "two conflicted souls, a Negro and an American." Lewis (1993) reviewed the graduate curriculum that Du Bois followed at Harvard. He concluded that seminars under the preeminent psychologist and philosopher William James probably shepherded Du Bois's thinking about the general complexity of human consciousness. However, as Lewis aptly points out, a lifetime in America's "psychic purgatory [was] fully capable by itself of nurturing a concept of divided consciousness" (96). In any event, the notion of double consciousness implies that there are at least two sets of forces shaping the minds and behavior of African Americans. One set of socializing influences is rooted in European-American culture. The second domain of influences is endemic to black culture.

Over half a century later, others (Cole 1970; Jones 1991; Boykin 1986) have partitioned the socializing forces in black life into three spheres: African cultural influences, influences growing out of contact with mainstream European-American culture, and events that are part of being on the receiving end of racial oppression. Boykin has termed this matrix of influences a triple quandary. He proposed that any model specifying the causes of behaviors of African Americans should consider complex interactions among forces emanating from these domains.

Clearly, disparate forces comprise the fabric of black life. The phenomenological field of people of African descent—that is, their moment-to-moment experience—is, indeed, as multifaceted and rich as Du Bois's 1903 prose suggested. It follows that clinical judgments regarding the mental health of individuals who are subject to these forces are potentially complicated. That is, the clinician can construct the basis for diagnosis from values or standards that exist in any one domain of influence. She or he may, on the other hand, use standards from a combination of the experiential realms. The problems that emerge are quite perplexing. For example, an individual of African descent may scrupulously avoid buying from most black businesses because of generally "higher prices and lower quality." If we judge the behavior based on mainstream values, we may consider the individual pragmatic and frugal. The behavior is normal and healthy. However, if we consider the vectors of influences that are part of the experience of racism, we will reach a different diagnostic conclusion. Behaviors that collude with oppressive conditions—in this case, consumer behaviors growing out of individual self-interest—are pathological. Pragmatic and frugal according to this analysis are seen as thin veils covering disordered cognitive structures. The Solomonic task is to synthesize a nosological system that would tend to treat, somewhat evenhandedly, the diagnoses that emerge from each perspective. The alternative is to employ several systems in a complementary fashion.

The diagnostic approaches offered by two constructionistic African psychologists acknowledge the existence of mainstream, oppressive, and African cultural influences on black life. They attempt to set ground rules for determining if the psychological "dogged strength" (Du Bois, 17) has insulated the individual African sufficiently from a complex array of threats to mental health. These systems are mere sketches, especially when compared to the voluminous DSM. However, each contains seminal elements that should stimulate the thinking of others interested in classifying disorders among the racially oppressed.

Akbar's nosology

Na'im Akbar (1991), in a concise paper, provided a definition of mental illness and four general classes of disorders. First, Akbar proposed that we view psychopathology as "the presence of ideas or forces within the mind that threaten awareness and mental growth" (342). The previous discussion of traditional definitions of psychopathology leads us to consider two aspects of Akbar's approach. One, Akbar avoided the use of the word *dysfunction*. He opted to locate the source of illnesses in cognitions and "forces." Perhaps the latter term is too vague and mysterious. Certainly, forces may encompass disease states. Also, forces would have to include instincts and drives. The term is imprecise and adds little to the definition except to admit that cognitive events are not the only source of mental illness. In fact, Akbar rejected the notion of mental "illness" in the traditional framework of the medical model. He voiced his agreement with Thomas Szasz (1960), stating that "one cannot assume a disease entity [is] present for the production of certain specific behaviors" (Akbar 1991, 342).

It is very significant, on the other hand, that "ideas" figure prominently in Akbar's definition. Ideas—in the form of values, preferences, and attitudes—are among the products of "normal" information-processing activities. They are structured from schemata. As we have seen, normal human information processing within a Manichean society will generate pathological schemata. Thus, Akbar provides a link between normal information processing and psychopathology.

The second noteworthy aspect of this definition emerges from the position Akbar takes regarding the basic tendency of the human personality. Here he is discussing a tendency that exists when pathology is absent. For Akbar, the human personality is an organic process that is in a continual state of growth. The personality is moving toward increasing apprehension and appreciation of the self. This is consistent with the thinking of many humanistic psychologists (Rogers 1961, Maslow 1962, Maddi 1989). Akbar places this concept within an African frame of reference. That is, the self includes the collective, living and dead, and is not restricted to the individual.

The idea of an organic, growth-oriented self whose functions are consistent with the collective good is most intriguing. Akbar and other humanists see humans as doing more than surviving in a static sense.

We generate and expand an increasingly rich appreciation of ourselves and those from whom we have descended. For Akbar, this is an essential process that characterizes the ordered or healthy mind. It provides the basis of a stringent and universal standard by which one can judge the relative impact on mental health of racism and other forms of social oppression. That is, according to Akbar, we are to gauge the impact of racism not only in terms of the presence of glaring pathology and bizarre behaviors. Subtle alterations of patterns of growth in the human personality and disruptions of the trajectory of the natural tendencies constitute a highly sensitive standard to be used in making clinical judgments.

Akbar (1991) described four classes of mental disorders among African Americans. Arguably, he set forth three of these in a hierarchical structure. He defined alien-self disorders as mental conditions characterized by the presence of values and ideas that are "contrary to (one's) nature and survival" (343). The examples Akbar provided include an acceptance of materialistic values and compulsive strivings for close social and physical proximity to people of European descent. The anti-self disorders are structured on the alien-self disorders in that self-deprecating ideas and values reside at their core. However, those suffering from anti-self disorders experience more extreme forms of self-destructive ideation. Hostility, both covert and overt forms, is pathognomonic of this disorder. The objects of the hostility are people of African descent. Akbar suggested that we can locate individuals suffering from these disorders in diverse settings. He noted that over-zealous law enforcement officers, black scholars who appear to be on a quest for accolades from the Western academic world, and driven business people concerned only with the "bottom line" all suffer anti-self disorders.

The self-destructive disorders are even more extreme. Individuals who suffer from these disorders have extended self-deprecation far beyond the cognitive realm. Their dominant patterns of behavior threaten their own survival as well as the lives of people around them. Here Akbar mentions individuals involved in the drug trade or prostitution and those addicted to substances as likely candidates for the diagnosis of self-destructive disorders. However, he made some surprising and paradoxical statements about the prevalence of self-destructive disorders and the cognitive processes involved in them.

First, Akbar shows that self-destructive disorders will exist among those who find the "doors to legitimate survival blocked" (347). There is something of a class notion implicit in this view of these forms of mental disorders. In fact, one might conclude that Akbar sees alien- and anti-self disorders as common in the relatively more affluent classes of African people, while self-destructive illnesses exist among the "wretched." However, by including substance abusers, psychotics, and drug pushers in the self-destructive categories, Akbar shows that a class analysis is not thoroughly compelling. Obviously, we find individuals who engage in these destructive lifestyles in all segments of black society.

Even more striking is Akbar's analysis of certain cognitive features of these disorders. He argued that those suffering self-destructive disorders "have refused to accept (or have not had the opportunity to develop) the alien self-identity" (347). Further, he posited that pimps and addicts have opted for their patterns of behavior out of a refusal to accept "alien" definitions of African humanness. If this characterization of the mental process involved in self-destructive disorders is not incorrect, it is certainly debatable. Clusters of individuals among the oppressed will opt for a lifestyle that transgresses the larger society's legal mandates. We should not conclude that these transgressors have resisted the core values and ethos of Western racist society. It is likely that pimps, pushers, and other hustlers possess cognitive schemata that place an inordinate value on material gain. Certainly this materialistic orientation is consistent with the Western ethos and, by extension, alien-self disorders.

Black prostitutes and addicts are not in close contact, *as an extension of their disorder,* with a "spiritual core" (Ani 1994) and natural growth tendencies (Akbar 1991). Similarly, materialistic middle-class black professionals are not in touch with African core values *as an extension of their mental illness.* In both instances, the disorders move individuals away from an African mind-set. There is a clear distinction between the mind seized by a self-destructive disorder and one with the schemata out of which resistance or "authentic upheaval" against oppression will emerge. The latter firmly rejects the core values of the "alien" culture. We can infer that an individual has assumed a truly resistant mental posture when she or he shows a rejection of core Western values. We should not base this inference on the fact that one has exhibited flagrant, illicit, and destructive patterns of actions. Dr. Akbar's text is somewhat misleading on this point.

The final class of disorders in Akbar's system—organic disorders—constitute a kind of appendage to the system. It is a catch-all category at best, made up of a heterogeneous set of disorders. Researchers have identified underlying physiological causes for these disorders. Akbar mentions senility, severe intellectual deficiency, and schizophrenia as examples. He argues that the organic conditions that cause the disorders can result from behaviors that are part of a self-destructive mind-set. Accordingly, physical abuse, poor nutrition, and addiction may be partially responsible for the onset of an organic disorder.

It is difficult to provide an overall assessment of the nosology Akbar outlined. One advantage of the system is that Akbar expanded the causes of mental disorders to include cognitions that are not "mental dysfunctions" in a general sense of the term. Perhaps the most compelling aspect of Akbar's discussion of nosology is that it includes a definition of the healthy personality in its definition of pathology. The criterion for judging the impact of racism on the mental health of African people is definite and stringent within his system. Pathology exists not only where behavior is bizarre, harmful, or threatening. Pathology is present also when various factors have truncated or altered the growth processes that are inherent in the healthy human personality.

On the other hand, a general assessment is difficult because Akbar provides only a basic outline of the disorders themselves. He is far from exhaustive in his designation of subclasses. The descriptions are rudimentary. This facet of the Akbar nosology begs a detailed exploration of manifestations of the disorders. Until others take up this gauntlet, clinicians are likely to find Akbar's system interesting but of minor assistance in classifying disorders.

Azibo's nosology

Daudi Azibo (1989) extended and embellished some aspects of Akbar's system. Other aspects of the Azibo nosology are a significant departure from the thrust of Akbar's thinking. The definition of mental health that Azibo provided is replete with terms that require further explanation. He proposed that psychological wellness is "psychological and behavioral functioning that is in accord with the basic nature of the original human and its attendant cosmology and survival thrust" (177). The prelude to the definition establishes that the "natural order" for humans is the root of an African cosmology. This cosmology characterizes the human-environment relationship as being harmonious to the point of unity. That is, the universe and all of its elements are orderly and divine. Humans in a healthy state are part of that order. The survival thrust involves a self-preservation instinct, where self comes to include others of African descent or of "greater biogenetic commonality" (178).

For Azibo, the distance between cosmology and biology is a short one. The survival thrust was a governing, biogenetic determinant of the actions of early humans. In a description of a nearly idyllic scene, Azibo proposes that the original humans existed in a harmonious state. Parenthetically, he states that these original human beings "had mental health" (177). This health was part of the biogenetic blueprint that matures into African cosmology. Still, it is easier to see "when and where" a survival thrust enters the genetic blueprint than where and how a complex African cosmology is reduced to this blueprint.

In this respect, Azibo and Akbar choose different paths. Akbar's central principles of mental health include growth, increased awareness, and self-acceptance. He describes them in broad terms. Akbar considers growth, awareness, and self-acceptance to be natural tendencies in humans. However, he carefully avoids discussions of genetic determinants. Not only is Azibo willing to charge into this discussion of biogenetics, he proposes that cultural values and ethos are genetically based. This position, while courageous, is not without pitfalls.

Locating the source of values and ethos in biology is a risky if intriguing enterprise. Genes are not necessarily the exclusive determinants of traits and patterns of behaviors even if these manifestations have existed for generations in human populations. Values, behavioral styles, and even a more amorphous quality like ethos can be transmitted tacitly as part of the socialization process. As we argued in chapter 5, the mechanisms involved in learning, memory, and the acquisition of a behavioral repertoire can operate subtly and in an unconscious fashion. To be sure, in the end the reductionists might wear us down with the argument that all mental events are biological, since we are, in part at least, corporal beings. They might add that the heritability estimates for a wide range of traits are tending to climb as researchers report more and more evidence (see Plomin and McClearn 1993).

However, I doubt that Azibo and other constructionists who make the genetic argument (see Kambon 1992; Nobles 1986) wish to argue that environmental forces, as opposed to genetic factors, play a minor role in determining behavior. Obviously, following Azibo's characterization of the environment of early sentient hominids, a mutual shaping process occurred. That is, proximally speaking, these hominids were shaped by their environment. However, they shaped their environment through the creation of culture (Triandis 1994). Those early, African-rooted creatures were likely, as Azibo said, to seek the survival of themselves and their kind and to function in harmony with natural laws. They also transmitted information and techniques. When language developed, they told stories and relayed their perceptions of the environment to their offspring. A complex mix of causal forces from social, psychological, and biogenetic realms was born.

In this respect, culture, if it is ultimately anything, is ultimately everything. That is, if its roots are biogenetic, they are also psychogenic, spiritual, and sociogenic. I see the emphasis on biogenetics as unbalanced and an oversimplification of interacting causes in Azibo's framework.

Azibo, like Akbar, specifies the nature of mental health and the criteria by which we can ascertain the health status of African people. The Azibo nosology (1989) sets forth four major classes of disorders. The first and fourth classes amount to broad categories. In the first, peripheral personality disorders are mental illnesses that would be identifiable in the traditional DSM. They would include biogenetic disorders and "psychotic" illnesses. The defining characteristic of the latter is a loss of contact with reality. A nonexhaustive list of "other Black personality disorders" (187) comprises the fourth category. It includes a range of troublesome behaviors including the self-destructive disorders from Akbar's system, organic disorders, and depression related to the loss of material goods. The common thread among these disorders is that they would be far less likely to occur in an environment free of white supremacy.

Azibo struggles to distinguish between the second class of disorders, psychological misorientation, and the third, disorders of mentacide. He defined psychological misorientation as a cognitive disorder where non-African concepts and beliefs are abundant. Azibo contended that it is appropriate to place both alien-self and anti-self disorders in this category. Pervasive destruction of the African elements of consciousness characterizes disorders classed as a product of mentacide. Wright coined the term *mentacide* (1981). Wright defined mentacide as the systematic destruction of the minds of a people.

Though Azibo takes pains to draw distinctions between the disorders in these classes, he is not altogether successful. The aggressive, destructive actions that those suffering from Akbar's anti-self disorders direct toward African people seem to be exactly what Azibo sees as the effects of mentacide. Mentacide as an effect is more severe than misorientation. The severity seems to be measurable with two processes. The first is the tenacity with which one is willing to embrace

European people and their values and norms. The second is the level of aggression they will mobilize against African people and culture. This is precisely the distinction Akbar makes between alien- and anti-self disorders. Although within the same class, anti-self and alien-self disorders differ to a large extent in severity. Severity is the principal distinguishing difference between misorientation and mentacide. Therefore, one must either abandon the distinction between misorientation and mentacide or place the alien- and anti-self disorders in separate classes.

The yield of the constructionists' nosologies

In some respects, both nosological systems are rudimentary. Both authors give very general descriptive outlines of the disorders. The clinician is not provided anywhere close to enough information to guide diagnoses in a heterogeneous group of individuals. The most fascinating aspect of both systems is that, ultimately, they establish beyond any question the need for a diagnostic system for those living under the heel of white supremacy. Each in its own way does this by discussing the nature of psychological health and mental illness. If the descriptions of the various disorders are foundational, the discussions of the definitions of mental health and disorders are classical. This is especially the case in Akbar's liberalizing of the source of mental disorders to include ideas and cognitions that are not necessarily bizarre, unexpectable, or atypical; they are simply alien to the natural disposition of the individual.

In summary then, these systems advance our thinking along two lines. First, they provide explicit definitions of mental health and illness. Both Akbar and Azibo articulate the value structures of their systems. As we have seen, values will be part of any nosological system at a variety of levels. Each author maintains that core African values exist and will saturate the healthy African personality. Together they depict an organic and spiritual core personality that in its healthy state thrives and seeks a harmonious relationship with the universe. They define the disorders in terms of an absence of these values in the personality and partially by the salience of Manichean values. This is an excellent point of departure for the detailed study of the kinds of disorders that emerge in postmodern racism.

The second contribution of these systems is that they recognize the complex fabric of modern African life. Azibo and Akbar make their judgments of the status of mental health with the African cultural base as the hub. Other aspects of black life, including the impact of racism, especially, and of African cultural retentions, are acknowledged. In fact, the disorders emerge as a function of racism and the imposition of mainstream Eurocentric values on the African core personality. Hence the "triple quandary" (Boykin's term, 1986) of black existence is treated implicitly in the systems. Most likely, Cole, Boykin, and Du Bois would be pleased.

Suggestions for further work

This would constitute a summary of observations on nosology I have made thus far: (1) The traditional Western approach to nosology has refined the understanding of mental illness. However, its current trajectory does not suggest it will ever generate a system relevant to understanding disorders growing out of racism. This is to say, the DSM has come a long way, but it has a long way to go. Further, it may be veering in the wrong direction. (2) Black life in modern society is a patchwork quilt of influences. Disparate arrays of input converge on the individual. The ultimate sources of these are the dominant European cultural value system; a rich, if besieged, African cultural base; and a developed system of white supremacy. We must consider all three sources when structuring a classification system for people of African descent. (3) The constructionists have shown it is best to see the healthy human personality as other than a stagnant entity, free of pathology. Rather, personality is a dynamic, expanding process that functions in harmony with its environment and strives to know and preserve itself, its kind, and its world.

Among black psychologists, the constructionists have taken the lead and embarked on a journey into developing a nosology. Now it is fitting that a cadre of black clinicians and nonclinicians who are concerned with the impact of racism on the African mind join them. Without a doubt, a system for classifying and understanding disorders is essential. The good diagnostic system allows us not only to classify patterns of behaviors; it also tells us where to look for further knowledge of various disorders. This is part of the heuristic function of diagnostic systems. It is an extension of this function that makes nosology useful as we strive to anticipate the impact of a Manichean world on the behavior of African people. In the future, a band of energetic clinicians and basic researchers will emerge. They will dedicate themselves to pushing forward the task of refining a classification system for mental disorders related to white supremacy. The remaining comments are meant to spur on, encourage, and direct those efforts.

The analysis of racism detailed in this book encourages an examination of the impact of racism on three separate cognitive regions. In the first chapter, we designated a cultural and historical region. The individual with a healthy African personality will treasure knowledge of the African people who preceded her or him. They will view Africans as subjects of their own history, not as peripheral elements of European history (see Asante 1987). These healthy individuals will hold precious African cultural values and will structure their lives around them. Therefore, mental illness exists where this cultural and historical region of cognition fails to unfold and actualize along lines where the individual fails to appreciate, in a broad sense, African ancestors and values. It is likely that scholars will identify several related illnesses within this category. Often they will be the byproducts of cultural racism and will be transmitted through the educational system and the popular media.

Where cultural racism is a dominant dynamic in a society, clinicians should not construe the failure to grasp and appreciate one's history and culture as either an adjusted or a neutral event. This failure to embrace these facets of one's background may be common, but it is not healthy. This position may appear to be strident and unyielding. However, the schemata related to African cultural values and history provide the bedrock of the healthy African personality. Cultural racism attacks these relentlessly. Where this attack has caused psychological damage, at best a change-worthy circumstance exists within the personality. Deprecation of one's history and culture represents a form of refusal to accept oneself. Therefore it is pathological.

We have yet to see the clear delineation of the forms this particular set of disorders will assume. In many instances, *lack of exposure* to cultural values and history will represent a core element of the pathology. Other individuals show an obstinate *refusal or an inability to accommodate* cultural and historical information that may contradict preexisting Manichean schemata. There is a need to identify the subclasses and specify the various disorders that are related to the schemata in the cultural and historical region. The general alien-self and misorientation disorders described by Azibo and Akbar are an excellent start. The challenge is to explore the details.

Second, we know that, indeed, it is healthy when humans come to acknowledge certain personal limitations as part of their normal development. We come to know that there are tasks we will never perform efficiently and forms of information we may never fully comprehend. Further, we begin to admit to ourselves, once the whirlwind cognitions of youth dissipate, that we are, each of us, mortal. Our time of transition will come. However, even in the face of these concessions, it is healthy to regard oneself and one's people as having a moderate amount of general competence and more than a modicum of efficacy. Further, when the mind is healthy, we come to know (perhaps to assume, when racism is absent) that we are rooted in people who can see to the meeting of life-sustaining needs. One comes to know that they are an extension of people who developed and improved on this process through the ages. We have seen that racism sets up conditions where this sense of competence and efficacy is less likely to emerge in the cognitive schema of the oppressed. Where this failure to develop a general sense of individual or collective competence exists, a mental disorder is present.

To be sure, there are subsets of symptoms within the set of disorders we would link to the competence and efficacy domain. In chapter 1 we proposed that real disparities between the environmental conditions of black and white people are one major source of racist input. These disparities lead one to develop racially based "doubt" or crises related to competence. We located another source of this input in the formal educational system. Theoreticians may elect to identify several types of "competence disorders" that tend to exist within a Manichean order. Alternatively, a competence vector or dynamic may be inserted into the available categories of alien-self or misorientation disorders. In either case, as this dimension is included in a diagnostic system, it will be important to determine the nature of input that drives the cognition. Scholars may organize subsets of symptoms organized around these.

The following point may be subtle, but it is not unimportant. An African growing up in a predominantly white setting may have a fairly limited number of experiences with other black people and institutions. An increasing number of black individuals in the United States are raised in settings of this kind. The presentation of history and culture by the educational system and various media sources shapes schemata related to competence and efficacy. Herrnstein and Murray's *The Bell Curve* (1994) is one of the recent perseverative outbursts from the academic community questioning the intellectual competence of African people (see also Rushton 1994; Itzkoff 1994). The popular media gave this book an astoundingly high profile. Here there was an interesting convergence of the educational and popular media sources of racist input. Schemata in the minds of African people, born of this kind of input, without direct experiences, may be of a unique quality and deserving of a separate diagnostic slot.

Where direct experience with real disparities has primed or reinforced media and educational input, a rather different pathological schema may emerge. Recall that the manner in which we interpret disparities is a function of the context in which they occur. Consider an instance in which an individual simply has not been provided an analysis of the root causes of disparities between services a black versus a white business can provide. The pathology in the competence schema may be more a function of the decontextualization process than of the inculcation of false propositions. The kind of disorder based on real life experience may differ in quality from the kind developed primarily from academic encounters or exposure to popular media.

Again, we are arguing that a distinction be made between disorders within the same class. Ultimately, the schemata of those suffering from these will be more alike than different. Still, the differences may be important. For example, there may be a difference in the intractability of the disorders. Those competence and efficacy disorders that are steeped in real world experience of disparities may be more resistant to therapeutic intervention than the disorders rooted in vicarious and intellectual encounters. The immediate challenge is to determine if the argument for this distinction is valid; that is, if the subclasses of disorders related to competence and efficacy are meaningful. Subsequently, research will have to answer the questions related to differing clusters of symptoms and prognosis in the subclasses.

Fanon (1967), in an existential moment, defined humans as motion toward self and toward one's likeness. The natural human growth process that Akbar described as part of his definition of the healthy personality must include an acceptance of (motion toward) our own physical bodies. Thus, mental disorders, by definition, interrupt this psychological motion. The domain of body image, then, is the third region of cognitive content clinicians should inspect for mental disorders. In chapter 1 we argued that the media blast the physical dimensions of Africans through their presentation of subtle and less than subtle images extolling the Caucasian aesthetic. We alluded to an interaction between race and gender in this process. That is, the

249

attack on the physical aesthetics of the African woman is much more vicious and unrelenting than the attack on the African man. Nosology should be sensitive to the effects of this barrage of images.

Again, we expect that manifestations of disorders related to body image will vary. On one hand, individuals may despise the African elements of their own appearances. Others may focus their disdain on the physical characteristics of other African people. It may be useful to distinguish between disorders where extreme individual self-deprecation exists and those where one tends to disparage the physical dimensions of other people of African descent strictly along Manichean lines. These tendencies may not be related in a linear fashion. That is, as one increases, the other may or may not change. Figure 5 proposes four outcomes of these tendencies. Only in the upper right quadrant do we find Fanon's notion of motion toward self and like. All other quadrants represent a form of pathology.

Research must be conducted before it is possible to describe the complex manifestations in the remaining three outcomes in figure 5. For example, it is quite plausible that an individual whom nature blessed with a good measure of skin melanin, full lips and nose, and strong, tight hair might, quite rightly, consider himself attractive. At the same time, he may have learned to ridicule these characteristics in others. There is an interesting analogue to this situation in the

FIGURE 5. Possible Evaluations of African Elements of Body Image in Self and Others

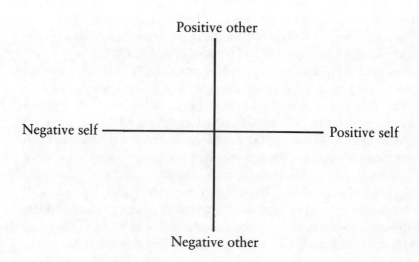

"racial identity" literature. Researchers have shown that one's black identity—that is, reference group identity—does not correlate with one's self-esteem or personal identity (see Cross 1991). Apparently, individuals tend to separate evaluations of themselves from those of the racial group to which they belong. This appears to be the case, at least, when researchers use gross and surface measures like paper and pencil tests and preferences for dolls or pictures to measure identity. Of course, when we raise the body image question clinically, we must go beyond gross measures and employ more detailed analyses of schemata. What cognitive mechanisms allow an individual to respond positively to a physical characteristic in oneself and negatively to that characteristic in another? How does negative body image in any of the three combinations affect interpersonal attraction and relationships? Under what circumstances are these amenable to change? These questions and a host of others emerge when we make Manichean body image an organizing dimension in the diagnostic system.

Racism will affect a fourth broad area of human functioning. This is the physiological domain. When operating properly, physiological systems have an astounding capacity to regulate their levels of activation as environmental conditions and situational demands change. The body's capacity to maintain levels of activity within set limits is known as homeostasis. For example, blood pressure refers to the pressure exerted against the walls of the arteries as blood moves through the vascular system. The level of blood pressure varies from heartbeat to heartbeat. However, considering the radical changes in environmental demands, it remains rather constant. As situations may require, we stand, sit, yawn, climb stairs, and eat, but blood pressure levels remain relatively stable. That is, normally as we engage in these activities, all the major organs and tissues of the body, including the brain, receive sufficient amounts of blood. We feel no ill effects as we carry out these actions.

One cardiovascular mechanism that regulates blood pressure and keeps it constant involves the baroreceptors or pressor receptor systems (Berne and Levy 1993). Baroreceptors are sensory cells located at various sites in the arteries and are highly concentrated in the carotid sinus (at the upper portion of the neck). They sense the level of pressure on each heartbeat and send neural messages to the brain. In response to this message, the brain, primarily through the action of the vagus nerve, will regulate pressure *on the next heartbeat*. This is an example of the highly sensitive control mechanisms that keep the human system in balance.

Racism, not only in interpersonal but also in institutional and cultural forms, has the potential to interrupt the functioning of the homeostatic systems through direct and indirect avenues. The result will be a physical disease of disregulation. When individuals encounter events that either tax or overwhelm coping abilities, there is risk of an interruption of physiological homeostatic processes. An encounter with institutional or individual racism may initiate a chain of events beginning with psychological stress and ending in physical disease. In this case, the individual will consciously process the precipitating events. The event is generally a discrete circumstance, like work-related stress, though the person may come across it chronically. Anderson et al. (1992) presented a model postulating a sequence of events and mechanisms that begins with psychological stress and ends in elevated blood pressure or hypertension in African Americans. I proposed a model some years ago showing another possible pathway leading from psychological stress to hypertension (see Harrell 1980). This model included a reduction in the sensitivity of the baroreceptors. Over the years, doctoral students have helped me construct a program of research that examines the physiological consequences of racism. We have measured blood pressure, heart rate, digital blood flow, and facial muscle (electromyographic) changes that occur when African Americans imagine or view racism. These laboratory demonstrations have shown that for some, the physiological consequences of encounters with even mild forms of racism will be quite significant (see Sutherland and Harrell 1987; Jones et al. 1996; Morris-Prather et al. 1996). For various physiological systems and particular diseases, future research will specify the mediating cognitive and physiological events that begin with psychologically stressful situations and end in disease.

In other instances, these forms of racism, as well as cultural racism, may cause individuals to engage in self-destructive behaviors. Such behaviors include substance abuse and risky sexual behavior. Here the pathway from racist stressors to physiological disease is more indirect. The causal nexus is still clear. For example, substance abuse was common among many of the pioneers of the classical African-American musical form called jazz. Society ignored or belittled their genius and work during their lifetimes. Many of the innovators of this form suffered premature death, sometimes secondary to their abuse of substances. It is much less likely that these gifted individuals would have "self-medicated" with these poisons in a society that valued and cherished their creativity. This is to say that their premature deaths are directly attributable to cultural racism.

A wide gamut of disorders resides within this class. It may be useful to distinguish between them based on the underlying physiological mechanisms and on the type of racism that is part of their etiology. For example, as we noted above, the tenth cranial nerve, the vagus nerve, regulates cardiac and respiratory activity. It is part of the parasympathetic branch of the autonomic nervous system and is highly sensitive to changes in our behavioral commerce with the environment (see Porges 1995). There are branches of the vagus that originate with and function parallel with the muscles that control our facial expressions. That is, the emotional expressions we show are linked fundamentally to the mechanisms that regulate the activity of the heart. Researchers have shown that another physical system, the immune system, is quite sensitive to psychological events. The immune system is responsible for destroying entities that threaten the integrity of the body. Intriguing findings demonstrate that natural killer cell levels change as a function of events including classically conditioned stimuli and caretaking of relatives (see Cacioppo 1994; and Ader 1981). Cardiovascular diseases (including hypertension and heart disease) as well as disorders that signal a breakdown in the immune system (including cancer, lupus, and arthritis) ultimately have stressful events in their etiology. Hence, racism may be part of the matrix of causes of these diseases. The classification system should accommodate these disorders. Research on autonomic and immune-related disorders that grow out of racism are but one exciting research frontier those constructing a nosology of racial oppression disorders will chart.

Reprise

The purpose of refining a nosological system for mental disorders suffered under white supremacy must go beyond the descriptive function. If the classification system only describes the pain or the suffering of the oppressed in a more lucid fashion, then its purpose remains a low one. Even, perhaps especially, in modern, more subtle forms, racism is a scourge. Those living under its heel know this well enough. The most cogent reason for refining a diagnostic scheme is that the system will have a prescriptive function. For this reason alone, we should not allow the work of the constructionists Azibo and Akbar to lie fallow.

* * * * * * * * *

What if the cadre of scholars had undertaken and finished the efforts I am calling for during the lifetime of my friend William? What if there had been a more appropriate diagnostic system for classifying the kinds of disorders that emerge when people of African descent negotiate that very perilous and precarious existence racism creates? To this day I wonder if we would have recognized William's dilemma and pain. Could we have done something about it? Some will reply that the version of the DSM available then would have been suited to the diagnostic task if someone had employed it properly. I seriously doubt that it would have been. I am talking about a diagnosis that a clinician would have made long before any sign of depressive affect surfaced. But the answers to these questions, of course, were sealed away a long time ago. Closed forever on a cold gray morning in a sparsely populated valley, where sad words told me that William was no longer with us.

References

Achebe, C. 1959. *Things Fall Apart*. Greenwich, Conn.: Fawcett.

Ader, R. 1981. *Psychoneuroimmunology*. New York: Academic Press.

Akbar, N. 1984. *Chains and Images of Psychological Slavery*. Tallahassee, Fla.: Mind Productions.

———. 1991. Mental Disorders among African Americans. In *Black Psychology*, 3d ed., ed. R. Jones, 339–52. Berkeley: Cobb and Henry.

American Psychological Association. 1980. *Diagnostic and Statistical Manual for Mental Disorders*. 3d ed. Washington, D.C.: Author.

———. 1987. *Diagnostic and Statistical Manual for Mental Disorders*. Rev. 3d ed. Washington, D.C.: Author.

———. 1994. *Diagnostic and Statistical Manual for Mental Disorders*. 4th ed. Washington, D.C.: Author.

Ani, M. 1994. *Yurugu: An African-centered Critique of European Cultural Thought and Behavior*. Trenton, N.J.: African World Press.

Asante, M. K. 1987. *The Afrocentric Idea*. Philadelphia: Temple University Press.

Azibo, D. 1989. African-centered Theses on Mental Health and a Nosology of Black/African Personality Disorder. *Journal of Black Psychology* 15: 173–214.

Baldwin, J. (Kambon, K. K. K.). 1991. *The African Personality in America: An African-Centered Framework*. Tallahassee, Fla.: Nubian Nation Publications.

Berne, R. M., and Levy, M. N. 1992. *Cardiovascular Physiology*. 6th ed. St. Louis, Mo.: Mosby-Year Books.

Boykin, A. W. 1986. Triple Quandary and Schooling of African-American Children. In *The School Achievement of Minority Children: New Perspectives*, ed. U. Neisser, 57–92. Hillsdale, N.J.: Erlbaum.

Bulhan, H. A. 1985. *Frantz Fanon and the Psychology of Oppression*. New York: Plenum.

Cacioppo, J. T. 1994. Social Neuroscience: Autonomic, Neuroendocrine, and Immune Responses to Stress. *Psychophysiology* 31: 113–28.

Cole, J. B. 1970. Culture: Negro, Black and Nigger. *Black Scholar* 1: 40–44.

Cross, W. E. 1991. *Shades of Black: Diversity in African-American Identity*. Philadelphia: Temple University Press.

Du Bois, W. E. B. 1903. *The Souls of Black Folk: Essays and Sketches*. Chicago: A. C. McClurg.

Fabrega, H. 1992. Diagnosis Interminable: Toward a Culturally Sensitive DSM-IV. *Journal of Nervous and Mental Disease* 180: 5–7.

Fanon, F. 1967. *Black Skin White Masks*. New York: Grove Press.

Hare, R. D. 1985. Comparison of Procedures for Assessment of Psychopathy. *Journal of Consulting and Clinical Psychology* 53: 7–16.

Harrell, J. P. 1980. Psychological Factors and Hypertension: A Status Report. *Psychological Bulletin* 87: 482–501.

Herrnstein, R. J., and Murray, C. 1994. *The Bell Curve: Intelligence and Class Structure in American Life*. New York: Free Press.

Itzkoff, S. W. 1994. *The Decline of Intelligence in America: A Strategy for Renewal*. Westport, Conn.: Praeger.

Jones, J. M. 1991. Racism: A Cultural Analysis of the Problem. In *Black Psychology*, 3d ed., ed. R. Jones, 609–36. Berkeley: Cobb and Henry.

Jones, D. R., Harrell, J. P., Morris-Prather, C. E., Thomas, J., and Omowale, N. 1996. Affective and Physiological Responses to Racism: The Roles of Afrocentrism and Mode of Presentation. *Ethnicity and Disease* 6: 109–22.

Kambon, K. K. K. (a.k.a. J. Baldwin). 1992. *The African Personality in America: An African-centered Framework*. Tallahassee, Fla.: Nubian Nation Publication.

Lewis, D. L. 1993. *W. E. B. Du Bois: Biography of a Race*. New York: Henry, Holt and Company.

Maddi, S. R. 1989. *Personality Theories: A Comparative Analysis*. 5th ed. Pacific Grove, Calif.: Brooks/Cole.

Maslow, A. H. 1962. *Toward a Psychology of Being*. 2d ed. New York: D. Van Nostrand.

Morris-Prather, C. E., Harrell, J. P., Collins, R., Leonard, K. L. J., Boss, M., and Lee, J. W. 1996. Gender Differences in Mood and Cardiovascular Responses to Socially Stressful Stimuli. *Ethnicity and Disease* 6: 123–31.

Nobles, W. W. 1986. *African Psychology: Toward its Reclamation, Reascension and Revitalization*. Oakland, Calif.: Black Family Institute.

Plomin, R., and McClearn, G. E. 1993. *Nature, Nurture and Psychology*. Washington, D.C.: American Psychological Association.

Porges, S. W. 1995. Orienting in a Defensive World: Mammalian Modification of Our Evolutionary Heritage: A Polyvagal Theory. *Psychophysiology* 32: 301–18.

255

Rogers, C. R. 1961. *On Becoming a Person*. Boston: Houghton-Mifflin.

Rushton, J. P. 1994. *Race, Evolution and Behavior.* New Brunswick, N.J.: Transaction.

Spitzer, R. L. 1991. An Outsider-insider View about Revising the DSMs. *Journal of Abnormal Psychology* 100: 294–96.

Spitzer, R. L., and Endicott, J. 1978. Medical and Mental Disorder: Proposed Definition and Criteria. In *Critical Issues in Psychiatric Diagnosis,* ed. R. L. Spitzer and D. F. Klein, 15–39. New York: Raven Press.

Sutherland, M. E., and Harrell, J. P. 1987. Individual Differences in Physiological Responses to Fearful, Racially Noxious, and Neutral Imagery. *Imagination, Emotion, and Cognition* 6: 133–50.

Szasz, T. 1960. Myth of Mental Illness. *American Psychologist* 15: 113–18.

Triandis, H. C. 1994. *Culture and Social Behavior.* New York: McGraw-Hill.

Wakefield, J. C. 1992a. Disorders as Harmful Dysfunction: A Conceptual Critique of DSM-III-R's Definition of Mental Disorder. *Psychological Review* 99: 232–47.

———. 1992b. The Concept of Mental Disorder: On the Boundary between Biological Facts and Social Values. *American Psychologist* 47: 373–88.

———. 1993. Limits of Operationalization: A Critique of Spitzer and Endicott's 1978 Proposed Operational Criteria for Mental Disorder. *Journal of Abnormal Psychology* 102, 160–72.

Weiner, B. 1974. An Attributional Interpretation of Expectancy-value Theory. In *Cognitive Views of Human Motivation,* ed. B. Weiner, 51–70. New York: Academic Press.

Wright, B. E. 1981. Black Suicide: Lynching by Any Other Name Is Still Lynching. *Black Books Bulletin* 7: 15–17.

CHAPTER SEVEN

Treatment

The young man looked better suited to singing in the choir at an A.M.E. church than to serving a ten-year prison sentence for armed robbery. He and I had been talking about the pilot program in which he was participating. In this program, a carefully selected group of forty inmates would participate in a novel, rehabilitative approach to incarceration. If all went well, government officials might implement the program on a larger scale. The pilot program gave officials the opportunity to evaluate the effectiveness of various facets of the intervention. This young man especially liked the nutritionist and the exercise physiologist. These consultants were teaching the residents the difference between bulging muscles and true health and fitness. He found the readings that the teachers were assigning in the classes on African and African-American history long and difficult. He said he was not accustomed to reading so much. Still, he enjoyed them. He showed me his heavily highlighted copy of Lerone Bennet's *Before the Mayflower*. On the other hand, like many of the other inmates, he was not sure about the "psyche man," the staff psychologist. He complained that the guy asked a lot of strange questions and gave few answers. Psyche man always had some test he and his fellow inmates were required to complete. However, another psychologist, the substance abuse specialist, was cool.

My young friend talked for a long time about the tall, quiet brother who played the harp. He was showing the residents how to use music as a way of finding peace. This music therapist was unlike any individual this young person had ever in his life encountered. "He seems calm all the time," the young man told me.

I strongly suspect that many African-American men who are not in prison feel at least a little bit queasy when they visit one. Without a doubt this is true in my case. As we rush toward the end of this century, the republic seems more and more prepared to place large segments of the black male population behind bars. This cold and barbaric attitude may be one source of our uneasiness. My involvement with this large prison on the southeastern coast of the United States had been from a distance. That was quite all right with me.

A very innovative black psychologist was given the task of designing a comprehensive substance abuse and rehabilitation program for the inmates of this facility. Over 95 percent of the inmates were black men. This psychologist asked me to write up a stress management course for the men in the pilot program. The objectives of the course included teaching them about the nature of psychological stress and providing them with ways of handling it. The writing had gone well, and I had trained some staff to serve as instructors for the module. All of this I had accomplished without setting foot in the prison. But now something had changed. The program director requested my presence, behind prison walls, for a series of meetings with the staff and the residents. It was time to prepare for the next phase of treatment.

Only after my discussion with the young resident did I appreciate the truly comprehensive nature of the pilot program. The psychologist-creator had considered the whole person—the spirit, the mind, and the body—as he developed the treatment regimen for these individuals. He had applied elements of knowledge and practice found in traditional clinical psychology, as well as reconstructionistic and constructionistic theories within black psychology. I had not witnessed a more skillful fusion of these paradigms into a practical, working program. Then the designer journeyed outside the field of psychology, beyond the behavioral sciences, and brought in experts in physiology, nutritional sciences, spirituality, and music therapy. The fields of knowledge of the experts, all women and men of African descent, were vastly different. But all agreed with the program director on two things. First, something had gone terribly wrong in the lives of the men who were residents of this prison. Second, to correct this unfortunate present set of circumstances, the team of therapists would have to make radical changes within the minds of these men.

Indeed, the residents of the prison had made great progress. We reviewed the objective test results that each specialist had included in her or his module. Aerobic capacities had increased as a function of an exercise program that deemphasized the accumulation of muscle mass and focused on cardiovascular fitness. Dietary habits had improved, and reading-level scores had increased. The staff psychologist reported that the men were handing conflicts in a more appropriate manner. Further, according to the test scores from my module, the conceptual understanding of the nature of stressful events had improved markedly. For the most part, urine samples had been "clean" for some time. (Even the most naive of us outsiders knew that illegal psychotropic substances are available in prisons in the United States.) The men seemed resolute. Each, including the young person who should have been in the choir, had a plan for changing his life. All had pledged to avoid further contact with the department of corrections.

Still, the designer of the program, along with those who worked as counselors for the men and knew them best, appeared to be altogether unimpressed. His words were piercing and sobering. To paraphrase: "Once these guys get out of here, back on those streets, into that world that sent them here in the first place, all bets are off. They have changed, they are sincere, but the things that happen to them when they move beyond these walls and gates are more formidable than anything we can construct in here. We have to prepare them to struggle against forces that defeated them when they met earlier. Our men are stronger, but the forces have become much stronger too. And each side knows who won the last encounter."

Our treatment efforts had yet to receive their first real test. As a naive academician, I was impressed by the comprehensive nature of the program. With flawless symmetry it brought to life two decades of largely theoretical work in black psychology. But the front-line practitioners had a better fix on what we were up against. We had best not underestimate this opponent.

It is appropriate that the present study close with a word on treatment. Fresh out of graduate school, I would have written this final chapter with a great deal of energy, assuredness, and optimism. Perhaps the aging process and my experience with the prison program and others like it have made me much more cautious. I will proffer no panaceas for changing Manichean mentality. There are no surprises here, and no superheroic therapeutic technology will burst forth. Instead, I will present a broad outline for multimodal intervention. First, the chapter will discuss the psychological and political goals of the treatment of disorders that are an outgrowth of racism. Subsequently I will make comments on the focus of psychological treatment strategies. In correcting the impact of the Manichean order on the oppressed, one can stress the modification of responses, cognitive events, and stimulus situations. We have seen that all three are part of the equation of racist oppression. Toward what ends should we direct therapeutic interventions? I will present two examples of strategies that focus on the modification of symptoms. A discussion of approaches that are concerned with modifying cognitive processes follows. The chapter closes with a discussion of strategies that target the modification of the stimulus input, that is, with changing the nature of racist environments.

Ultimately, Fanon's thinking informs our approach to therapy. We will discuss the changing of both psychobehavioral and social structural realities. "The black [man] must wage his war on both levels: Since historically they influence each other, any unilateral liberation is incomplete, and the *gravest mistake would be to believe in their automatic interdependence*" (Fanon 1967a, 11, emphasis mine).

The goals of therapy

For our purposes, therapy will be defined as a two-pronged process. Therapy is any corrective action directed toward the prevention, mitigation, or eradication of mental illness. At the same time, the thrust of therapy is to propel the individual toward a state of health and wholeness. This is a broad definition. It allows us to subsume a wide gamut of interpersonal encounters under the heading *therapy* or *therapeutic*. These interactions may take place in a hospital or clinic, in the school or home, or in community settings. The activities can take the form of highly structured and formal encounters between an individual and a trained or licensed professional. Traditional psychotherapy that a clinical psychologist or psychiatrist would carry out in an office or clinic is an example of a structured form. In other instances, therapeutic encounters are quite informal and unstructured.

Meetings with mentors and elders are examples of less formal but potentially highly therapeutic interactions. In addition, as we "wage war on both levels," the therapeutic process becomes less individualized and may not involve an encounter between a patient and a therapist at all. That is, therapy can take the form of an in vivo, social process. As part of this process, individuals or groups mount an active struggle against oppressive institutions, practices, and conditions. Therapeutic activities saturate social activism. This is the case for reformist as well as revolutionary actions. Hence, though dissimilar in form, individual counseling sessions, community rites-of-passage programs, and armed resistance to oppressive conditions are forms of therapy. The restorative and healing intent of the activities places them under the same rubric.

In the very broad sense, the intent of therapy is corrective. However, it is more difficult and contentious to identify specific goals of the therapeutic process. One's definition of mental illness and mental health will determine, to a large extent, the ultimate goals she or he establishes for therapy. For example, influenced by Wakefield's definition, we may view mental illness as "harmful dysfunctions" (see chapter 6). From this perspective, the goal of therapy might be the correction of the dysfunction, a mitigation of the harm resulting from it, or both. We might consider therapy for one suffering from a substance abuse disorder involving crack cocaine successful when several conditions are evident. First, multiple measures of drug use, including urine analyses, self-report, and reports from significant others, suggest that the individual is no longer using the substance. Second, the individual is able to use personal and interpersonal resources to develop a sense of mastery over cravings for the substance. Third, the client has gained insight into situational factors that increase her or his likelihood of drug use. Additionally, the patient has mastered strategies for mitigating the impact of these environmental influences. Fourth, therapy has succeeded in identifying and modifying deep-seated personality traits and dynamics within the addicted individual that increase vulnerability to drug use. Finally, the therapeutic process has repaired some portion of the harmful effects of the addiction on interpersonal relationships, especially those involving family and close associates. The theoretical orientation of therapy will determine if and in what order the change agent will address each of these therapeutic goals.

On the other hand, in chapter 6 we showed that Akbar's definition of mental disorders differed in several significant ways from the DSM definition and Wakefield's definition. The therapist will find it necessary to amend the specific goals of therapy if this definition forms the underpinning for the therapeutic enterprise. Akbar viewed mental disorders as internal events that tend to block inherent processes of self-acceptance, self-knowledge, and growth within the human personality. From this perspective on therapy, one might argue that treatment must include, but not be limited to, the removal of internal causes of mental illness and the mitigation of harm caused by these illnesses. The healing process should ensure that the growth and actualizing processes that are elements of normal or natural personality functioning are restored. Thus it is insufficient for one to simply remove pathological elements or to correct the disorder without "reinitializing" the growth process in the personality.

One might counter that if Akbar's central "growth and discovery" tendencies within the personality are truly inherent, once the therapist dispels the mental illnesses, these processes will resurface automatically. According to this argument, the processes are strong currents within the mind that will resume their previous course of flow once therapy removes the diverting obstacles. This is a strongly optimistic position on the resilience of the inherent growth tendencies in the personality. Even if one rejects it in the strong form, she or he need not abandon Akbar's view of mental illness. Again, Akbar's perspective is that within humans there are inherent tendencies to embrace the self and for the personality to blossom. It is not inconsistent to argue that therapy may have to nudge, tweak, reinvigorate, or resuscitate these inherent tendencies after the therapist has treated the mental disorders and their harmful effects. Hence, an additional goal of therapy is to revive the growth and unfolding processes within the human personality that mental disorders have interrupted. Take again the instance of the person addicted to crack cocaine. Now therapy includes helping the individual locate those positive forces that operated in the personality before either the addiction or the development of the dysfunction that resulted in the addiction.

Another aspect of the goals of therapy is worthy of consideration. Treatment is not a politically neutral process. Frantz Fanon learned this when he functioned in a clinical capacity in Algeria. However, in 1956 Fanon submitted his letter of resignation from his position as medical director at the Psychiatric Hospital of Blida-Joinville in Algeria. For three years he treated mental disorders in Algerian people only to release the healed into a French colonial environment he described as "systematized de-humanization" (Fanon 1967b, 53). At the end of three years, he had seen enough. As a psychiatrist, Fanon came to believe that treatment could be executed "in the social scheme of things" only under circumstances in which the clinician is "convinced of the excellence of the society" (54). Clearly, Fanon has identified another goal of the treatment process when it takes place within the context of oppression. It is cowardly and dishonest to attempt to repair the psychological damage that is an outgrowth of racism or other forms of social oppression while taking a "no comment" position regarding the oppressive conditions themselves. Within the context of white supremacy, therapy, if at all comprehensive, must include politically critical elements. Therefore, two additional related therapeutic goals emerge. First, therapy should provide the individual, at the very least, with insight into the social forces and conditions that played a putative role in the development of the mental disorder. Second, treatment should give the individual some methods for developing a cognitive screen against these forces. The more courageous variation on the theme of this second goal will include providing individuals with strategies for routing these forces wherever they surface.

I am suggesting that we consider an addendum to Akbar's definition of mental health within the context of modern racial oppression. The mentally healthy individual of African descent will exhibit two cognitive markers. He or she will manifest the self-awareness, self-acceptance, and growth tendencies that Akbar described. Additionally, the healthy individual will operate with cognitive schemata that are capable of offering a compelling critique of the environmental input that leads to the development of a Manichean mind. Mental health has to involve some component of awareness of pathogenic forces and processes in the environment. Therapy must alert individuals to the presence of these forces and provide them with some means of mitigating their impact. Ideally, therapy will point the way toward the out and out destruction of sources of dehumanization.

In summary, the goals of treatment will be an extension of the prevailing definitions of mental health and mental disorders. The theoretical orientation of the treatment will generate guidelines for prioritizing these goals. Some interventions will emphasize the removal of symptoms, while others will concern themselves with modifying underlying personality structures thought to be responsible for the appearance of the symptoms. Still others may focus on repairing relationships and social systems that actions stemming from the mental disorder may have harmed. This may include fixing interpersonal dynamics within the family and on job settings. Using Akbar's approach to mental health and disorders, additional goals of therapy will center around reviving growth processes in the personality that the mental disorder may have disrupted. Finally, therapy that remains politically neutral supports prevailing dehumanization. Where mental disorders are an outgrowth of racism, insight into these conditions, as well as methods for coping directly or indirectly with them, should be included in the goals of therapy.

Treating Manichean disorders

At the level of the symptom

The most common forms of therapy for behavioral problems are highly personalized encounters. Usually, the troubling or destructive behavior of one person is brought to the attention of a mental health professional, who uses specific techniques to curb the behavior. Hayes (1991) published an interesting manifesto that urged African-American psychologists to eschew elaborate causal explanations of behavior. These explanations sculpt complex, nonobservable mental structures and propose that they are the primary units of analysis for the study of behavior. For example, the Freudians propose that elaborate unconscious processes cloak motivational processes that are the root of our behaviors (Freud 1952). Trait theorists claim that basic, enduring structures exist within the human personality and that they cause our behaviors to be consistent across time and place. Hayes's allegiance was to a school of thought known as radical behaviorism (Skinner 1964). He encouraged an analysis of behavior that focused on the individual's responses or overt behavior and the environmental consequences.

In the therapeutic context, this highly individualized approach requires that one specify the problematic behavior or symptom and identify the impact of this behavior on the environment. This is the "functional analysis of behavior" articulated by B. F. Skinner in the 1940s and 1950s. It reached a pinnacle of popularity in the late 1960s. Hayes took pains to draw a distinction between discussions of the *consequences* versus the *causes* of behavior. Consequences are environmental events that control or maintain behavior. They are observable and, in most instances, malleable. Therefore, behaviors or symptoms can be eliminated or accelerated by the manipulation of their consequences. If an individual is addicted to a substance or abuse of his or her spouse, the therapist's task is to identify and remove the reinforcing consequences of these undesirable behaviors. The original causes, whether they are cognitive schemata that were acquired during childhood or personality structures that emerged through an interaction between environmental and biological factors, remain moot within this framework. Indeed, how important are these original causes—that is, internal structures of any kind—if the behavior or symptom can be controlled by systematically manipulating consequences?

Obviously, "radical Black behaviorism" as outlined by Hayes obviates the need for much of the material discussed in this book. The exception is some of the matters related to conditioning that chapter 4 outlined. Mental events are superfluous at best when "the control of black people's *behavior* is . . . the bone of contention over which blacks and whites struggle" (Hayes 1991, 75, emphasis mine). However, it is very risky for therapists to be unconcerned with mental activity, even though we cannot apprehend it with our senses and it proves to be a slippery subject for scientific examination. People construe and appraise the environmental circumstances that they encounter. Seventy years ago, psychologists knew that if people are a function of their environments, then environments too are a function of people (see Ekehammar 1974). A reinforcing consequence for me in one moment may not be reinforcing several moments later. When my children were young, they worked with a mathematics software program that would reinforce each correct response with the spoken phrase "good job, _____" (the child's name). However, after some time the children began to grow weary of the little voice. Soon they began to search desperately for a way to turn off the squeaky reinforcing verbalization. Actually, they began to dread getting the correct answer for fear of hearing "good job, _____." The consequences for correct responses remained the same; however, the manner in which the children appraised these consequences had changed.

There is an interminable theoretical argument that surfaces when psychologists engage in discussions of the functional analysis of behavior. The radical behaviorists argue that if a reinforcer or punishment, for whatever reason, loses its controlling function over a given behavior, it is, quite simply, no longer a reinforcer. It is the therapist's job to find out what consequence is now controlling behavior. Thus, the discussion of mental events remains unnecessary. This line of thinking leads to regressive, if not dangerous, outcomes. For example, when poor people in the United States break a law, the consequences almost invariably involve punishment by imprisonment or death. Recent trends would suggest that the more frequently the state imposes punishment, the higher the rates of crime. Some argue that prisons are too soft. They maintain that they have lost the qualities that, in the past, made them punishment. This argument contends that society has to make its prisons a bit more "cruel and unusual." The pitfall in this line of thinking is that the focus remains on the environmental consequences. Those designing this form of public policy are circumventing a very disturbing question. What life circumstances lead a significant portion of the population to construe the risk of the loss of one's freedom as anything but a consequence one must avoid at almost all costs? The answer to this question can be uncovered only by exploring the cognitive schemata of these individuals. Obviously, there is little inclination to do so.

The therapist must attend to the mental activity of those being treated, even though this activity is elusive and the content sometimes ephemeral. Indeed, the overt symptoms that the victims of white supremacy evidence are salient and compelling. Nevertheless, change agents must consider other meaningful content. Notwithstanding the important environmental consequences (and antecedents) of these overt symptoms, causes and effects reside in another domain. The therapist, at some level, is all but compelled to consider the impact of white supremacy on the thinking patterns of the oppressed.

Frances Welsing (1991), writing in a therapeutic mode, outlined a program that focuses on symptoms. In this respect it is similar to the program of the radical behaviorists. Still, she did not belittle the role of mental events in her analysis. Although her prescriptive statements are almost distressingly simple, Welsing maintained that an "ability to analyze ourselves, our behavior and our reality critically is one of the signs of true mental health" (239). For Welsing, treatment of mental disorders related to racism must begin with work in the cognitive domain. She (Welsing 1991) pronounced what ring forth almost like commandments for those living in a racist environment. These behavioral directives, quite well known within the African community in the United States, are targeted obviously to all who have been on the receiving end of white supremacy. They include, "Stop name calling one another; stop cursing one another; stop using and selling drugs to one another." These and others she puts forth as tenets to be taught to black children to help develop a basis for self-respect in a racist environment.

On the one hand, Welsing's theory of white supremacy (see chapter 1) is open to criticism for what appears to be a lack of parsimony. The theory may provide a needlessly complex explanation for phenomena related to racism. As argued in chapter 1, the status of her theory of white supremacy is unclear because most scholars have tended to ridicule or ignore it rather than provide a critical analysis. On the other hand, at first glance her therapeutic injunctions seem to be too simplistic. How do we correct disorders related to white supremacy? The answer: "don't kill, don't gossip, and don't behave in a group negating fashion." However, the "simplicity" criticism is inappropriate.

Welsing's call to modify the behavioral output constitutes a focus on symptoms. However, it follows the cognitive work of uncovering the motives and methods of racism. For example, Welsing counsels African people in the United States to delay marriage and procreation until the third decade of life (262). She sets forth this behavioral directive, aimed at reducing the rate of teenage parenting, within a context of reeducation and emotional preparation. She urges young African people to use the delay interval to hone their ability to function in a complex postmodern society and to sharpen their capacities to understand and parry the influences of white supremacy. Hence, at first, Welsing's clinical prescriptions appear to be very much symptom-oriented. However, she embedded them in a theoretical context that acknowledges both environmental and cognitive influences on behavior.

In conclusion, critics will be quick to point out that changing the behaviors of individuals while ignoring underlying causes may be problematic for two related reasons. The first involves the permanence of the changes. Prescriptions that instruct or induce one to modify particular behavioral patterns may have a temporary effect only. Eventually, underlying causes of the behaviors will reassert themselves. The problematic behavior, or one similar to it, will surface again. In a similar vein, one might criticize these techniques for their apparently superficial treatment of the effects of racism. Rather than get to the core of the problem, the therapeutic intervention has busied itself with modifying manifestations only.

Both criticisms are valid. However, they are not dismissive. In many instances, it will not be possible to modify underlying, deep-seated causes of symptoms until the therapist can preempt disruptive surface manifestations. For example, clinicians know that where anti-self disorders exist, they may find it necessary to modify violent or aggressive behavior using behavioral techniques. Subsequently, one can begin changing underlying schemata that mediate the aggressive actions. Similarly, the therapeutic agent may find it necessary to instruct parents not to allow children to watch negative programming on television. Neither the children nor the parents may be aware of the subtly toxic elements in this programming. That is, they may not fully comprehend the reasons the therapist is asking them to change their behavior. Still, this modification of symptoms tends to halt the development of racist cognitive structures. Also, in a small way, it pulls the plug on one source of support for those who manufacture the programs. Corrective social movements find their genesis in the protests of small cadres of individuals. Therefore, it is not hard to envision a significant role for the therapeutic interventions that tend to focus on symptoms alone. Dr. Welsing's prescriptions and techniques within the behavioral therapies may prove useful adjuncts.

At the level of the mind

As we noted, radical behaviorism alleged that private mental events are not an important part of the therapeutic process. In fact, clinical psychology's flirtations with the strong form of this thesis were shortlived. If thinking ranks among the significant concomitants of overt human behavior, it will ultimately figure into the therapeutic process. Accordingly, mental health clinicians have witnessed an explosion in the number of cognitive therapies over the past twenty years.

Traditional cognitive therapy. Dobson and Block (1988) distinguished among several therapeutic techniques that alter or modify cognition in order to effect changes in behavior. They placed these procedures under the broad heading of cognitive behavior therapy. These techniques share three assumptions, according to Dobson and Block (1988, 4). The first and third are causal assumptions. The second is related to the accessibility and malleability of cognition. Specifically, cognitive behavior therapies assume that (1) thinking affects behavior, (2) thinking can be monitored and changed, and (3) behavior can be affected by changing one's thinking.

Indeed, the cognitive approaches have enjoyed tremendous growth in the past two decades. However, Mahoney (1988) noted that Kelly's (1955) personal construct theory and Frankl's (1963) logotherapy were the early, sometimes overlooked precursors of cognitive behavior therapy. More proximal foundations are in the therapies of Aaron Beck and Albert Ellis. Beck's (1967) cognitive therapy with depressed patients has influenced a generation of clinicians. Similarly, Ellis's rational emotive therapy (1962) has proved to be a useful clinical tool. However, beginning in the 1970s, clinicians generated a deluge of treatment techniques that entail cognitive restructuring, coping skills development, and problem-solving training (see Mahoney 1988).

Therapists tend to conduct cognitive behavior therapies in phases. Initially, therapists show clients how important thought processes are in determining our actions. They also introduce clients or patients to the notion of metacognition. This involves showing clients how to monitor their thoughts. Finally, cognitive behavior therapists work with the cognitive arsenal of the individual. This final phase involves modifying thoughts and adding skills where appropriate (see Meichenbaum and Genest 1980; Goldfried and Goldfried 1980).

Mahoney (1988) argued that the growth of cognitive behavior therapies is part of a new emphasis on cognition in the behavioral sciences. However, the emerging techniques are distinguishable in several important respects. Mahoney proposed that cognitive therapies in the *rationalist* and *developmental* camps differ philosophically, theoretically, and practically. The rationalistic theories are more absolute in their view of reality. They contend that human reasoning processes make real truth known. Thus they embrace theories of "cerebral primacy" over emotions (373). The intellect is ultimately the seat of wisdom. Practically, the rationalists are problem and goal focused. The clinician, in the role of a technical instructor, directs the therapeutic process. The therapist, then, has a clear notion of the purpose and ultimate aim of treatment.

On the other hand, Mahoney (1988) proposed that developmental cognitive behavior therapies see construing processes as central determinants of reality. Thus their ontological approach is relativistic. Reality becomes an individual phenomenon. The developmentalist's theoretical approach to the client is holistic, avoiding mind-body dualism. Emotions as well as cognitions are essential and healthy elements of being. Finally, therapy itself is process oriented. The therapeutic relationship is one in which client and therapist explore more effective ways for the client to meet environmental challenges.

The prototypic rationalistic approach to therapy would be Ellis's rational emotive therapy. Ellisonian therapy is renowned for its businesslike, pedagogical approach to clients. The therapist lectures the client on the irrationality of her or his belief (Haaga and Davison 1988). Conversely, Guidano and Liotti's (1983) structural psychotherapy is similar to Beck's (see Beck et al. 1979). In both instances, the therapist's job is to assist the client in abandoning cognitions that are not adaptive. This leads to a personal transformation. The individual, with the aid of the therapist, finds a more adaptive belief system. These latter techniques belong under the developmental rubric.

Are the cognitive therapies feasible for modifying Manichean cognitive schemata? Indeed, they have provided some important technical advances. Perhaps the most important feature they offer is the emphasis on metacognition. A number of the cognitive therapies instruct clients to *listen* to their own thinking and to monitor "self-sentences." An essential step toward modifying Manichean schemata is to make the individual aware that he or she uses them. Therefore, insofar as we are able to make certain racist beliefs conscious, cognitive therapies may be helpful.

In addition, cognitive therapists borrow many techniques from the other approaches. Some of these, used as adjuncts, will prove helpful in modifying Manichean schemata. Role playing using new or old thinking styles should be valuable. Therapists can use role playing to illustrate to the client how old and destructive or new and generative cognitive strategies operate. In addition, systematic desensitization (see Paul 1966) may prove valuable in reducing conditioned emotional responses. Some components of these may be "precognitive," as we discussed in chapters 4 and 5. Desensitization coupled with cognitive restructuring may help the therapist effect a more comprehensive modification of the change-worthy cognitions.

Clinicians developed the cognitive strategies almost exclusively to treat distressed individuals. The schemata of the troubled individuals were causing them to be anxious, depressed, or generally ineffective people. In chapter 6 we saw that often Manichean schemata will not cause the client a great deal of distress. In fact, these thought patterns will be consistent with the currents of thought that the larger society tends to applaud. Therefore, in many cases the impetus to change Manichean schemata is not because they have failed to serve the individual. From a pragmatic perspective, they are often quite adaptive. Rather, those who use the cognitive behavior therapies will have to reconstruct the rationale for modifying cognitions. The schemata are change-worthy *because* they are adaptive in the short run. However, in a broad view, they are destructive to the person and to African people as a collective.

Herein lies the challenge for the therapist. Treatment must lead the individual to become aware of racist cognitions. Part of motivating the individual to abandon these will involve restructuring an underlying value system. The skilled therapist will have to demonstrate the ultimate value in placing long-term personal and collective benefits above short-term gain. Often the therapist can accomplish this through the discussion of biographies of significant African individuals. Convincing the client of the negative personal and collective consequences of this thinking is always a challenge. Of course, in those cases in which the Manichean cognitions have led the individual to destructive and disturbing consequences, the therapist's task is simpler. The most difficult challenge for the application of cognitive therapies will be where the Manichean schemata appear to be serving the individual quite well.

Ntu therapy. Ntu therapy fuses elements of an African-centered philosophical orientation with humanistic psychology. Ntu is a hub or central force that, in some African traditions, provides existence with an underlying unifying force (Jahn 1961). The result of this fusion is an interesting and promising approach to treatment. Frederick Phillips (1990), a past president of the Association of Black Psychologists, formulated Ntu therapy. Its philosophy and goals are quite lucid. The techniques are less discernible from Phillips's presentation. Therapists will require a clear statement of these procedures to achieve praxis and therapeutic goals.

Phillips (1990) referred to five core principles that comprise Ntu therapy's philosophical foundation. These core principles should saturate the therapeutic environment. Because the therapy is relationship oriented, the therapist must manifest each principle. *Harmony*, the first principle, characterizes the internal and external relationships healthy humans will share with all of existence. There should be no cleavage between the major forces within humans, that is, between mind, body, and spirit. Humans should also evidence a harmonious relationship with external forces. *Balance* is the second organizing principle of Ntu therapy. It directs individuals to permit expressions that are seemingly contradictory in nature. Hence, one should give focused striving and flexible recreational behaviors equal expression. *Interconnectedness* is a more formal statement of the Ntu concept. It is inappropriate with this treatment strategy for individuals to view themselves as separated from any other facet of existence. The interrelatedness of the various human systems symbolizes the connectedness of all elements of existence.

Phillips advanced *affective epistemology* as a formal therapeutic principle. The implication is that processing occurs through "an integration of both feeling experience and verbal cognitive" modes (59). Interpersonal relationships under optimal circumstances will be characterized by an expanding *authenticity*. This principle refers to one's ability to be in touch with others and willingness to express to them one's essential being. Finally, Phillips integrated *cultural awareness* into the philosophical fabric of Ntu therapy. He emphasized the importance of knowing and accepting one's "cultural self." Though he does not define cultural self explicitly, the term seems to include one's ancestral background. Phillips endorsed Azibo's (1983) and Baldwin's (1981) insistence that an acceptance of core African values is essential to the mental health of African people.

The goal of Ntu therapy is to help the client function in a harmonious fashion. The healthy client manifests this harmony internally and externally. The internal harmony encompasses biological, psychological, and psychosocial functions. That is, mentally healthy people bring physiological systems into effective interactions with biological challenges. They tend to be more healthy physically. Also, the psychological systems of healthy people interact efficiently with the demands and challenges that social structures, interpersonal events, and personal limitations may present.

The goal of establishing harmony also relates to external functions. Ntu therapy specifies the value system or code by which African Americans should conduct their lives. Phillips selected the value system Karenga distilled in the late 1960s. The system is known as the Nguzo Saba, Kiswahili for seven principles. The values include unity (intra- and interpersonal), self-determination (collective and individual), collective work and responsibility, cooperative economics, purpose, creativity, and faith. One who lives according to these principles will achieve harmonious relationship with others.

Phillips (1990) described the process of the therapeutic relationship. The quality of the relationship between the therapist and client is crucial. Clients begin to view the Ntu therapist as committed to their mutual growth. As contact in the sessions continues, the client becomes aware of personal limitations, potentials, and resources. Therapy also involves an "alignment" phase. Here the client faces anxieties and fears with the help of the therapist. New modes of handling difficult situations are generated. Clients "practice and experiment with new attitudes and behaviors" (71). This is the actualization phase of therapy. Finally, clients achieve an integration of the therapeutic products into their personalities. The principles of therapy become part of their lives.

Regarding technique, Ntu therapy is eclectic. Therapists use guided imagery, relaxation techniques, prayer, role playing, and libations to accomplish the therapeutic tasks. There are specific tasks associated with the therapeutic values. Family budgeting, physical exercise, and cultural studies are all part of the therapeutic technology. Hence, it is probably best to view Ntu therapy as a compilation of techniques that are directed toward clearly stated ends.

Ntu therapy has considerable promise for the treatment of disorders related to racism. At the same time, there is a pressing need for a comprehensive technique manual. Relatively mild, alien-self disorders are appropriate candidates for Ntu therapy. Self-destructive disorders are equally good candidates for treatment. However, surely the technology that a change agent might use in these instances would differ. The manual would suggest the particular treatment strategies a therapist might use.

The goals of Ntu treatment would be identical for the mild and the severe pathologies that are an outgrowth of racism. Ntu therapy approaches mental health with the "cultural agenda" on the table. It provides an intriguing approach to treating Manichean schemata because it focuses on constructing a value system rather than modifying bizarre or distressing behaviors. Therefore, Ntu therapy is equipped to deal with subtler forms and manifestations of racism's effects. Once its developers specify the therapeutic technology, it may prove to be a powerful treatment adjunct.

Hord's literary approach to treatment. Hord's *Reconstructing Memory* (1991) is a work of literary criticism and more. In some respects it constitutes a detailed preface for a cognitive therapy manual. The clients for this therapy would be those suffering the ravages of cultural racism. While Ntu therapy is vague on the nuts and bolts of technique, Hord's approach is very specific. He argues that young people of African descent, even those who are part of the current postmodern era, have only a sketchy appreciation of their history. In addition, he suggested that they tend to deny or disclaim their African heritage. Hord calls this phenomenon a loss of cultural memory. He maintained that by using selected authors who are part of the national literature, teachers can regenerate the cultural memory of their students. He focused on the national literature of African Americans, but clearly his approach can be generalized to other parts of the African diaspora.

Hord (1991) draws heavily on the pioneering studies of Fanon, Albert Memmi, and Amilcar Cabral. All three authors emphasize the role of national culture as colonial people struggle for liberation. It is this culture that colonial powers attacked ruthlessly. Hord concludes that colonial regimes structure institutions that "deracinate the past of the colonized, or at least . . . disfigure the collective memory" (4). This is the core of the cultural racism that James Jones (1972) described. Hord pointed to educational institutions as the primary purveyors of cultural racism. Therefore he views the curricula of Western institutions as nurturers of Manichean schemata. Modifying these curricula should prove therapeutic.

The details in Hord's analysis are impressive from the standpoint of therapy. He encourages an examination of the works of Frederick Douglass, Paul Laurence Dunbar, Ralph Ellison, John Killens, Sonia Sanchez, and Haki R. Madhubuti. These authors differ widely on an ideological spectrum. Certainly, Dunbar and Ellison left readings that assume a less nationalistic posture than those of Sanchez, Madhubuti, or Killens. Hord demonstrates how exploring the works of all these individuals can be therapeutic. His criticism enhances the regenerative aspects of each work.

For example, Hord shows how valuable a careful study of Douglass's *Narrative of the Life of a Slave* can be. In this short book, Douglass described the depths to which slavery sent people. Hord does not encourage us to shrink from a discussion of these symptoms. On the other hand, Douglass paints unforgettable pictures of the awesome power of black resistance. These images are essential to reconstructing the cultural memory.

In summary, the thrust of Hord's approach is to instill values and vision in the oppressed through the study of literature. Obviously, his focus is on repairing the minds of high-school and college students. Still, his approach can be generalized to other authors who may be appropriate for other grade levels. Indeed, a creative and literate therapist could extend this approach to younger children. There is a burgeoning black children's literature (see the works of Lucille

Clifton, Eloise Greenfield, and Mildred Taylor) that teachers might use toward these ends.

Finally, the focus need not remain on repairing or reconstructing memory. African people everywhere must begin to use their literature of national culture to promote generative values and perspectives. This process of instilling the proper information must start on the first days of contact with formal education, in order to beat cultural racism to the punch. The nurturing and healing properties of literature, written or spoken, are evident. What remains is the dynamic task of specifying the authors, sources, and bodies of thought in which we must begin to steep developing African minds.

Altering input

Vincent Harding (1975) argued that in 1954, a singular event dealt a serious blow to white supremacy and European world domination. Many people associate 1954 with the landmark *Brown v. Board of Education* decision. The *Brown* decision outlawed segregation in public education facilities in the United States. However, the event to which Harding was referring took place far from U.S. shores. In that year, the people of Vietnam handed the French a decisive and stunning military defeat at a place called Dien Bien Phu. Harding maintained that this event shook the colonial world to its very foundations.

Perhaps for some, Dien Bien Phu signaled the downfall of white supremacy. A nation of colored people had soundly defeated a modern colonial power. The rotten, racist structure was about to crumble. Others, no doubt, reacted in a cautious and more sober fashion. They concluded that the fall of the political structures of colonialism showed that certain facets of white supremacy were vulnerable and transient. However, through institutional transformations, oppression might persist in their absence. Sadly, the latter view proved correct.

Earlier we asserted that Fanon was prophetic when he said that it would be most beneficial to treat the psychological consequences of racism on several levels. Of course, it is only humane and appropriate to help the sufferer. As we have seen, in treating the afflicted individual we focus on the symptoms and cognitions of the individual. At the same time, the therapist should not allow the causes of the symptoms to go unchallenged. The community psychologists joined Fanon in this effort by calling for the "primary prevention" of mental disorders.

Surely, the years since the midpoint of this century have brought significant changes in the social and political institutions that once buttressed white supremacy. Since Dien Bien Phu and since the time that Fanon walked the streets and alleys of Algeria, Paris, and Martinique, many of the old legal and social institutions that supported white supremacy have crumbled. Indeed, the remaining structured white supremacist government in South Africa was forced from the world stage in the early 1990s. One who left the United States in 1962, when Du Bois did, would find its racial landscape far different upon returning in the middle 1990s. In view of the changes in the oppressive forces that support racism, is the focus on causes still necessary? Is the clarion call for simple reform in the socializing institutions and circumstances of people of African descent necessary? Does the need for radical or revolutionary change persist? Consider in serial fashion each of the three sources of racist cognition that we identified in chapter 1.

Disparities. Perceiving the decontextualized disparities between the circumstances of black and white people fosters racist thinking in a unique fashion. There are four significant properties of this mode of inculcation. First, often there is no agent or identifiable perpetrator of the crucial event or circumstance that leads to Manichean thinking. Ostensibly, things just seem to happen. Second, there appears to be no intent to do harm to the perceiver. Though the conditions are often deplorable, they exist independently of the individual perceiver. Third, the impact of the information is subtle. Indeed, we have argued that people may not consciously process many of the disparities that they meet. Finally, if the impact of the decontextualized disparities is subtle and preconscious, the disparities themselves are at the same time pervasive and ubiquitous.

Given these characteristics, therapeutic intervention should proceed along two lines. The first operation is for the therapist to modify the context, which social institutions have altered cleverly. The second, the more difficult course of action, is to eradicate the disparities themselves.

In fact, the first mode of intervention is not preventive in the strictest sense of the word. It involves the cognitive restructuring that I have discussed in the previous section. Authentic primary prevention entails modifying the external causes of mental disorders. A therapist, or the individual, embarks on a journey to modify the causal attributions one makes after coming across disparities. The transformational process is gradual and involves a series of steps.

The first step in providing a context to economic, developmental, and ambient disparities is to increase the *perceptual gain* on the disparities themselves. That is, the therapist must make the negative conditions more salient by calling attention to them. Once the disparities lie in stark relief, therapist and client can begin the work of deciphering their core causes. The aim is to replace the causal network that the client is using with an attributional network that includes a more accurate description of core causes. As we noted in chapter 1, the client will ultimately tend to attribute the cause of the disparities to failings and faults of those victimized by the negative conditions. It will be necessary, as part of treatment, to discuss the fallacies and limitations of this attributional system. Through discussions, guided academic explorations, and re-education, change agents can show the individual the power of alternative causal schemes. This process may shake the value structure of the client. For example, one may see the grips of unbridled materialism and individualistic thinking loosen as the individual develops a deeper appreciation of the need to restructure belief systems. Hence, the process of therapy for disorders related to the perception of disparities would take place in stages. It is likely to involve alterations of proximal and distal cognitive schemata.

Take, for example, my personal struggle with the disparities between the status of democratic institutions in the West and those in continental Africa. Postcolonial political conditions in many African countries are particularly troubling. Witnessing the coups and the rise of demagogues through mainstream media has been more than annoying. Old-line colonialists and racists shake their heads knowingly. The implication, of course, is that anything, even white rule, is preferable to these tragic events. For me the situation is analogous to writers with the perspectives of Jensen and Herrnstein cataloging the failure of black children to thrive in the educational system. The situation is rife with potential for psychological damage in the competence/efficacy cognitive region.

Initially my therapy came in the writings of Chancellor Williams. They helped provide a context for the current conditions. Dr. Williams showed that traditionally African governing institutions have been intrinsically democratic. The evidence that Counter and Evans (1981) provided after their meetings with African societies in Surinam supported Dr. Willliams's argument. These societies have preserved African traditions and are both democratic and fiercely independent. The corruption, the despots, and the horrible wars find their roots in colonial oppression. The colonists were masters in capitalizing on human foibles. Still, my troubled consciousness aches at the facts of the matter. The wars rage on and many tyrants rule.

The thinking of K. Ajyei Akoto (1992), a master educator, helped me take a therapeutic step forward. He noted that the status of African political systems should not surprise the discerning individual. Africans are ruling out of the decaying political structures and institutions that the colonialists left behind. European oppressors prescribed even the borders between the existing nation states. Confusion should be expected. For me, these remarks helped modify the decontextualized status of the disparities between European and African political institutions. They embellished the therapeutic context.

Indeed, therapy often is like sowing seeds in a field. Both placement and timing are important. This is true when one strives to change the context surrounding the disparities between the living conditions of the privileged and those of the racially oppressed. Insightful information that a therapeutic agent provides at the proper moment, or phrases proffered memorably, may alter one's cognitive schemata and life trajectory immediately. This insight may occur in formal therapy, or an individual may derive it from a book, a poem, a song, or a rap. On the other hand, there will be times that the therapeutic encounter will simply plant a seed. No germination will take place until other conditions are present. People of African descent, acting as therapeutic agents, should recognize that the beneficial impact of any encounter they have with another African can be far removed from the time and place of the encounter. Therefore, it is only on rare occasions that one should shrink from the opportunity to assist another black person in recontextualizing the disparities in development, economics, or ambience that he or she may perceive. One should provide the dissenting voice in even light conversations where the fault for these disparities is placed *exclusively* at the door of the victims of racism. In this fashion, one might plant therapeutic seeds. Insofar as one changes the context in which disparities are embedded, she or he has effected a measure of prevention.

Ultimately, the second preventive approach to cognitive effects of disparities will prove most effective. This approach involves taking direct action against the conditions themselves. It is this work that thrusts many people of African descent into the role of therapist. The scale of activity ranges from individual efforts to national movements. Some efforts will be self-conscious challenges to the structure of white supremacy. Others may be more spontaneous extensions of culture or personality. Regardless, each day dedicated service people clean streets and buildings in and around black communities. Resilient business people strive to develop commerce. A host of institution builders persist in their attempts to nurture educational, communications, and informational infrastructures. All are engaging in psychotherapy for the masses. Booker T. Washington, Marcus Garvey, and Elijah Muhammed recognized the therapeutic effects of constructive efforts within the black community. Du Bois's appreciation of this notion had matured by the 1930s (see Cruse 1987). The scale and the level of consciousness of activities will not be uniform. Still, we will be able to mark a significant therapeutic step forward where individuals and groups transform conditions in which African people live.

Chinweizu (1987) identified a problem related to development that those involved in constructing infrastructures within African communities will face. Capitalistic societies whet the appetites of individuals for glossy and novel goods and convenient services. In many instances, African people live close to or in the midst of modern conveniences and goods. Rarely are they in control of the mechanisms that produce these. Still, proximity and advertisements induce Africans to strive to obtain them. Obviously, people of African descent consume VCRs, DVDS, automobiles, and the services of major hotel chains. They struggle to consume but are, at best, involved only peripherally in the production of these products.

In fact, as Chinweizu points out, the African institutional structure that will lift black people from this consumer status will not appear in a flash. Construction will inch forward in small steps. Singular institutions will struggle to survive for years. Many will not endure. Media outlets and schools will open to some fanfare and then fade and close if conditions for prospering are not nurturing. But ultimately, the problem essentially becomes a cognitive one. This is Chinweizu's point. African people must hone their appetites so that they prefer and consume their own perhaps less glossy but self-generated products over sophisticated "cargo" from external sources. It is necessary to instruct the masses in the science of nurturing their budding institutions. This will permit the taking of small steps that reduce the disparities between ambient developmental and economic conditions in black and white environments.

Popular culture. The "war of images" people of African descent wage within popular culture burns like a subsurface fire in a municipal dumping facility. The ground is hot to the point of smoldering. Occasionally, flames erupt and reach skyward. One thing is certain. The terrain is far from settled.

From a therapeutic perspective, much is at stake in this battle. The struggle is to generate an authentic representation of African people and their cultural products inside a commercialized popular culture. Creative people—the writers of all genres, performing and visual artists, and filmmakers—have a strong hand in shaping the cognitive schemata of the masses. The question becomes, what forces will vie for control over those who generate cultural products? Two philosophies shape approaches to this problem.

The "mere presence" philosophy argues that increased numbers of people of African descent within the cultural apparatus will automatically prove ameliorative. That is, more black journalists, black characters on daytime television dramas, and black megastars in entertainment and sports will serve to heal minds victimized by racism. This healing occurs because the presence of these people provides the hope that a more open opportunity structure will recognize the talents and competence of African people. The ideological posture of the participant is not important within this approach. African people are not either ideologically or culturally monolithic. The argument is that with adequate presence, all perspectives will be represented.

This argument has a measure of hidden power. We have maintained that unconscious processing of environmental input can affect social behavior significantly. The mere presence approach amounts to a kind of "color-blind casting" of black people in entertainment and journalistic roles. Black people smoothly execute roles and functions that ordinarily whites would perform. This provides a strong challenge to Manichean schemata in the competence and efficacy cognitive regions. Without fanfare, African people see themselves in variegated roles. In a subtle fashion, where white supremacy might threaten cognitive processes, these images constitute a therapeutic counterweight.

However, the mere presence approach to modifying racist input is fatally flawed from a therapeutic perspective. Substituting black faces to execute white functions is only a peripheral challenge to white supremacy. It is analogous to pruning a tree that bears poisonous fruit. The most compelling example of the failure of this approach is in television journalism (see Thorton 1990). Salt-and-pepper anchor teams exist in television newsrooms all over the United States. In all fairness, for the most part they mount only occasional critiques to white supremacy. Their mere presence demonstrates that black journalists can provide as shallow and decontextualized a presentation of "top 40" news as their white counterparts. Thus their therapeutic impact is limited.

On the other hand, a second philosophical approach insists that attempts to challenge oppression and white supremacy from the popular culture must be "self-conscious" (Semmes 1992). Here the artist or writer produces information or an image that is an authentic representation of black life. In the process, the product challenges both white supremacy and African responses to it. This is the essence of cognitive therapy. It provides the consumer of the image with richer and more complex conceptual categories. Schemata emerge that transcend the old standard Manichean representations.

Semmes (1992) recognized several stages that creative artists in the African-American community traverse. They move through these stages as cultural forces shape their work and as they respond to economic pressures. Initially, the indigenous, if hybrid, culture of the African-American community gives birth to the artist. The artist generates products that tend to "express and advance the cultural ethos and aspirations" of the black community (229). The African-American community is the primary consumer of these products. In the second stage, the wider community becomes aware of the creative efforts of the artist. The market for these products begins to extend to the expanded market. The process of "crossover" is germinating. Semmes maintained that at this stage, the artist strives to service the internal market as well as the new market. However, the new market is often more lucrative. The artist may slide into the third stage, where she or he courts this market actively. Now significant alterations in the cultural product become evident. One is able to discern the artist's efforts to "accommodate the perspective, expectations, economic potential and legitimating power of the external market" (229). Authentic African cultural images will emerge from artists located in the first and second stages only. These will resist the distortion of the black image, sometimes spontaneously, but more often in a self-conscious fashion.

Consider two examples of the self-conscious, therapeutic use of images. Those that produced these images were functioning out of Semmes's second stage. Both are taken from the television genre. Until the network canceled it in 1994, the television program *Roc* provided glimpses of the good and rough times experienced by a black working-class family in Baltimore. Dignified, lazy, corrupt, insightful, patient, and impulsive black characters interacted in this series. That is, the characters reflected the fabric of black life. To be sure, the performers in this unusual series were accomplished stage actors, and in fact they actually performed many of the programs live. The program was therapeutic because it pandered to authenticity only. The challenge to white supremacy and to Manichean thinking emerged from its unflinching portrayal of black life. We saw burned-out, racist cops and teachers. Additionally, we laughed at the antics of grown siblings still vying for the attention of their parent. The program also showed that old folks were to be treated as elders and that black men and women can work together to build family and community.

The *Eyes on the Prize* series I and II were highly engaging documentaries of inestimable therapeutic potential. They chronicled the recent history of the struggle African people in the United States waged against racism. The shows are remarkable for their flowing prose and smooth editing. However, most significant is the uncompromising perspective that the filmmakers take. They offer no apologies for the actions of the oppressors. In cool tones they depict white supremacy as the utter scourge on humanity that it is. In addition, the filmmakers do not oversimplify the search for solutions to the dilemmas posed by racism. Resistance has taken many forms. *Eyes on the Prize* leaves the viewer with an appreciation of the many facets of the struggle to overcome the effects of racism. Therefore, from a therapeutic perspective, it girds schemata in the cultural-historical and competence-efficacy region against Manichean input. One comes to see how black culture has informed the historical process of resistance to racism in the United States. On a larger scale, the series shows how this resistance struggle has influenced the struggles of oppressed people around the world. African people become actors and agents and not pawns of history. Viewing this in the powerful television medium is highly therapeutic.

Creative artists in the black community are irrepressible. Their healing instincts are sharp even in the face of cultural cooptation and hegemony. Currently, elements of hip hop culture are beginning to find and fuse with their bebop and jazz roots. Together they will produce important postmodern images of the African locked in a struggle to express humanness. In addition, I have met African-American dancers who are treating troubled black youth in our major cities. These dignified artists describe the therapeutic use of rhythm and movement in terms every bit as clear as trained clinical psychologists detailed the use of systematic desensitization therapy when I was in graduate school. Young filmmakers continue to slip healing films into the mix of Hollywood's offerings. The self-conscious attempts to plant therapeutic seeds in the forms of images will remain pivotal in the healing of African people.

Formal education. Education for the racially oppressed is the prototypic double-edged sword. In chapter 1, formal education emerged as a pivotal source of racist information and cultural hegemony. However, as Hord's (1991) book shows, wielded properly, education can prove to be just as therapeutic and ameliorative as it is destructive and oppressive. The challenge for teachers and communities is to structure a generative curriculum that is prophylactic and corrective. Indeed, the object is to turn the blade toward the vitals of white supremacy.

Presently, several approaches that are critical of traditional Western education are visible. Multicultural and Afrocentric approaches to education vie for the attention of those who educate black children in the United States. McLaren (1994) described several of the approaches within multicultural education. He revealed how these approaches differ with respect to the treatment of differences between cultures. *Liberal multiculturalism* stresses or imposes a kind of sameness across cultures, according to McLaren. *Left-liberal multiculturalism* places cultural differences in bold relief. The *critical multiculturalism* that McLaren promoted provides a substantive critique of white norms for establishing cultural hierarchies. This form of multiculturalism is comfortable with cultural differences, though it does not center itself around them. It actively challenges oppressive forces within the society.

Sixty years ago both Carter Woodson and W. E. B. Du Bois urged educators to center the education of African Americans around the experiences of African people. In an address at Fisk University in 1933, Du Bois is clearly on the same page as Woodson (1933), who published his *Miseducation of the Negro* in the same year. Du Bois argued that the education of African Americans should be "founded on a knowledge of the history of their people in Africa and in the United States, and in their present condition" (Du Bois 1973, 93). The call for African-centered education today (see Asante 1991) echoes the sentiments expressed a half century earlier.

The contentious status of the relationship between multicultural and African-centered educators is unfortunate. When offered sincerely, multicultural education provides the student with an appreciation of the varied manifestations of human culture. There is no dichotomy here. African-centered education strives to engender in

283

students an appreciation of human culture. It simply initiates its curriculum in the center of the child's culture.

Historically, the road to realizing the therapeutic value in African-centered pedagogy is full of ironies. Du Bois himself would appreciate these. In hindsight, he recognized that his old foe Booker Washington had centered the education of black children properly. "The industrial school founded itself and rightly upon the actual situation of American Negroes and said: 'What can be done to change this situation?'" (Du Bois 1973, 94).

Again paradoxically, Marcus Garvey, another unfortunate foe of Du Bois, contributed to African-centered education. His publication *The Negro World* concerned itself with both literacy and literary issues. Hence, besides being politically oriented, the publication had an educational thrust. A number of writers reviewed books from a myriad of disciplines in this African-centered journal. Zora Neal Hurston, Alain Locke, Claude McKay, and a host of others contributed to the publication (Martin 1983). Thus the largest of the African-centered movements in American history included a broad-based educational component. The irony of history is that it seemed to fit Du Bois's prescription for education perfectly. *The Negro World* began where the reader or student lived and opened horizons of thought as broad as the world. Its therapeutic potential, therefore, was formidable.

Presently, the issue becomes, what educational approach is the most effective in countering cultural racism? Obviously this is an empirical question. However, the body of thought in favor of an African-centered approach is compelling (Shujaa 1994). The African centered approach is an independent intellectual tradition in the black community. Orthodox educators take great pains to discourage its growth. Still, in Semmes's words, its "revitalizing" potential is great. African-centered curricula place the child at the core of the educational dialogue. Carol Lee (1994) echoed Du Bois's sentiments in her powerful defense of the African-centered thrust in education. She noted that the benefits of an African-centered approach are not limited to the enhancement of "self-esteem, historical accuracy, values clarification and community empowerment" (300). Lee cited research pointing to the importance of centering education around the cultural life of the community. Preexisting cultural schema will serve to "enrich and diversify the network of association [children] are able to construct around specific concepts or skills" (300). Lee, in this passage, gave a cognitive spin to Du Bois's directive to begin education where the child lives.

Clearly, for the African child, African-centered education constitutes an effective preemptive strike against cultural racism. It debunks
notions of the superiority of European culture and history. Thus, this
form of therapy secures the cultural and historical cognitive regions
against racism. In addition, because the conceptual knowledge in
African-centered education is linked to cultural knowledge, as educators refine this approach, the academic performance of African
children will improve. The efficacy and competence regions will flourish as African children observe their collective academic success.

A final word about treatment

Disputes about the level at which we should concentrate treatment
for the psychological ravages of racism are baseless and futile. Interventions must be multilevel and coordinated. Change agents will find
it necessary to arrest or decelerate pathological behaviors that some
oppressed persons, as a function of wretched conditions, are likely to
exhibit. Treatment strategies directed toward cognitions or toward
modifying input may not be feasible until therapists help distressed
individuals control these behaviors. There is no inherent tension
among the treatment agents. Those who treat behavioral symptoms
should be among the most vocal supporters of the individuals who
dedicate their lives to dismantling social structures that undergird
white supremacy. The admiration should be mutual.

One can readily identify the levels at which therapists can treat the
effects of racism. However, launching a coordinated treatment effort
is quite another matter. A truly comprehensive program consists of
efforts from a number of disciplines and orientations. Educators, social critics and activists, psychotherapists, and all other agents of
change in the black community must broaden their visions and
appreciate the complementary nature of their roles. The unified, coordinated therapeutic effort will be a product of individuals transcending their preferences for intervention strategies.

Initially, this chapter described a prison treatment program that
targeted for change troublesome behaviors, self-destructive cognitions, and toxic forms of environmental input. The stumbling block
was that therapists could not control a treacherous environment outside the walls of the institution. Highly sophisticated psychotherapeu-
tic techniques are not entirely worthless when the social environment

is beyond the reach of the therapist. However, the long-term effectiveness of these techniques will remain under siege until proactive interventions lead to a restructuring of the environment of African people. This is the meaning of coordinated intervention.

Finally, at each level of intervention, treatment of racism and its effects is a process that introduces fundamental, if not revolutionary, changes. Many of these alterations will move against the thrust of Western culture and ethos. They will contradict roundly the prescriptions white supremacy advances for the behavior of African people. Therapists will help clients construct cognitive screens against an environment that is polluted with racist information. Change agents will challenge mythology, symbols, and perspectives that emanate from the society's principal socializing institutions and mechanisms. These are not the actions that compromising and obliging individuals will execute. For treatment to be successful, teachers will have to lead African children to embrace their culture and value an African perspective on history. Therapists who help clients restructure their views of the world cannot shrink from providing them biographies of those who offered racism no concessions. Often these individuals are those that the larger society would rather African people despise and repudiate. Those who challenge and seek to deflect the input from media and educational centers will have to be adamant in their efforts. An intransigent society will call them paranoid and extremist as they identify subtle elements of racism that emanate from these institutions.

At all levels, the work of reconstructing the minds of African people requires enormous courage—enormous, but not unprecedented, courage. The nameless ones at Nueva España in 1537 found it when they said "No more." Harriet showed it when she said again and again, "Let's go." Rosa was saturated with it when she didn't move to the back. Louis exuded it when he said "one million men," and it echoed in the grass roots when a million women went to Philadelphia.

Each day, despite the designs of a Manichean world, most African people rise, gird themselves, and push the human struggle onward. The healers among us will find strength and courage in the dignity of those people.

References

Akbar, N. 1991. Mental Disorders among African Americans. In *Black Psychology*, 3d ed., ed. R. Jones, 339–52. Berkeley: Cobb and Henry.

Akoto, K. A. 1992. *Nationbuilding: Theory and Practice in Afrikan-centered Education.* Washington, D.C.: Pan Afrikan World Institute.

Asante, M. K. 1991. The Afrocentric Idea in Education. *Journal of Negro Education* 60: 170–80.

Azibo, D. A. 1983. Some Psychological Concomitants and Consequences of the Black Personality: Mental Health Implications. *Journal of Non-White Concerns* 11: 59–65.

Baldwin, J. A. 1981. *Afrikan (Black) Personality: From an Afrocentric Framework.* Chicago: Third World Press.

Bandura, A. 1969. *Principles of Behavior Modification.* New York: Holt, Rinehart and Winston.

Beck, A. T. 1967. *Depression: Clinical, Experimental and Theoretical Aspects.* New York: Harper and Row.

Beck, A. T., Rush, A. J., Shaw, B. R., and Emery, G. 1979. *Cognitive Therapy for Depression.* New York: Guilford.

Chinweizu. 1987. *Decolonising the African Mind.* Lagos, Nigeria: Pero Press.

Counter, S. A., and Evans, D. L. 1981. *I Sought My Brother: An Afro-American Reunion.* Cambridge, Mass.: MIT Press.

Cruse, H. 1987. *Plural but Equal: A Critical Study of Blacks and Minorities and America's Plural Society.* New York: William Morrow.

Dobson, K. S., and Block, L. 1988. Historical and Philosophical Bases of Cognitive-behavioral Therapy. In *Handbook of Cognitive-behavioral Therapies,* ed. K. S. Dobson, 3–38. New York: Guilford Press.

Du Bois, W. E. B. 1973. The Field and Function of the Negro College. In *The Education of Black People: Ten Critiques, 1906–1960 by W. E. B. Du Bois,* ed. H. Aptheker, 61–82. New York: Monthly Review Press.

Ekehammar, B. 1974. Interactionism in Personality from a Historical Perspective. *Psychological Bulletin* 81: 1026–48.

Ellis, A. 1962. *Reason and Emotion in Psychotherapy.* New York: Stuart.

Fanon, F. 1967a. *Black Skin White Masks.* New York: Grove Press.

———. 1967b. *Toward the African Revolution.* New York: Grove Press.

Frankl, V. E. 1963. *Man's Search for Meaning: An Introduction to Logotherapy.* New York: Washington Square Press.

Freud, S. 1952. *A General Introduction to Psychoanalysis.* New York: Washington Square Press.

Goldfried, M. R., and Goldfried, A. P. 1980. Cognitive Change Methods. In *Helping People Change: A Textbook of Methods,* 2d ed., ed. F. H. Kanfer and A. P. Goldstein, 97–130. New York: Pergamon Press.

Guidano, V. F., and Liotti, G. 1983. *Cognitive Processes and Emotional Disorders: A Structural Approach to Psychotherapy.* New York: Guilford.

Haaga, D. A., and Davison, G. C. 1988. Cognitive Change Methods. In *Helping People Change: A Textbook of Methods,* 3d ed., ed. F. H. Kanfer and A. P. Goldstein, 236–82. New York: Pergamon Press.

Harding, V. 1975. The Black Wedge in America: Struggle, Crisis and Hope: 1955–1975. *The Black Scholar* 7: 28–46.

Hayes, W. A. 1991. Radical Black Behaviorism. In *Black Psychology*, 3d ed., ed. R. Jones, 65–78. Berkeley: Cobb and Henry.

Hord, F. L. 1991. *Reconstructing Memory: Black Literary Criticism*. Chicago: Third World Press.

Jahn, J. 1961. *Muntu*. New York: Grove Press.

Jones, J. M. 1972. *Prejudice and Racism*. New York: McGraw Hill.

Karenga, M. 1980. *Kawaida Theory: An Introductory Outline*. Los Angeles: Kawaida Publications.

Kelly, G. A. 1955. *The Psychology of Personal Constructs*. New York: Norton.

Lee, C. D. 1994. African-centered Pedagogy: Complexities and Possibilities. In *Too Much Schooling, Too Little Education: A Paradox of Black Life in White Schools*, ed. M. J. Shujaa, 295–318. Trenton, N.J.: African World Press.

Mahoney, M. J. 1988. The Cognitive Sciences and Psychotherapy: Patterns in a Developing Relationship. In *Handbook of Cognitive-behavioral Therapies*, ed. K. S. Dobson, 357–86. New York: Guilford Press.

Martin, T. 1983. *African Fundamentalism: A Literary and Cultural Anthology of Garvey's Harlem Renaissance*. Dover, Mass.: Majority Press.

McLaren, P. 1994. White Terror and Oppositional Agency: Towards a Critical Multiculturalism. In *The Politics of Human Science*, ed. S. Miedema, G. Biesta, B. Boog, A Smaling, W. Wardekker, and B. Levering. Brussels: Vubpress.

Meichenbaum, D., and Genest, M. 1980. Cognitive Behavior Modification: An Integration of Cognitive and Behavioral Methods. In *Helping People Change: A Textbook of Methods*, 2d ed., ed. F. H. Kanfer and A. P. Goldstein, 390–422. New York: Pergamon Press.

Paul, G. L. 1966. *Insight vs. Desensitization in Psychotherapy*. Stanford, Calif.: Stanford University Press.

Phillips, F. B. 1990. Ntu Psychotherapy: An Afrocentric Approach. *Journal of Black Psychology* 17: 55–74.

Prunier, G. 1995. *The Rwanda Crisis: History of a Genocide*. New York: Columbia University Press.

Semmes, C. E. 1992. *Cultural Hegemony and African-American Development*. Westport, Conn.: Praeger.

Shujaa, M. J. 1994. Education and Schooling: You Can Have One without the Other. In *Too Much Schooling, Too Little Education: A Paradox of Black Life in White Schools*, ed. M. J. Shujaa, 13–36. Trenton, N.J.: African World Press.

Skinner, B. F. 1964. Behaviorism at Fifty. In *Behaviorism and Phenomenology*, ed. T. W. Wann, 79–97. Chicago: University of Chicago Press.

Thorton, L. 1990. Broadcast News. In *Split Image: African Americans in the Mass Media*, ed. J. L. Dates and W. Barlow, 389–418. Washington, D.C.: Howard University Press.

Welsing, F. C. 1991. *The Isis Papers: Keys to the Colors*. Chicago: Third World Press.

Woodson, C. G. 1933. *The Mis-education of the Negro*. Washington, D.C.: Associated Publishers.

Index